'Highly recommended text for any therapist or educator working with children or young people. The rationale, description and practical illustrations of drama and play therapy methods are developmentally grounded, cultural inclusive and usefully specific.'

Jacki Short, *Director of Sydney Centre for Creative Change, President of the Australian Play Therapists Association, Registered Counselling Psychologist and Supervisor, Registered Play Therapist and Supervisor*

'The content of this book provides inspiration and motivation for a fulfilling life for every individual, from early childhood, adolescence, the period of preparation for parenthood and pregnancy, to adulthood and old age. Through both theoretical and practical perspective, it defines valuable and effective approaches of the NDP method in an individually tailored and culturally inclusive environment. Therefore, it is highly recommended for therapists and professionals from various fields who work with children, adolescents and families.

The text is especially recommended for professionals interested in the application and exploration of innovative, developmentally grounded, creative and expressive therapeutic approaches, particularly those focused on play and dramatic play in various contexts. These approaches, through a performative process and communication channels that go beyond verbal strategies, stimulate imagination, creativity, self-expression, experience, embodiment, distancing from distress, and the exploration of new narratives based on satisfaction, hope and trust. They encourage transformation and integration.

This book makes a significant contribution to the theory of NDP and includes exceptionally useful, well-founded and cross-culturally tested methods for working with children and young people who have experienced trauma, attachment issues, and emotional or behavioral regulation difficulties. From an educational perspective, it is also highly recommended for parents and professionals working with parents, as it fosters self-empowerment and the acceptance of responsibility.

The book offers valuable insight into rediscovering childhood through play, curious playfulness, and performance. It provides readers with innovative approaches, knowledge, and practical examples of the NDP method to support holistic psychophysical, emotional, and cognitive development, interpersonal relationships, and spiritual awareness. In today's era of societal changes and increasing mental health challenges, this is particularly relevant.

The content of this book can deeply resonate with and is recommended for all readers who are exploring the significance of reconnecting with themselves, their inner child, and the fundamental essence of nature and humanity.'

Urška Novak, *Founder and Director of a Private Institute for assisting children, adolescents, and families in Celje, Slovenia; vice president of the Slovenian Association of Art Therapists; professor of defectology; Master of Science in Special and Rehabilitation Pedagogy; master of Creative Art Therapies; doctoral student in Marriage and Family Therapy; licensed personal and NLP coach; licensed master of hypnosis; certified birth and postpartum doula*

'This collection of writings opens the doors to the rich experience of therapists that are using the Neuro-Dramatic-Play (NDP) in practice. It highlights specific applications of NDP in a variety of needs and settings from early care to elder care, children, teenagers, adults, psychiatric, forensic and young onset dementia. We get to see and understand the myriad manifestations of Attachment-based Play, NDP and Theatre of Resilience (ToR). Voices from across cultures attest to the universality of NDP and its effective use in healing, restoration and development, from Romania to Malaysia and Hong Kong, from Ukraine to India and UK. It is wonderful that the pioneer, Dr. Sue Jennings adds her voice, recounting the evolution – 'Roots and Branches' of NDP and its application in neurodiversity. Chapters carefully span across theory and practice, elucidated with actual experiences and cases from clinical settings. An informative, reflective, and applied collection of international experiences of NDP.'

Aanand Chabukswar, *Applied Theatre and Arts-based Therapy (ABT) Practitioner, India Author of Creative Rites of the Recovering Mind: Arts-Based Therapy for Persons Living with Mental Illness*

'This is a book to cherish. An absolute must for therapists and practitioners working with children and families in a modern culturally diverse landscape. As with all of Sue's work, practitioners will find this resource both accessible and enduring.'

Anna Hodgson, *Charity Director at Clear Sky Children's Charity and Chair of the Oxfordshire Schools Mental Health and Wellbeing Network.*

The Handbook of Neuro-Dramatic-Play

An innovative contribution to our understanding of research and practice behind Neuro-Dramatic-Play (NDP), this book demonstrates how readers may apply this attachment and play-based approach to teaching, parenting, and therapy. This essential book will provide guidance on new techniques and methods, enhancing their practice and providing potential solutions to problems they may be encountering in their work with clients.

Filled with diverse contributions from a team of multi-cultural authors, this book is divided into five distinct parts:

- Section 1 begins by considering the roots and development of NDP, including the science and evidence supporting it as a practice.
- Section 2 covers applying NDP to work with children and young people, including neurodivergent children and those who have experienced trauma.
- Section 3 explores how readers can integrate NDP practices into art, drama, and play therapy.
- Section 4 moves on to discuss international perspectives on NDP, including NDP practice within a range of different geographical and cultural contexts.
- Section 5 concludes the book by examining case studies of work with diverse populations, including pregnant women, forensic settings, and people with young-onset dementia.

Written for clinicians and therapists of all specialisms, this is a compelling read for any mental health practitioner seeking a practical approach to develop (or re-develop) attachment experiences for individuals who have experienced loss, neglect, rejection, or abuse.

Clive Holmwood is an associate professor, lecturer, researcher, author, and doctoral supervisor in the Discipline of Therapeutic Arts at the University of Derby, UK. He is a consultant dramatherapist with 30 years post-qualifying experience working in the public and voluntary sectors and in private practice as a director of Creative Solutions Therapy Ltd.

Sue Jennings is Professor of Play (European Federation); Distinguished Scholar at the University of Witwatersrand, South Africa; Senior Research Fellow, The Shakespeare Institute, University of Birmingham, UK; and a retired play therapist and dramatherapist. She is the originator of Neuro-Dramatic-Play (NDP) and is a pioneer of dramatherapy around the world.

Neuro-Dramatic-Play: Creative Interventions in Attachment-based Practice
Series Editor: Sue Jennings

In the Neuro-Dramatic-Play® Series, series editor Sue Jennings, founder of NDP, and other NDP practitioners aim to produce an array of books on a range of NDP topics. There is a growing literature on the arts and well-being, and in the recent years play has been increasingly included and recognized as an intrinsic piece. The developing neuro-aesthetics discipline clearly demonstrates play as both an art form and a therapy, as well as a developmental process, and acknowledges the ways it can make an important contribution to healing, whatever the age! This series aims to be at the heart of this developing literature. A relatively recent new approach to teaching, parenting and therapy, NDP emphasises children, professional adults and parents in the creative healing process. It is an attachment-based intervention that uses play and drama to emphasise a combination of basic trust, security and ritual, with stimulation, exploration and risk. Enabling people to become more playful and to think 'outside the box', NDP in turn helps people to be more independent and self-reliant and affirms their identity and self-esteem. It is an ideal approach for working with children who have been traumatised, neglected or abused. In a world where rapid changes with families, schools and the care system, the Series fills a great need for practical resources to address the well-being of children and adults.

In this series:

The Handbook of Neuro-Dramatic-Play
Cross-Cultural, Attachment Based Play for Clinicians and Practitioners
Edited by Clive Holmwood and Sue Jennings

The Handbook of Neuro-Dramatic-Play

Cross-Cultural, Attachment-Based Play for Clinicians and Practitioners

Clive Holmwood and Sue Jennings

Routledge
Taylor & Francis Group

LONDON AND NEW YORK

Designed cover image: @getty

First published 2026
by Routledge
4 Park Square, Milton Park, Abingdon, Oxon OX14 4RN

and by Routledge
605 Third Avenue, New York, NY 10158

Routledge is an imprint of the Taylor & Francis Group, an informa business

British Library Cataloguing-in-Publication Data
A catalogue record for this book is available from the British Library

ISBN: 978-1-032-80709-6 (hbk)
ISBN: 978-1-032-80708-9 (pbk)
ISBN: 978-1-003-49820-9 (ebk)

DOI: 10.4324/9781003498209

Typeset in Sabon
by Apex CoVantage, LLC

To all children, everywhere, especially those who have struggled or continue to struggle in their development and growth.

Contents

Acknowledgments   *xiv*
Foreword   *xv*
Editor biographies   *xx*
List of Contributors   *xxi*
List of Figures   *xxv*
List of Tables   *xxvii*

SECTION 1
NDP the basics   1

1 The 'roots and branches' of neuro-dramatic-play:
   An introduction   3
   SUE JENNINGS

2 The performativity in the beginning of life and psychotherapy   13
   STELIOS KRASANAKIS AND ERI ARGYRAKI

SECTION 2
NDP children and young adulthood   21

3 Neurodivergence and Neuro-Dramatic-Play (NDP) in
   children and young people   23
   SUE JENNINGS

4 Using Neuro Dramatic Play (NDP) in schools with children
   and young people post-Covid-19, developing positive
   attachments and good mental health   32
   CLIVE HOLMWOOD

5 I fit in by not being myself   45
   BER CARROLL

6 The expanded EPR framework and Theatre of Resilience for
   young adults – from theatre to the coming-of-age ritual in
   response to social trauma   53
   SHIU HEI LARRY NG

SECTION 3
NDP in therapy   73

7 Into the unknown – a young hero's journey from Ukraine   75
   ALISON CHOWN

8 The use and themes of water in NDP-informed Art Therapy   87
   BRIDGET REES

9 Hunter's journey back to his nest: Application utilising the
   NDP and EPR in parent and child nature-based play therapy   104
   CATRIONA O'NEILL-HAYES

SECTION 4
NDP and international perspectives   113

10 Unlocking healing through neuro-dramatic-play in
    Malaysia: A journey of empowerment   115
    JAFF CHOONG GIAN YONG

11 NDP in the jungle: Play, enjoy and get stronger   135
    ANDY HICKSON AND MING YANG

12 NDP and performance training in Greece: Rediscovering
    childhood: Learning to play again   142
    ROS JOHNSON AND NEIL JOHNSON

13 The journey of learning with NDP within a collective:
    Pre-pandemic, during and after the pandemic   153
    AKANSHA RASTOGI, LAVINA NANDA, ASHIMA KANDWAL, SUKARMA
    DAWAR, AND KAVITA ARORA

14 Neuro-dramatic-play and postcolonial African
theatre – performing resilience 170
DAVID EVANS

SECTION 5
NDP and diverse populations 183

15 Taking care of pregnant womens' mental health through
NDP, a model 185
ULISES MORENO-SERENA

16 Emotions neuro-dramatic play in forensic settings 204
ROWAN MACKENZIE

17 A research project considering the adaptation and practice
of NDP for adults with a diagnosis of young onset dementia 218
CLIVE HOLMWOOD, GEMMA COLLARD-STOKES, AND ALISON WARD

Afterword: The momentum of *The Handbook of*
Neuro-Dramatic-Play 234
PHIL JONES

Index *245*

Acknowledgments

To all our families and friends, all the many participants who have attended our courses, and the NDP community from across the globe.

We thank you!

Foreword

Cathy A. Malchiodi

The fields of expressive arts therapy and creative arts therapies have long known that action-oriented and imagination-driven approaches are restorative for body and mind. But long before the formal discipline of psychotherapy and arts-based therapies appeared, humans incorporated these practices within ceremonies, rituals, and performances as ways of transforming difficulties when confronted by crisis, tragedy, or loss. As a species, we have been turning to the healing factors found in these experiences to confront and resolve distress for thousands of years. These actions emerged not only as individual forms of reparation but also as social engagement, capitalizing on connection with others and community as agents of repair. In this century, play therapy and various forms of therapeutic enactment have been acknowledged as effective methods to address and resolve trauma, loss, attachment problems, and more.

As a psychotherapist who specializes in working with traumatic stress, I regularly see individuals with disabling reactions that interrupt their daily lives. For those whose lives are impacted by adverse events or complex or chronic trauma, this human right to play, enact, and express does not necessarily feel natural or possible. As children, they simply may not have had the opportunities to play due to neglect, lack of caregivers, or social and environmental barriers. Even as adults, opportunities to safely experience playfulness, pretend, and imagination to counteract loneliness, fear, anxiety, grief, and loss may not be available, present, or possible.

When I first began to work with children and adolescents who had developmental trauma, a topic highlighted in this book, I noticed a sharp contrast in how imagination was expressed compared to individuals without adverse experiences. Some children and teens simply did not know how to interact with toys, art materials, drums, or puppets because they never had these experiences early in life nor the guidance from a supportive adult caregiver. Many were just too fearful of repercussions or punishment to freely play, pretend, improvise, or make art. These same fears were present in their parents and caregivers. I quickly realized that it would be a challenge for these individuals to engage in the very processes that I believed would bring about reparation and a sense of well-being because their ability to imagine was essentially impaired. Despite these challenges, using drama and pretend play are, in my experience, the most effective ways to work with anyone stuck in unproductive trauma stories and in need of the "magical moments" for change.

Performative change: the foundation of transformation and restoration

When it comes to dramatic enactment, it is impossible to separate play from drama or acting from play and imagination; they are complementary agents of change. They enable individuals to embody various characters, use distancing to pretend, provide opportunities to personify others, and most of all, a chance to imagine new scenarios. They are key approaches that support the transformative work necessary to help individuals make sense and eventually make meaning in their lives. Within the array of creative and expressive arts approaches, drama, enactment, roleplay, and playful improvisation are the only ones that provide this type of transformative container to literally alter painful life narratives.

As a trauma specialist, I believe the kinds of restorative cognitions, emotions, and sensory experiences we want to make "stick" with clients when using art-based approaches are key to eventually helping them imagine new narratives post-trauma. In other words, if we do not eventually assist individuals in moving away from distress, we leave them with thoughts, feelings, and sensations that will not support new narratives of pleasure, confidence, and hope. This premise is also emphasized in current somatic approaches that redirect body and mind toward regulation and support resilience through engagement with the body (Malchiodi, 2022). Within the field of expressive arts therapy and creative arts therapies, therapeutic applications of dramatic enactment are powerful strategies that uniquely integrate multiple pathways for encouraging novel and reparative stories and restoring health and well-being in a uniquely action-oriented way.

But just why is enactment such a powerful method? I think there is one obvious answer to this question – it helps individuals find reparation through *performative change*. That is, individuals are engaged in a multi-layered, action-oriented process that taps many levels of expression and transformative experiences. Whether improvisation, role play, theatrical reading, or actual performance on stage, dramatic enactment generally integrates movement, gesture, sound, voice, playfulness, visual experiences, and storytelling. It provides the opportunity to try out new narratives not only through language but through the embodiment of a character.

Performative change is central to taking on any dramatic role or "pretend" play. But, equally important, when experienced as part of a group of individuals, there are the added elements of relationships as well as social engagement, attunement, and co-regulation with others. These experiences encourage individuals to take risks through pretend roles and novel identities. When an audience (whether other group members or the therapist) is part of the dynamic, the element of being witnessed is an additional part of the experience for both the individuals playing roles as well as the viewers. What is unique about dramatic enactment in any form is the element of witnessing in the form of an audience; in a therapy session, the therapist becomes the viewer.

Resensitizing body and mind through play and enactment

So many individuals we see in practice are literally haunted by a "theater of sensations" in their own bodies, unable to control or articulate how those sensations impact them in multiple and adverse ways. Because of my background in expressive arts therapy, I am always looking beyond distressful reactions and past adverse events, trying to understand clients from a different perspective. Creative approaches provide channels of communication that are not found in language-based strategies. More importantly, they also offer moments of empowerment, self-agency, and mastery.

There are numerous reasons for adding play and enactment to support re-sensitization of body and mind in psychotherapy, attachment work, and trauma intervention. Three concepts that are particularly important when it comes to expanding capacity through expressive and play-based experiences include:

Coming to our senses: Neurobiology has recently taught us that we need to "come to our senses" in developing effective components for psychotherapy for both mind and body (Malchiodi, 2020). Introducing play and enactment makes "sense" because it involves visual, tactile, olfactory, auditory, vestibular, and proprioceptive experiences not found in talk alone. It is exteroceptive (the sensing of external stimuli); in the expressive arts, it is multisensorial, depending on the medium. For example, encounters with music or percussion not only involve sound but also include vibrational, rhythmic, and movement-focused experiences. Drama and play may include vocalization, visual impact, and other sensory qualities. When introducing art expression within the context of play, various smells of media and tactile sensations, such as fluidity, stickiness, dampness, hardness, softness, or resistance, expand awareness of the senses.

Restoring our aliveness: The success of any therapeutic work is intricately connected to how we restore a sense of aliveness in individuals, especially those experiencing traumatic stress. By aliveness, I mean not just existing and surviving but living life with vitality, joy, and connectedness.

Play-based approaches have a unique role in restoring a sense of vitality and joy because aliveness is not something we can be "talked into." It has to be experienced in both mind and body. This experience of vitality and joy is also strengthened where there is a relationship between "players." It is a unique type of energy that circulates through singing, dancing, performing, laughing, and playing together. Our ability as therapists to help resensitize mind and body in playful ways may be as, or even more powerful, than anything we can say to our clients with words alone. These moments become internalized sensations of animation, vigor, and passion because playing affirms that we are alive (Malchiodi, 2022).

"Shift Happens" through Play: To play and pretend is not always easy for those in distress due to acute or multiple traumas, attachment difficulties, or emotional disorders. It requires a sense of feeling safe, and that is something not easily possible, especially in the earliest stages of therapeutic work. But, over time, introducing playfulness, whether through expressive arts, toys or props, silly games, or enactment, inevitably, a "shift" that happens. It is a synergy that takes on a life of its own, with one expressive movement, gesture, image, or sound leading naturally to others. The shift has manifested when a person walks into the therapy session with a different rhythm or vibe, an upbeat step, a palpable change in prosody, or even ready with a joke to tell – all signs of reparative change. We can encourage that shift by introducing playful experiences described throughout this book, helping our clients once again learn to be within the joyful experience of an "unscripted moment."

Finally, when we bring play and enactment into therapy, we support clients in moving beyond a "window of tolerance" (Siegal, 2009) for distress, detachment, and disabling emotions. In order to truly repair and recover, we need moments that involve something beyond enduring and coping. By including expressive in sessions, it becomes obvious that repair and recovery are not necessarily found through expanding the ability to tolerate reactions. They come through supporting tangible, sensory, and somatic experiences of efficacy, resourcing, and *resilience*. The authors of this book explain not only how repair and recovery take place through the reduction of distress but also how to replace the uncomfortable sensations of hyperactivation in pleasurable and joyful ways. This is a transformation felt in the body as empowerment, mastery, and enlivenment when encountering distress and disruptive events. These are just a few of the qualities in play and enactment – natural sources of restoration for body, mind, and spirit.

Neuro-dramatic play works

Play, at its core, is essentially a form of reparative dramatic enactment. This is a natural pairing that is almost inseparable because through dramatic enactment, the play-driven, multi-sensory "theatre of imagination" emerges. It is this theatre that has been a core in human recuperation and restoration for thousands of years through rituals, ceremonies, and procedures for health and well-being. It is also central to the human capacity for play as exploration and curiosity, a way of resensitizing body and mind to mastery and self-agency, enlivenment, resilience, and joy.

This book demonstrates that by engaging clients in Neuro-Dramatic Play, practitioners have the opportunity to observe and support the capacity of individuals while engaging in actions that lead to experiences of joy, enlivenment, curiosity, attunement, and, most importantly, playfulness. As therapists, when we put the principles of NDP into practice, we can instill sensory, emotional, and cognitive capacities for flexibility and connection to others.

As Dr. Jennings says, "Through acting, people are empowered to act" (Jennings, 2023). When I first read that statement, I realized it implies much more than empowerment. The NDP model integrates not only the many restorative dimensions of playfulness and dramatic enactment but also brings together brain and body, sensory processing, and attachment. These are the foundations for synchrony and attunement within oneself and with others. I believe what this book communicates is that when we are playing, whether through pretend scenarios, enjoyable movements, making sounds, or self-expression, an inner harmony manifests. Within that harmony, we begin to see the world with curiosity and unrestricted vision. May this book and its authors take you on a journey that supports this harmony, curiosity, and unrestricted vision in your restorative work with people of all ages.

Cathy A. Malchiodi, PhD
Founder and Director, Trauma-Informed Practices and
Expressive Arts Therapy Institute, Louisville, KY, USA

References

Jennings, S. (2023) *Managing Social Anxiety in Children and Young People*. London: Routledge.

Malchiodi, C. A. (2020) *Trauma and Expressive Arts Therapy: Brain, Body, and Imagination in the Healing Process*. New York: Guilford Press.

Malchiodi, C. A. (2022) *Handbook of Expressive Arts Therapy*. New York: Guilford Press.

Siegal, D. (2009) *Mindsight*. New York: Norton.

Editor biographies

Clive Holmwood PhD (UK) – is a Neuro-Dramatic Play practitioner and trainer and dramatherapist and Deputy Director of NDP Ltd. He is also an Associate Professor in the Discipline of Therapeutic Arts at the University of Derby. He lectures and researches in Dramatherapy and Creative Arts Health and Wellbeing. His PhD in Education from the University of Warwick was published by Routledge in 2014 as "Drama Education and Dramatherapy." Amongst many other publications, he is the co-editor of Three International Handbooks with his colleague Dr Sue Jennings. His first practice-based book on NDP, *Games for Building Secure Relationships in the Early Years*, was published by Hinton House in 2023.

Sue Jennings PhD (UK) – is known internationally for her pioneering work in Dramatherapy and Play Therapy and for her many publications on those topics. Her doctoral fieldwork research was with the Temiars who inhabit the Malaysian rainforest. She is a founder-member of the International Attachment Network. She holds various honorary posts overseas, including to Children First, New Delhi, Romanian Association of Play Therapy and Dramatherapy, AEON Dramatherapy Institute Athens, Greece, and Ouch Theatre, Nanjing, China.

Contributors

Eri Argyraki (Greece) – is dual trained as a psychologist and dramatherapist.

Kavita Arora (India) – is a psychiatrist with an Advanced Diploma in NDP and is a part of Children First India. The team works leading an early intervention service that attempts to combine the neurobiological understanding of childhood and developmental needs with therapeutic approaches rooted in playfulness and respect and wonder for neurodiversity.

Ber Carroll (Ireland) – has over 30 years' experience working with children. She has a BA in humanities and a first-class honors degree in Psychology and English Literature. She is a qualified play therapist, parent mentor, and sensory attachment practitioner. Ber has established the 'Circle of Care' intervention and training. She holds the Advanced Diploma in Neuro-Dramatic-Play.

Jaff Choong Gian Yong (Malysia) – is a counsellor registered under the Board of Counsellors, Malaysia, and a Certified NDP Trainer from the UK. He practiced therapeutic play in his work for the past 13 years in educational, hospital, and welfare settings (including juvenile schools, orphanage homes, and prisons). He is also currently a Psychology Lecturer at the Asia Pacific University of Technology and Innovation (APU) whilst having his own private practice in Silver Lining Psychology.

Alison Chown (UK) – is a highly experienced play therapist, specialist education practitioner (SEMH), supervisor, and trainer holding Post Graduate Diplomas in Play Therapy and Special Educational Needs and a Master's in Education. She has pioneered outdoor play therapy in the UK since 2010, writing *Play Therapy in the Outdoors* in 2014, *The Practical Guide to Play Therapy in the Outdoors* in 2017, and has chapters in *The Routledge International Handbook of Play, Therapeutic Play and Play Therapy*. She is the co-founder and facilitator of The Collaboration of Outdoor Play Therapists (COOPT) and devised and delivers their Best Practice Certificate course, a key strand of which promotes a greater connection to nature for therapists working outdoors. She was awarded an honorary diploma in Neuro-Dramatic-Play for her services to Play Therapy in the outdoors.

Gemma Collard-Stokes PhD (UK) – is an interdisciplinary performance art-ist and researcher with over 20 years of experience in participatory arts, arts for health, and professional performance. Her work explores how somatic movement practices and eco-somatic approaches can foster recon-nection and re-enchantment during transitional life experiences, such as birth trauma, aging, dementia, and climate crises. Through interdiscipli-nary collaboration in dance, poetry, and visual arts, she investigates how creative interactions with nature support well-being and a deeper sense of connection to the world.

Sukarma Dawar (India) – is a developmental psychologist with an Advanced Diploma in NDP and is part of Children First India. The team works leading an early intervention service that attempts to combine the neu-robiological understanding of childhood and developmental needs with therapeutic approaches rooted in playfulness and respect and wonder for neurodiversity.

David Evans PhD (Nigeria) – For 16 years, David regularly attended Yoruba performance events, including marketplaces, family celebrations, street performances, masquerades, and touring theatre. David then trained as an actor for three years at the Bristol Old Vic Theatre School and went on to join the company for a nine-month season. As a professional actor, David felt the transformative imperative of Yoruba performance was missing from his theatre experience. Four years in English theatre were followed by training as a teacher and the founding of Imùlè Theatre in 1990, where David combined his environmental concerns with a Yoruba performative aesthetic.

Andy Hickson PhD (UK) – is currently Artistic Director of Actionwork The-atre and former Professor and former Faculty Dean of an independent international university. He has a diploma in Neuro-Dramatic-Play and contributes to the teaching program.

Neil Johnson (UK/Naxos Greece) – Neil is co-founder of Naxos Creative. Until recently, Neil was heading up the performing arts dept in one of Britain's leading specialist music schools. He now runs presentation skills and business development training in the UK, Asia, and Greece. He spent many years working as an actor in theatre and television, following three years of training at the Guildford School of Acting. Neil has worked as a presentation consultant with board-level executives from BT, Ameri-can Express, Balfour Beatty, Lego, Lever Brothers, and General Motors.

Ros Johnson (UK/Naxos Greece) – Ros is co-founder of Naxos Creative. She trained at the Central School of Speech and Drama as a teacher and voice coach. She is a counsellor and trained life coach. She worked as assistant director at the Crucible Sheffield with the late great Clare Venables and then at the RSC, working with the celebrated voice coach, Cicely Berry.

After the RSC, she went to the National Theatre as Assistant Director to Sir Richard Eyre and was involved in several West End transfers.

Ashima Kandwal (India) – is a developmental psychologist and has an Advanced Diploma in NDP and is part of Children First India. The team works leading an early intervention service that attempts to combine the neurobiological understanding of childhood and developmental needs with therapeutic approaches rooted in playfulness and respect and wonder for neurodiversity.

Stelios Krasanakis MD (Greece) – is Psychiatrist, Psychotherapist-Dramatherapist, Lecturer in the National and Kapodistrian University of Athens, and Theatre Director.

Rowan Mackenzie PhD (UK) – is both a practitioner and academic, working with specialized communities. Her doctoral research used spatial theory as a framework to examine global theatre practices with incarcerated people and people with mental health issues, learning disabilities, and experiences of homelessness. She has a Diploma in Neuro-Dramatic-Play. She is Founder and Artistic Director of Shakespeare UnBard, which facilitates collaborative theatre companies in a number of UK prisons, and Co-Chair of the Shakespeare Beyond Borders Alliance. She is the recipient of many national and international awards for her work, including the prestigious Butler Trust award. She has published numerous chapters and essays on Shakespeare within prisons, Shakespeare with learning-disabled actors, and the heterotopic potential of applied theatre. Her monograph Creating Space for Shakespeare was published by Bloomsbury Arden in March 2023.

Ulises Moreno-Serena (Mexico) – is the Coordinator at Teatro Aplicado CDMX, holds a B.A. in Theatre, an M.A. in Psychology, is a candidate for a Ph.D. in Mental Health, and is also doing post-doctoral studies in trans-disciplinary research and pursuing the alternative training path to become a Registered Drama Therapist for the North American Drama Therapy Association. He has taken as a life goal the promotion of Applied Theatre and Drama Therapy in his country. Two of his articles have been published in Spanish: "Intentionality in Applied Theatre and Mental Health" and "Resiliency upon disasters: training in stress inoculation as an opportunity of primordial prevention." His professional experience has been developed both in clinical and organizational settings for the past 22 years.

Lavina Nanda (India) – is a developmental psychologist, therapeutic play practitioner, has an Advanced Diploma in NDP, and is part of Children First India. The team leads an early intervention service that attempts to combine the neurobiological understanding of childhood and developmental needs with therapeutic approaches rooted in playfulness and respect and wonder for neurodiversity.

Shiu Hei Larry Ng (Hong Kong) – is a registered drama therapist (NADTA) and theatre practitioner specializing in physical theatre, mime, and mask, with training in Lecoq's pedagogy and Decroux's Corporeal Mime. He is a certified Feldenkrais Method® practitioner and Jeremy Krauss Approach therapist, working with children with special needs. He actively practices Playback Theatre and has advanced training in Satir Transformational Systemic Therapy, Ericksonian hypnotherapy, Neuro-Dramatic-Play, and the Therapeutic Spiral Model of psychodrama for trauma. He holds a Master's degree in Drama Education, an MPhil in Philosophy, and an MA in Drama, Theatre and Performance Studies, and is currently pursuing a PhD in the same field.

Catriona O'Neill-Hayes (Ireland) – holds a BA in Applied Social Studies in Social Care. She is an Integrative Trauma-Informed Play Therapist and has 12 years of experience working in the private and public sectors. Catriona is also a Theraplay™ practitioner and a Forest School leader and has recently obtained her Advanced Diploma in Neuro-Dramatic-Play. Catriona has extensive experience working in the area of trauma and attachment, having worked with children, teenagers, and parents for 23 years in various roles. Catriona is currently undertaking a master's degree in creative psychotherapy (Humanistic and Integrative modality) with The Children's Therapy Centre in Ireland.

Akansha Rastogi (India) – is a developmental psychologist, has an Advanced Diploma in NDP, and is part of Children First India. The team leads an early intervention service that attempts to combine the neurobiological understanding of childhood and developmental needs with therapeutic approaches rooted in playfulness and respect and wonder for neurodiversity.

Bridget Rees (UK) – is an HCPC registered Art Psychotherapist working with people of all ages in her independent practice in a rural area of Somerset in the UK. She is Founder and Director of the Somerset Arts Therapies Centre, which offers all creative arts and play therapy modalities. Bridget trained in MA Art Psychotherapy at The University of South Wales and has a background in art teaching. She has completed the Diploma and Advanced Diploma in NDP and, at the time of writing, is working towards becoming an NDP Trainer.

Alison Ward PhD (UK) – is Deputy Director for Research, Evaluation, and Impact at Dementia UK. Alison has extensive research experience in the field of dementia, with a focus on using creative methods as an intervention and research method. She is also the lead UK researcher for an international collaboration using lifelong learning with people with dementia.

Ming Yang (UK) – is a freelance journalist and media consultant. She has a diploma in Neuro-Dramatic-Play and works as an NDP assessor. With Andy, she is a parent of two young children.

Figures

4.1	Sam	35
4.2	Annie placing the figures in the puddle of water	36
4.3	Anxiety Loop	40
7.1	A rectangle of low block walls with a doorway inside a right-angled pair of small bridges set on a tarmac play area	84
8.1	A face and tonsils made from Play-Doh	95
8.2	Two baby dolls in a toy bath on a table	96
8.3	Two hands pressing down on a tabletop, rubbing paint over the tabletop. The hands are covered in paint	99
8.4	Paint smeared on a tabletop with swirling patterns, same on the left and right side, looking a bit like a human brain	99
9.1	The Nesting Tree	108
10.1	The Tree of Life: Piṭṭam (Buttock) Tree	128
10.2	The Rainbow: 天使和恶魔的诞生 (The Birth of Angel and Devil)	129
10.3	Spectogram: GTA Animal 5P VS GTA Animal King	129
10.4	Mask Making: Journey to the West	130
13.1	Imaginary ball warm-up activity	162
13.2	Group Collective Experience	163
13.3	Messy Play	164
13.4	Mask Work	164
13.5	Reflections	165
15.1	Landscape map of the author's own elaboration for you to get inspired!	195
15.2	Mandala layout (own elaboration)	197
16.1	Image from Obun's cartoon book image 1	210
16.2	Image from Obun's cartoon book image 2	211
Afterword.1	What dialogues can occur between different cultures of play and NDP?	236
Afterword.2	Interconnected questions	237
Afterword.3	NDP and development	237

Afterword.4   How can a case study approach contribute to wider
             knowledge in NDP?   239
Afterword.5   How can individual experiences contribute to wider
             knowledge in NDP?   240
Afterword.6   How can NDP further enhance its engagement
             with, and empowerment of participant responses
             and 'voices'?   242

Tables

6.1 Different intermediary play organized according to types of
   transitional function   61
6.2 Session plan/record for the final season   67
8.1 EPR as defined by Sue Jennings   90
10.1 Sample of Planned Sessions   124
15.1 Experienced stressors by pregnant women   186

Section 1

NDP the basics

Chapter 1

The 'roots and branches' of neuro-dramatic-play

An introduction

Sue Jennings

The context

Dramatic performances through rituals and ceremonies have an ancient and respected past. These performances are usually for celebration (of histori- cal events or famous people), or the transition to a new status, otherwise known as a *'rite de passage'*. Other rituals may accompany seasonal planting and harvest, as well as fertility rites. There are also dramatic enactments for health and healing. This is particularly the case in non-Western cultures.

However, in the UK and The West, drama has had a chequered develop- ment, and actors for many years were considered vagabonds and of ques- tionable reputation. Theatre started within the church's Easter Mass as a four-line interaction between Mary Magdalene and the Angel Gabrielle. The Romans also brought theatre to the UK and built large auditoria. There were 'Mummer's Plays', and Morality and Mystery Plays, all based on Christian themes. However, the ambivalence towards actors and theatre has continued throughout history.

While Peter Slade (1965) was pioneering Dramatherapy within educational drama, it was Moreno who pioneered the theory and practice of Psycho- drama in the clinical world. He said 'Psychodrama is the scientific explora- tion of truth through dramatic method', quoted in Fox (1987). Although some Western Dramatherapists also train in psychodrama, the roots of dram- atherapy lie in theatre-in-education and Peter Slade's early work.

Other leading figures in the field, such as Dorothy Heathcote, Gavin Bol- ton, and Brian Way, were describing drama work with what we would now term 'neurodivergent' groups, but it was never referred to as therapy. Initia- tives by the Sesame Institute and the Institute of Dramatherapy began the process of putting dramatherapy firmly on the therapeutic map. This was approximately at the same time as the other arts therapies: art, music, and dance-movement.

However, there was a curious dichotomy. For example, in Art Therapy, the art-making process as well as the created art objects have significance in the therapeutic experience. With Dramatherapy, the drama-making process

DOI: 10.4324/9781003498209-2

is significant, but usually, the created object, the culmination of the drama work – theatre – is not addressed!

When I was appointed leader of the yet to be set up, Dramatherapy training course in Hertfordshire, I included various theatre subjects in the syllabus: theatre visits, history of theatre, performance skills, and the study and performance of plays. People who applied for the course, if they had no theatre experience, had to go away and get some! Unfortunately, this has gradually been eroded and, generally, people don't study theatre and performance. The only performance they are usually involved in is the autobiographical solo show, which is performed as part of their final assessment at some training schools. Drama and theatre are not part of their entry requirements either. Just imagine someone being accepted into a music therapy training if they were unable to play an instrument or sing or read music!

It was not until the 1970s that moves began to enable dramatherapy to become a recognised practice and profession, which would eventually lead to State Registration. There were two main pathways from the Sesame Institute, which emphasised drama and movement in therapy, with a strong grounding in Jungian theory, and the former Institute of Dramatherapy which believed in a theatre model and an emphasis on performance. This model was based on the developmental paradigm 'Embodiment-Projection-Role' or EPR.

The State Registration body said that there could only be one application, so any organisations running dramatherapy courses had to combine together. Since all the dramatherapy courses were being run in non-university colleges, it was felt that it was important for them to also gain post-graduate accreditation. It was a time of immense activity as well as rivalry between the different art therapies.

With the lack of a theatre and performance model, dramatherapy has become closer and closer to psychodrama. I would not be surprised if Dramatherapy and Psychodrama combined some time in the future.

When I was designing and implementing the Hertfordshire training, I also felt it was very important for practitioners to have a working understanding of social anthropology in order to understand cross-cultural themes and rituals, but the subject has now become mainly an optional extra. We need to understand ritual within the context of culture and dramatic presentation. It can be used in a preventative or curative practice and accompanies the belief system of society. However, we live in an era that emphasises psychotherapy rather than socio-therapy: the individual over the group.

There is no doubt in my mind that Dramatherapy is treated differently; maybe things could have more of an arts therapy basis if we had named it Theatre Therapy? Sadly, we shall never know!

Since these two core principles were no longer at the heart of dramatherapy – theatre and ritual – I decided it was time for me to step back and re-appraise where it was all going and, indeed, where I was going!

Since I developed the Embodiment-Projection-Role (EPR) paradigm for Dramatherapy, the noticeable gap in our 'dramatic development' has become a yawning chasm in society generally. Even if dramatic playfulness is accepted as important at the beginning of life, it is soon diminished when children are told to 'stop playing about!'

Since the innovation of Peter Slade and the optimism of the '60s when theatre-in-education groups abounded, most schools had a drama teacher, and there was even a drama advisor at County Hall in London; sadly, there has been a major shift. The arts in education have been severely cut; there are very few theatre in education companies, and we no longer have drama advisors. Drama, again, is seen as less important despite the obvious links between forms of play and STEM education (science, technology, engineering, maths). I made the decision to focus on the beginning of life and, where possible, bring some ideas to bear on pregnancy play.

I was already looking at early infant development following on from my doctoral research with the Temiar people in the Malaysian rain forest. We were living alongside people who were making babies, surviving pregnancy, and then giving birth in my house or next door. This gave me the opportunity to observe infants from the beginning.

It was now that I was observing that 'mimicry before language' was the order of development and that dramatic interaction before birth enables the infant to be born 'dramatised'. As well as the nurturing between carer and infant, most of the interactions are imitative, as adults and babies imitate each other's expressions and sounds. There is an appreciation through nods, smiles, and handclaps, with a sense of these communications being performative. So, performative playing, a personal solo show, with a mother or adult attachment person being the audience!

'Through acting, people are empowered to act' (Jennings, 2023).

When I was developing the basis of Neuro-Dramatic-Play and looking at the people who contributed to the innovation of attachment theory and practice, I was immediately struck by the influence of the personal experiences of the authors. John Bowlby was very vocal regarding the loss of his beloved nanny and his early dispatch to boarding school. Erik Erikson was also influenced by his distorted parenting, and he invented and wrote *Identity, Youth and Crisis* (1968). I suffered trauma at the age of 4 and again at 10 years old, so it was not surprising that much of my childhood memories have seemed irretrievable. Careful and steady therapy has freed much of that experience, and I have been diagnosed with ADHD. It is obvious to say that my focus now is a result of my early trauma!

Fortunately, my work at the Royal London Hospital in the Department of Obstetrics and Gynaecology in the 1980s gave me the opportunity to observe during pregnancy and the first year of life. This, together with my Temiar observations, led me to the realisation that there were some serious gaps in the EPR model I had researched and created. Whereas the Embodiment stage included small and gross body movements, it did not include sensory play. Nor did it give sufficient focus to rhythmic play, commencing from early heartbeats and growing into chants, clapping games, and 'dancing on the lap'.

Without realising it, I had been cutting off the Embodiment-Projection-Role development from its roots in early play and attachment. Basically, I had been pioneering a model that already assumed a playful beginning! It was time to take stock of what I had learned from the Temiars and increase my observations of early child development (Jennings, 2011).

The result is Neuro-Dramatic-Play, with a focus on water, rhythmic, messy, dramatic (interactive), and performative play. NDP is where drama and theatre and, therefore, dramatherapy, begin!

Differentiating early forms of play

The following NDP forms are not sequential; they occur in parallel play, both before birth and during the first year of life after birth. It is important to remember that rhythmic play provides predictable security and feelings of safety, whereas messy play is the opportunity for exploration and discovery.

The following are some broad play headings that we need to be mindful of, and all these forms of play need to be present in the early years. Play *is* learning and development and will lead to other learning. It serves as a foundation for physical, mental, and spiritual growth.

One important stage needs to be noted, and that is the transition from mimicry from birth and 'let's pretend' at about six months. Let's pretend it is observable through the game of Peekaboo, which is usually enjoyed from six months onwards.

Water play

During pregnancy, babies have a 9-month relationship with water. They are growing in slimy water until the moment when the waters break, and the journey to the world of light begins. Unless babies have been dipped in water to make them breathe, most babies have a positive relationship with water, especially if they are born in a birthing pool. Playing with bubbles is also important.

Rhythmic play

Babies need to adjust to their circadian rhythm in the early weeks: it differentiates light and dark and night and day. Research has shown that breast milk also responds to this rhythm, with more stimulating hormones in the morning and calming ones in the evening!

Our earliest felt rhythm is our heartbeat and our mother's heartbeat. Small babies often change their heartbeat to their mother's or primary carer's when held against the left shoulder.

We have a natural response to move in a rhythmic way, whether marching, skipping, or dancing. Mothers and babies spontaneously rock together, helped in the olden days with rocking chairs and cradles, and time. Rocking is soothing and predictable, originating in the womb, where a baby feels rocked in water when the mother is walking or dancing.

We also experience music before we are born and can recognise the same music after we are born. Rhythm is important in soothing after a meltdown or shock.

Messy play

Childbirth itself is a slimy, sticky, and watery journey following nine months of darkness in slippery water. Doctors and nurses these days are less in a hurry to 'wash and weigh' and place babies on their mother's chests where they can still sense their mother's heartbeat and have skin-to-skin contact. Washing and cutting of the cord are delayed, and babies can feel secure in their mother's arms, the second circle of attachment, the first being the womb itself (Jennings, 2011).

The adult and child, or child alone, play with clay, mud, finger paints, pastry, flour and water, lotions, and potions. Make sure there is a floor covering and that the rules for containing the mess are clearly explained and agreed. Maybe the activities can include real cooking as well as pretend cooking. All children enjoy pretend cooking and serving meals to other children or their toys or accompanying adults. This is not only imaginative play, but also rehearsing, balance, coordination, and social play.

The first year of life has a lot of mess: dribbling milk, sticky eating, bubbles, and splashing in the bath, for example. And from mess gradually comes form; out of mud comes mud pies or chocolate pudding!

If children are to learn to create form, build, or model, they need to start with the mess. They experience a myriad of physical actions and coordination, as well as most of their senses, and, very importantly, creating form. Creating form can also lead to monsters, the dark shadowy side that can be controlling or controlled. Children can communicate their fears and nightmares through Monster Messy Play. They are giving form to wafting and startling images that can feel overwhelming. It is important that adults do not dismiss the child's fears about Monsters: a child's talk of Monsters may be a first step to the disclosure of monstrous behaviour.

Parents, teachers, and carers immediately wish to clear up mess, and wet wipes feature heavily on people's shopping lists! There are adults who are averse to mess and wet textures, even avoiding wet contact in training courses! Cleanliness is a sign of civilisation, not sanitised living!

Current practice to prevent further pandemics is to sterilise the toys or have a personal set of toys for each child. Surfaces and door handles need to be bleached, and the floor surface needs to be appropriately cleaned.

Outdoor Play: Includes all the different play elements: messy, physical, challenging, curious, interactive, solitary. Children need to be able to explore and construct. In outdoor play (Chown, 2014), children become attuned to the rhythms of nature, the cycle of life, and the balance between self and environment. They become aware of the bigger world.

Dramatic Play (or Interactive Play): You and the child interact with each other through the play, such as Pooh sticks, echo play (adult and child echo each other's sounds, words, or gestures); role play (playing simple parts in stories or rhymes, sometimes with dressing up); finger games (This Little Piggy went to Market, Round and Round the Garden, Hide and Seek). Dramatic play is also intrinsic to puppet play.

Hide and Seek: For many children, the most important thing about Hide and Seek is that they are found! This simple game is reassuring for children who may have suffered abuse or abandonment. The message is, 'I am important enough to be found!' Many children coming to therapeutic play ask to play Hide and Seek many times. Usually, if children want to repeat a game over and over again, they are seeking safety, predictability, and the known and not the unknown (Jennings, 2023).

Exploratory Play: Children are allowed and encouraged to explore without adult interference or direction. This can be a piece of wild garden or somewhere in the woods or some rocks and pools at the seaside or grandma's button box or a pile of cardboard boxes. Remember that it is important for self-direction, curiosity, and exploration to be a part of all playing.

Brain Play: The adult and the child play board and card games, chess, and guessing games (this type of play belongs to Projective Play, but it may be a safe starting point for anxious children).

All these forms of play create a balance between order and disorder, as we seek safety but need to develop and discover. And all these forms of play need to be encouraged during the early years (Holmwood, 2023).

Having established that dramatic play is the forerunner of drama and theatre, I was now asking myself how we could understand the significance of theatre performance and whether its emergence can be observed.

Mothers talk to their unborn children during pregnancy and will sometimes 'role-reverse': talk to the child and then answer themselves *as if* they are the child. At birth, there is a significant few hours when mothers and babies try to imitate each other's expressions (facially and vocally). Mother or carer and child are imitating each other, and mimicry is the beginning of theatre. Our dramatic development includes the capacity to role reverse or play 'as if' we are the other. This also enables us to show empathy.

When babies 'dance' on the adult's lap, they continue to get a sense of performance (from about 6 months). The late Richard Courtney (1968) observed that the special moment when an infant begins to imitate someone else occurs at 10 months. From then on, we get more glimpses of performance, imitation of story characters, and creating voices for dolls and animal toys. However, it is rarely a sustained performance until 6 or 7 years old. There seems to be a shift from dramatic play to drama 'for real'; there is more sustained enactment and a growing critical awareness.

I have termed this 'Theatre of Resilience (ToR)'. Through growing performance skills, people (children and adults) are able to explore a character and maybe a scene, safely, keeping their own emotions intact. Nevertheless, this exploration makes an impact on the inner life of the participant, which results in changes and insight. The exploration of 'other', paradoxically, allows understanding and change of the self.

Neuro-Dramatic-Play (NDP), Embodiment-Projection-Role (EPR), and Theatre of Resilience (ToR) can now be integrated into a working model of Early Child Development based on drama and theatre: enactment and performance. This forms the basis of the art form of 'Theatre Art', which can be applied preventatively or curatively. This model can be adapted for all age groups, with appropriate adjustment of contents. The three paradigms can include application with those with developmental delay, post-trauma impact, neurodiversity, behavioural challenges, and disrupted attachments.

NDP is relevant in education, therapy, and clinical application as well as being appropriate for creative parenting and preventative work in school space and community. Its flexibility means it can be adapted for individual, family, or group work.

As we become more aware of the process of the drama theatre on our clients, and indeed on ourselves, our realisation of its impact on attachment becomes apparent. It can be quite startling to observe that so many plays, stories, epics, rituals, celebrations, and more are about individual or social attachments (Jennings, 2022).

Attachment-based play

There is a lot of literature on the subject of attachment, and most of it focusses on the early bonding between mothers and babies (including Jennings, 2011). Our primary attachment is usually to whoever cares for us after birth, which is usually the person who gave birth to us. We need to acknowledge the attachment that forms during pregnancy. This may be confused if we were abandoned or handed over too early to a child-minder or were neglected, abused, or born from a surrogate mother. Our birth mothers may have given birth to us on behalf of someone else, or we may be adopted very soon after birth. Over the years, there are many, many secondary attachments that develop, some of which are temporary, others that last years, and some, indeed, for a lifetime (Jennings, 2011).

Loss or estrangement of mothers is a major cause of grief and distress, not only for babies and small children but for individuals of any age. We become attached to pets, places, dwellings, gifts, inherited objects, and toys. We also become attached to our jobs and the colleagues with whom we work, which is why sudden redundancy can be traumatic. We join in rituals that emphasise our bond with others or acknowledge grief at our losses.

Older people experience feelings of sadness and loss of attachment when they make a transition into a home for older people and have to leave so many things behind. They may be leaving a home they have lived in for many, many years. Some care homes do not encourage individuality, and bedspreads and towels can be the same colour. Children and adults can become institutionalised if their own individual attachment needs are not considered, especially if there is an insistence that 'we all do things together'.

Certain addictive conditions can be seen as a distorted attachment, including eating issues and self-harming. The connection between addiction and attachment needs research and exploration (Jennings, 2018).

The most important aspects of attachment-based play are how it can be contained within circles and also manifest through water, messy, rhythmic, dramatic, and performative play; as I said earlier, the security and the exploration.

Although NDP focusses on pre-birth and early weeks, it's important to constantly remember that it can be applied with older children, teenagers, (Jennings, 2019) and adults if there has been developmental delay or attachment issues or sudden change or loss.

We need to acknowledge NDP's early roots in play, especially attachment and dramatic play. Rather than saying NDP can be applied to address attachment issues, we could consider that attachment 'is the dramatic play'. Then everything that becomes enacted either in performance or in everyday life is connected to the attachment process and can be resolved through an attachment-based intervention. This is a huge, huge statement, and one that needs further development.

The following is an example of an attachment story about two friends who are very different but have found a way to be friends. This example also gives ways in which we could apply the story therapeutically or educationally, or just to enjoy!

Moose and Mouse get Muddy!
It had been raining, and the path by the pine woods was very muddy, and there were big puddles. Moose said, 'My hooves and legs are getting very muddy! If the mud gets any deeper, I shall get stuck and not be able to move!'

'Oh, don't get stuck cos I will get stuck with you', said Mouse, who was in her usual place on the crown of Moose's head, in between his antlers. 'You stay where you are', said Moose, 'And I will get us away from the mud'. Moose continued to walk along the path, a little more slowly now, as the mud was sticking to his hooves. However, Mouse's private thought was that she would love to play with some mud!

The path became a bit drier, and Mouse said to Moose that she wanted to come on the ground for a little time. Moose stopped, and Mouse ran down his shoulder and leg, and she climbed over the mud on his hoof. She ran over to a small puddle that was quite muddy and began to splash in the water. What fun! Moose smiled at his little friend's happiness. He watched as she pressed her feet in the mud and splashed the water with her tail.

'Time for washing, I think', said Moose, 'We both need to get rid of the mud!'

'My feet are so heavy I can hardly walk', said Mouse. Mouse climbed with difficulty onto Moose's back, and he walked slowly forward to a small lake called the Small Water. 'This is where we can get rid of all the mud and play with the water!'

Mouse climbed down again, and she walked to the edge of the Small Water, paddled in the shallows, and splashed the water over her back. The mud soon came off her feet and fur. Moose walked slowly into the water and splashed some water over his back. Then he walked deeper until all his back was covered; he then turned and came back to the shore. He shook himself, and water sprayed everywhere! 'Stop it, Moose, I'm getting drenched', squealed Mouse.

So, Moose and Mouse had fun with the mud and the water, lots of water and lots of messy mud!

Exploration of the Story:

1. Walk with very heavy feet as if they are muddy.
2. Stamp your feet to get rid of the mud, then run around
3. Pretend you are Moose, and you are walking very carefully because Mouse is on your head.
4. Pretend you are Mouse and you are tiny, but you are running very fast!
5. Make a very muddy picture with crayons or finger paints.
6. Draw and colour Moose and Mouse and the water.
7. With a partner, show Moose and Mouse playing in the mud and then splashing in the water.
8. Find an opportunity to play outdoors in water and mud – listen to all the squelchy sounds.[1]

Note

1 Moose and Mouse is a series of books which explore difference and togetherness; they also tackle 'difficult' subjects for children such as 'Going into Hospital' and 'Going to the Airport'. You can also listen to Moose and Mouse stories on YouTube).

And HAVE FUN!

References

Chown, A. (2014) *Play Therapy in the Outdoors*. London: JKP/Hachette.

Courtney, R. (1968) *Play, Drama and Thought*. London: Cassell and Collier Macmillan.

Heathcote, D. and Bolton, G. www.mantleoftheexpert.com

Fox, J. (Ed.) (1987) *The Essential Moreno: Writings on Psychodrama, Group Method and Spontaneity*. New York: Springer.

Holmwood, C. (2023) *Games for Building Relationships in the Early Years*. Buckingham: Hinton House.

Jennings, S. (2011) *Healthy Attachments and Neuro-Dramatic-Play*. London: JKP/Hachette.

Jennings, S. (2018) *Working with Children and Young People Who Self-Harm*. Buckingham: Hinton House.

Jennings, S. (2019) *Working with Attachment Difficulties in Teenagers*. Buckingham: Hinton House.

Jennings, S. (2022) Through the fairy door to the land of stories. In *International Handbook of Therapeutic Stories and Storytelling*, eds. C. Holmwood, S. Jennings and S. Jacksties. London: Routledge.

Jennings, S. (2023) *Managing Social Anxiety in Children and Young People*. London: Routledge.

Slade, P. (1965) *Child Drama and Its Value in Education*. London: Educational Drama Association.

Chapter 2

The performativity in the beginning of life and psychotherapy

Stelios Krasanakis and Eri Argyraki

Working for almost 40 years as a Psychiatrist/Dramatherapist, I come across cases of adults whose majority of difficulties stem from an early age and an unhealthy primary attachment with their mother. This is the reason they choose dramatherapy to reinvent play and, through play, to recover and heal the traumas of childhood. I was, therefore, thrilled when Sue Jennings first talked to me about NDP and gave me her book *Healthy Attachments and Neuro-Dramatic Play* (2011).

I found in it an original conception, an inspiration, and a recognition of play before and after birth. I arranged for the book to be published in Greek, and I was the editor and supervisor of the Greek translation. I became involved with this book because it took me back to the 1980s, on the one hand, to my own relationship with the mother-teacher Sue Jennings, and on the other hand, to dramatherapy itself. This bond went through the phases of Messy Play, Rhythmic Play, Projective Play, and Interactive Play to evolve into Dramatic Play.

During the years that followed, I found out daily that most of our relationships go through these phases, not just the one with the mother. NDP influences, prepares, and shapes the future relationships we will develop in our lives. It is the mould, the matrix, the way we will relate for the rest of our lives. Therefore, NDP is useful for every psychotherapist, not just those working with children. NDP can have a wide use on many different populations, such as clients with dementia (Holmwood, 2021).

Psychotherapy comes to improve, change, and transform this interplay of relationships, our interaction with others, and our ability to give and receive emotions and love. Here, we should mention that in Greece, Dramatherapy and Play therapy are included and recognized as psychotherapies, both by the European Association of Psychotherapies (EAP) and by the Greek section of the EAP.

In this paper, I will first deal with the way the different phases of the NDP and the phases of each psychotherapeutic relationship relate to each other. Then, cases of applying NDP to children will be presented by Eri Argyraki.

DOI: 10.4324/9781003498209-3

In the third part, we will address specific issues like autism, adoption, and surrogacy.

In studying NDP, the psychotherapeutic relationship goes through similar phases. Here, I will first try to follow these parallel trajectories of NDP and psychotherapeutic process, which have a common feature: play, a kind of performativity and ritual that begins with the beginning of life and the beginnings of therapy, moving on to engagement and the process of change.

The therapist-client relationship is a performance for two involving the body, the senses, the brain and movements, sounds, rhythms, narratives, projections and roles, among many interacting roles. As Donald Winnicott noted, "psychotherapy is about two people playing together" (2009, p. 80).

At the beginning of the psychotherapeutic process, there is always a messy play between the therapist and the client. Lots of doubts, anxiety, insecurity, unstructured material, confused memories, and narratives until commitment and trust are established.

This chaotic phase must be endured by the therapist and client, just as the mother and the child must endure it in the NDP before and after childbirth. It must be understood that the building of chaos and its transformation into creative play will come slowly, that it takes time, and that chaos contains the materials of creation just as clay arises from water and soil.

How often, as psychotherapists, have we felt that we are involved in this messy play at the beginning of the psychotherapy process? How much do we try to delineate it within the psychotherapeutic setting, making use of the therapeutic contract? How awkward and nervous do we feel at every first encounter with a new case? How much do we understand the client's nervousness and awkwardness in the first meetings? What do we do to experience and make the most of this situation? Usually, we try to control it, to reduce it, which does not help in utilizing it and in bringing out important therapeutic material for the process to follow.

After we move past the messy phase and the client commits to the therapeutic relationship, the main psychotherapy process begins, where the client's issues, traumas, unresolved relationships, and difficulties with significant others come in. The therapist and the client slowly find a rhythm, and a rhythmic play begins. They find a dance to dance to. They try out different rhythms, accept each other, understand, and build on their therapeutic relationship. Through the alternating rhythms, their relationship becomes interactive, and an interactive play begins between them both on a physical level and on that of transference and countertransference; then we enter the core of the psychotherapeutic process with the central therapeutic demands emerging and being addressed through dramatic play, where the past meets the present, memory meets action and trauma meets its representation. The role system is reconfigured, the senses are brought into the here and now, and play helps mobility against fixation and apathy.

Play as a process, but also as a content, in psychotherapy is something that I have become increasingly interested in and appreciative of over the years of my clinical experience. Representing the play of life in the therapeutic scene is effective and creative. It brings to the foreground, develops, and evolves physicality and the senses, the great stakes of online communication in our online age.

Appreciating Sue Jennings' inspiration, I incorporated the NDP training into the Dramatherapy Institute's "AEON" program so that several drama-therapists could be trained in this new approach.

At the same time, I began supervising the use of NDP with children and adolescents from the first graduates of the NDP specialization programs. One of my supervisees, Eri Argyraki, provides here three case studies that demonstrate the potential and usefulness of NDP techniques.

First case study

George is a 10-year-old boy diagnosed with autism spectrum disorder. His parents' initial request was to reduce the increased tension he was showing at home and in other environments. The first year we worked together, he was in a group of three while having individual sessions with a colleague of mine.

This year, we began individual sessions together. Just before Christmas, we started working on the Neuro Dramatic Play Model.

At first, he played with water without being given any other objects. He used his hands to make sounds with it. From the beginning, there was only one rule. Try not to throw water out of the bowl. It was not completely achieved, but he did his best to follow that rule. We gradually added small objects for him to use in water play as well as liquid colours. The satisfaction on his face was evident. He left with a big smile and was looking forward to our next session.

In our next session, I suggested that he play with flour and water. I put a certain amount of flour in a small bowl and slowly added water so that he could feel the different textures that the flour formed with the addition of water. At one point, he complained that the flour smelled bad, and he could not stand the smell. There are liquid perfumes in the place where the sessions are held, and I suggested that he could add a few drops if he wanted to. He agreed, but it continued to smell bad to him. He then took the initiative and added the hand sanitizer to the mixture. It was a more bearable smell for him. However, he could not stand the texture on his hands for long and asked to wash them. He had soiled himself in several places on his pants. "My grandma will yell at my dad for getting me dirty," he said with a smile, "but I really like getting dirty," he added.

In the following session, upon entering the room, he asked me, "What are we going to play today? Should we play with sand?" In the space where

I work, we have quicksand, so I placed it in a basin, and we began. But before the game started, he asked me to turn down the lights in the room and put on some relaxing music. He began to vigorously dip his hands into the sand and let it fall from above. The sensation seemed to be overwhelming. He had indulged in the whole process with total concentration and attention. Just before this session ended, he asked me to play tic-tac-toe. It was the first time we stood closer to each other without making any move to avoid me.

In the sessions that followed, he sometimes asked to play with water or sand. Other times, when he came in tense and overstimulated, he would lie down on a small couch after turning down the lights and asking to listen to relaxing music. Then, he wanted to hear a story. Either a short story from the ones in the room or a story that he would ask me to improvise. In fact, I was actually telling him stories that I had previously read and thought would make some sense to him. Sometimes, he would ask himself, after the end of the story, to draw something. Sometimes, it was a specific form; sometimes, it was different colours, a form of abstract art.

George gradually learned to use ways to relax when he felt he was tense and overstimulated. He came to our sessions in a better mood, made jokes, and accepted jokes more easily himself. At a follow-up meeting I had with his parents, they reported that they had observed a significant reduction in the tensions he had in the home. He cooperates more easily and is more able to tolerate frustration.

Second case study

John is 5 years old. He is on the autism spectrum. The parents' initial request was to socialize him and to involve him in group work by following instructions and rules. In addition, his parents reported that he had tantrums, especially towards peers.

When we started working with John, he was loudly vocalizing and had various obsessions. After the first two exploratory sessions, we started working on Neuro Dramatic Play. Because of his age, I found it more constructive for him to first make a sensory bag. Inside this bag, I placed different kinds of sponges, legumes in different boxes, bells, scented soaps, toys with different textures (mostly soft), and small musical instruments. In the initial sessions, he explored the different objects in a playful way. He would touch the various beans with joy and enthusiasm on his face and then throw them high in the air, scattering them around the room. With the musical instruments, we often became an excellent orchestra. When I found that he had improved considerably on a sensory level, I gave him a large box of beans and suggested, if he wished, that he take off his socks and put his bare feet into this box. This he found thrilling.

In a subsequent session, I suggested he could use finger paints. He started using his fingertips to draw on a large piece of paper. Gradually, in the same session, he used two or three fingers and finally drew on meter paper with his whole palm. Finally, he put paint on both of his palms and began to rub his hands, smearing them up to his elbows. His joy and excitement were evident on his face.

Another time, I gave John a bowl of water to play in. He would dip his palms into the water and then lift them up sharply to get rained on. At the same time, it was also raining on me, and this caused him a lot of laughter.

For many sessions, he used a variety of sensory stimuli. At this point, I would like to add something that I think is quite important. In the first sessions, I gave John the chance to work through the room's various toys. One of these was a dollhouse with miniature dolls. His initial game was to pick up the dolls and bang them hard on the doll's house, and this was something he enjoyed. After several sessions using the sensory bag and messy play, he played with the dollhouse again. This time, his play was quite different. He took the miniature dolls and moved them around the dollhouse. He did not create a story but very short dialogues between the dolls, like "Hello. How are you?", "I'm fine, how are you?"

In late sessions, when he felt tired, he would ask to lie down on a mattress, and I would read him a story to relax.

John and I continue to this day with our sessions. In a follow-up meeting I had with his parents, they mentioned that he now participates in all the activities in the classroom, has made friends, and asserts what he wants in a polite manner. My own observation is that John has almost stopped sounding, and his obsessions have been curtailed, but they have not completely disappeared.

In our last sessions, he became more positive about playing board games and following instructions and rules. He enters each session with a smile, although in the initial sessions, he had separation anxiety and needed to enter the room with his mother until he felt safe and trusted me.

Third study case

Jim is 11 years old. At 3, he was removed from his parental family and placed in a child protection institution as his biological parents were deemed unfit to take care of him.

Jim lived and grew up in that home until a few months ago, when he was adopted by a couple. He has been living with his new family ever since.

The first meeting was with Jim's parents, who gave me as complete a history of the child as possible. They mentioned their concerns and the difficulties they had to deal with daily. They themselves seemed quite frightened and embarrassed regarding their new role.

The first session with Jim was quite exploratory. He scrutinized the space where we would be holding the sessions and asked to learn about the use of the various toys, materials, etc. He is a caring and kind child who tries anxiously to make the best impression on the adults. He is diagnosed with ADHD. In our first session, he was constantly talking about his mom and dad, his foster parents, and his everyday life with enthusiasm.

In the next session, I suggested that he play with the sand as long as he wanted to do so. At first, it seemed a fun activity for him. He would rush his hands into the sand, catch sand in his hands, and watch it fall from above. He asked me to play with him. For about 30 minutes, we played and laughed. Suddenly, the game stopped abruptly. He took his knees in his arms and put his head between them. There was complete silence in the room. The truth is that at that moment, I lost it. I felt embarrassed. I did not know whether to say something or just endure his silence. Instinctively, I reached out my hand after a few seconds and patted his head. For a few seconds, he tolerated it. Then he pulled away. He signaled me to stop. All I said to him just before the session ended was, "I'm here for whatever you need me for." He nodded his head affirmatively. A shocking moment! One of the most intense moments I have ever experienced.

The next week, Jim came into the room and asked to play with the sand again. This time, he got several objects in which he put sand. As he placed the sand inside the objects, he said, "I placed the sand carefully. Look at me. I am very careful." In subsequent sessions, the sand play continued. In one of the following sessions, he entered the room restlessly. I suggested we do some relaxation. He lay down on the mattress provided in the room and followed my verbal instructions for breathing. When he felt ready, he got up, and I gave him a big piece of paper and fingerpaints. He asked to draw with a paintbrush because he did not want to get his hands dirty. The picture he formed on the paper was of something very scary. A bright red mass in a phallic shape with his name and surname written around it, like a horror movie.

An important point I would like to add here is that Jim's older brother also grew up in the same institution, as it was discovered that his biological parents had sexually abused him.

At the time of writing this chapter, sessions with Jim are ongoing.

Running through the three cases shared by Eri, it is evident that the NDP allows for the remediation at different developmental stages of the deficiencies of previous stages, as it appears in the first two cases with severe sensory problems but also with unsuccessful bereavements as in the third case.

More clearly, we can see:

- How the therapeutic play starts.
- How it evolves through the interaction between therapist and client.
- How silences are used in the process.
- How trust and the therapeutic relationship are established.

We observe the therapeutic effect of storytelling in dramatic play (Krasanakis, 2022; Schubert, 2020) and the function of the doll's house as a space for projecting everyday life. In addition, the way the children approach materials such as water, sand, colours, pulses, and musical instruments is particularly revealing. How careful they are, how dirty they are, how wasteful they are, and how much they follow the rules (Goren-Bar, 2021).

In the first case study, NDP highlights the senses of smell, hearing, and touch and the problems encountered in these in autism (Seymour, 2017; Baron-Cohen, 2008). We also observe the interaction of the bodies through the game of tic-tac-toe.

In the second case study, the sensory bag proves to be very helpful. Working with creative supervision (Lahad, 2000), I wondered about the usefulness of a similar sensory bag in any psychotherapeutic approach. What does this metaphorical bag contain? Words, phrases, images, artwork, body movements or postures, a gaze. What is the metaphor's role that proves to be particularly fruitful and motivating?

In the third case study, we find the function of silence in the psychotherapeutic process and its mediation in the therapist-client relationship. Once again, we acknowledge the importance of art therapies in dealing with difficult and traumatic situations such as child abuse (Cattanach, 1992–2008) but also the therapist's embarrassment when such issues come up in therapy. Embarrassment also seems to exist on the part of parents in adoption cases. NDP comes to heal the difficulties of such a transition. In recent years, there has been much discussion about cases where there is a surrogate mother in homosexual or heterosexual couples. In these cases, the NDP comes to offer useful services to ensure continuity before and after childbirth, with different persons being asked to play the role of the mother in many cases, regardless of gender. This is a topic that needs special discussion in the future, and the NDP may play a leading role in this development.

To conclude, we note that as shown in the mentioned cases, what works therapeutically in NDP is freedom with limits that help to sort out the chaos: A goal that is set in every psychotherapeutic approach regardless of the therapeutic tools used.

References

Baron-Cohen, S. (2008) *Autism and Asperger Syndrome*. Oxford: Oxford University Press.

Cattanach, A. (1992–2008) *Play Therapy with Abused Children*. London: Jessika Kingsley Publishers.

Goren-Bar, A. (2021) *Ta mystika tis ekfrastikis therapeias meso technon kai coaching* [The Secrets of Expressive Arts Therapy and Coaching]. Athens: Kastaniotis Editions.

Holmwood, C. (2021) Older people, dementia and neuro-dramatic-play: A personal and theoretical drama therapy perspective. *Drama Therapy Review*, Volume 7 Number 1(Issue Older Adults), 61–75, April. https://doi.org/10.1386/dtr_00061_1. Accessed 27.8.2024.

Jennings, S. (2011) *Healthy Attachments and Neuro-Dramatic-Play*. London: Jessica Kinglsey Publishers.

Krasanakis, S. (2022) Myth – drama – narrative – performance. In *Routledge International Handbook of Therapeutic Stories and Storytelling*, eds. Holmwood, C., Jennings, S. and Jacksties, S. London: Routledge Editions.

Lahad, M. (2000) *Creative Supervision: The Use of Arts Methods in Supervision and Self-Supervision*. London: Jessica Kinglsey Publishers.

Schubert, M. (2020) *Itan kapote. Dramatotherapeia kai Afigisi* [Once Upon a Time: Dramatherapy and Storytelling], ed. Krasanakis, S. Athens: Parisianou Editions.

Seymour, A. (2017) *Dramatherapy and Autism*. London: Routledge Editions.

Winnicott, D. (2009) *To paidi, to pehnidi kai i pragmatikotita* [Play and Reality], trans. Kostopoulos, G. Athens: Kastaniotis Editions.

Section 2

NDP children and young adulthood

Chapter 3

Neurodivergence and Neuro-Dramatic-Play (NDP) in children and young people

Sue Jennings

Definitions

Neurodivergent: If we are neurodivergent, then our responses to any given situation may be individual. Neurodivergence comes in many shapes and sizes, and it is believed that all neurodivergent brains are unique.

Neurotypical: If we are neurotypical, we are considered to have 'normal' brain function; our brains function more or less the same as other people's brains, and our abilities are considered 'typical'.

Neuro-Dramatic-Play (NDP): NDP is the essential means of applying attachment-based play with children and young people, including those who are neurodivergent.

However, we need to remember that we use NDP as a major part of children's attachment development, initially commencing during pregnancy and continuing until 6 or 7 years old, play in all its forms is central. It may need to be repeated where there are attachment struggles, infant illness, rejection, or neurodivergence. It then repeats itself throughout the rest of life, albeit in various forms and with age-appropriate content.

This focussed form of play may be with individuals or groups. It may take place in school, a therapy centre, or a home. It can be built into an educational programme, or therapeutic interventions or be part of a firm parenting approach.

Neuro-Dramatic Play includes water play, rhythmic play, messy play, dramatic play and performative play. They are not sequential, but they can occur in parallel or are weaving through a child's early experience. They often reflect the child's feelings of needing safety or seeking adventure. For example, rhythmic play, which starts with the heartbeats, creates repetition, predictability, and, therefore, safety. In contrast, messy play is the opposite; it is unpredictable, and the outcome is unknown, so it creates a sense of exploration and helps to foster curiosity.

Some children may get wilder and wilder in their messy play, which adults often think is perverse and, therefore, should be stopped or even

DOI: 10.4324/9781003498209-5

banned. However, looking at the bigger picture, the child may well have been through a series of foster homes and schools, each one different from the last, and have no sense of attachment or belonging. An appropriate means of expressing their feelings is by making a mess, which is what their lives feel like: it may be through the wrecking of the playroom, throwing objects such as bricks, scattering the sand from the sand play tray, pouring all the paints out and mixing them together, squirting all the shaving foam until it is empty. One hopes that adults will take note of this communication and, therefore, do something about the situation. Wrecking the playroom is a different type of messy play than the exploring of mess that most children will go through. When a child first starts in therapy or education, the rules can be explained: yes, messy play is fine, but keep it on this table or in this corner.

For example, teenagers may baulk at the idea of Messy Play but will often readily participate in cooking activities. And we will make sure that they are suitably messy! Nevertheless, when working with older teenagers and young adults who had lived in institutions in Romania, I was warned by staff not to do messy play as the participants would feel it was childish. However, they felt differently and pleaded for us to include messy play! The results can be seen on YouTube in the film 'A Journey to Playfulness and Creativity'. They were all delighted to submerge their hands in flour and water and model various objects, including houses, cars, and flowers.

The application of NDP

It is often assumed that NDP is a form of therapy and that it may be a variation or a different model of Play Therapy. It is, first and foremost, an attachment-play intervention that can be applied in clinical, educational, social, or family settings. It can be applied as a therapeutic intervention, especially in play and the arts therapies with trained therapists.

However, it is equally valuable when teachers and teaching assistants build NDP into the curriculum or nursery activities. It can be spontaneously evoked in a situation that needs a change of gear.

For example:

Aiming for WHEW!
NDP practitioner David was teaching in a school that had a high pro-portion of neurodivergent children. One child, Robert, arrived at school, removed his socks and shoes, and started to run a circuit round the school: upstairs, across the landing, down the other side, and along the hall. And then round again!

A teacher and an assistant decided to pursue him, which, of course, Robert found very exciting, and ran even faster. David sat at the bottom of the staircase, and when Robert next came by, said to him, 'Hey, Robert, have you ever looked at your feet?' The child stopped in his tracks, and immediately, David began the game of 'This little piggy went to market!' This led to 'Round and round the garden' and other finger and hand games. Robert, who was now fully engaged with David, gradually sat down and visibly calmed. It was as if his whole body was able to go – Whew!

Some fun breathing exercises followed, blowing some bubbles that David just happened to have in his bag and doing the five-finger breathing exercise (see later on), and then Robert was ready to return to his classroom.

Children and young people who are neurodivergent need additional support with their Neuro-Dramatic Play and additional variations in application in order to support their individual learning patterns.

The importance of safety

A meltdown is a response to a feeling of danger: the individual does not feel safe and is overwhelmed by their feelings (not the same as a tantrum, which is a power-based reaction!). If we remember the F responses to a feeling of danger or as a result of past trauma, we can consider techniques to either anticipate a particular response, or address it once it is happening. The original F words were Flight, Fight, Freeze, to which Flock and Fawn have recently been added. I now include Fabling, where a child tells an impossible story in order to delay or avoid a dangerous event.

Safe and Secure: all people need to feel safe and secure, not just babies and small children. Children and young people who are neurodivergent have additional safety needs which need to be managed carefully. New routines, spaces, teachers, or expectations can all provoke anxiety in those who are neurodivergent and may result in meltdowns. Disruptions to usual routines or unexpected people, such as a temporary teacher, can create a lack of safety. This can alert the reactive part of the brain, which does not give pause for thought, red flags are up, and the response may well be a total withdrawal and shutting down, or a loud and physical powerhouse, often in a public place. The individual child is overwhelmed by their feelings and is unable to manage them and take control.

The following strategies may work:

- Remove the child from the place where it is all taking place
- Rub the back to soothe and contain
- Reassure the child they are safe and secure
- Quietly repeat a familiar song or chant
- Rock slowly, maybe back-to-back

The preceding actions are all rhythmic and will usually induce a feeling of calm. It is worth discovering the sensory responses that the child enjoys, maybe an essential oil (lavender and rosemary are very soothing; a Gipsy traditional remedy for child nightmares is to hang a bunch of fresh rosemary near the cot); moving objects to watch and track; special food that is associated with pleasure and calm; music, songs, and other sounds OR if sound is overwhelming, noise cancelling head phones; depending on the setting, if touch is allowed, then what sort of touch? Holding and rocking? Swaying back-to-back? Hand massage? Reassuring arm round the shoulders? All to be negotiated.

There are simple games that can be played in order to stay in close proximity, such as:

- Sit on the floor, roll a large ball between each other
- Stand up and bounce a ball to each other
- Roll yourself up in a blanket and see if you can roll across the floor
- Curl up inside the play tent or safe box and rest
- Play hide and seek
- Place an ice cube inside a cup; shake and feel it, and drink the cold water as it melts

These responses are not from the neo-cortex but are reactive and intuitive, often initiated by the amygdala part of the brain (which alerts us to fear) and then continued through other parts of the limbic system (including emotions and memories).

ADHD is one of the most frequently occurring manifestations of neurodivergent, and it includes sub-categories of:

Hyperactivity – the person who interrupts or talks non-stop or without thinking first; they also fidget or need to move around and seem restless. They are considered adventurous.

Daydreaming – the person who wanders off and cannot concentrate; they are considered inattentive but are often missed out as they are not drawing attention to themselves and may be considered withdrawn or shy.

However, we also have the 'hyperactive daydreamer' – the person who combines both the first two sub-categories at various times.

> Attention deficit hyperactivity disorder (ADHD) affects the functions of the brain that control emotions, concentration, organisational skills, memory, motivation and more. These functions impact behaviour. Despite its name, not all people with ADHD lack attention or are hyperactive – it's more complex than that!
>
> (Gooding, 2023, p. 40)

It is important that we accept ADHD within the spectrum of neurodivergency rather than seeing it as a deficit or disability. Then we can plan a programme of 'enhancement' rather than believing we need to 'remedy'. We can draw upon all the NDP skills when working with ADHD.

Neuro-dramatic-play in more detail

Neuro – enhances our brain activity and safety.
Dramatic – encourages interactive, creative communication.
Play – emphasises artistic playfulness for attachment and curiosity.

First stage – Nurture and Nesting (NaN) (conception – 6/12 months)
(Touching, rocking, skin-to-skin contact, water and messy play, bubbles, baby games, peekaboo, dancing on lap, clapping hands, singing, pulling faces, imitation, performative play, beginning of 'let's pretend')

Second stage – Embodiment-Projection-Role (EPR) (from birth – 6 years)
(Flour and water play, shaving foam, complex messy play, movement and music, dancing; drawing, painting, clay, construction, puzzles; puppets, dolls house scenes, enactment, storytelling, performance)

Third stage – Theatre of Resilience (ToR) (6 years onwards)
(Voice and movement, performance, improvisation, social theatre, enactment, mime, texts, performance, design, extended puppet play, props, masks, costume, lighting, effects)

How does a neurodivergent child benefit from NDP? (ADHD)

- Establishes a safe place and a safe base
- Encourages feelings of nurture and nesting
- Provides gradual experience of messy and rhythmic play
- Enhances lived experience
- Emphasises the normality of diversity!

These NDP stages will promote the development of attachment, empathy, and resilience, which in turn will reinforce:

- Emotional intelligence
- Cognitive development
- Social relationships
- Spiritual awareness

These NDP stages are formative in all child development and underpin growth and maturation throughout life. Children, young people, and adults who are neurodivergent may need to repeat these stages or undertake them at a slower pace. There must always be choices in the activities with no 'right way' to play, simply the setting of boundaries.

NDP theory draws on 'Attachment' (Jennings, 1990), 'Ritual and Risk' (Jennings, 1990), 'Polyvagel Theory' (Porges, 2021), and neuroaesthetic understanding of the impact of the arts on human emotions (Magsamen and Ross, 2023), NDP and Attachment (Jennings, 2023).

Water Play: infants spend nine months of gestation in the dark, in slimy, warm water. There is a continuation of the water in the womb and external exciting water play, whether in the bath or the garden! Bubble play can be an important part of water play. Pouring and splashing, blowing, and flicking are all important water play activities. Water play has been known to stop bed-wetting.

Rhythmic Play: infants respond to the heartbeats of themselves and their carer. Heartbeats are initially experienced during pregnancy and then through skin-to-skin contact. Heartbeats are reassuring and later transform into singing, clapping, music, and rituals of all sorts. An infant held on the left shoulder of the adult will immediately calm as they sense the adult's heartbeat.

Messy Play: the 'O dear' of NDP as parents visualise uncontrolled mess in their home and over their child! Messy play leads somewhere, eventually, to some kind of form – a picture or model or collage. Messy play encourages curiosity and adventure. It is the beginning of science and maths! Later, it is central to cooking, experiments, engineering, and many forms of art, including sculpting and painting.

Dramatic Play (or Interactive Play): imitative playing starts from birth when babies copy expressions and sounds that are close by, and this becomes interactive when parents echo the child's sounds. Dramatic play transforms our capacity to have flexible roles in life and work and also enables us to empathise with the roles of other people. At about six months, we notice that there is a change from imitative play to 'let's pretend' play. Very importantly, it evolves into drama, theatre-art, and performance.

Performative Play: infant and adult are performing for each other and gaining smiles and recognition, rewards, and affirmation. Initially at birth, it is imitative as they take it in turns to mimic each other; during 'peek-a-boo', an infant is learning 'let's pretend', a crucial skill in development.

Please Note: we need to be sure that the infant understands 'let's pretend' and that not all neurodivergent children are able to grasp this. It takes time, explanation, and practice, and even then, it needs checking out.

Neuro-Dramatic-Play: techniques and methods are adapted appropriately to the ages of the participants so that NDP is relevant to all age groups. Although many people apply Neuro-Dramatic-Play during pregnancy and early years, there is an increasing number of people who see its importance with young adults, older people, and those people with dementia. The same applies to people who are neurodiverse; NDP is applicable across the age range to the 'whole of life' experience.

Neuro-Dramatic-Play as a method for pregnancy and early years cannot be over-emphasised, and its application with children and young people who are neurodivergent is a real breakthrough in therapy, education, and parenting. It is particularly relevant for the following people:

- Foster parents and adoptive parents
- Parents and grandparents
- Teachers and SENCOS
- Adults working with neurodiverse children and young people
- Play therapists and arts therapists
- Child support workers
- All those working for the emotional well-being of neurodivergent children and young people

This chapter has mainly focussed on the application of NDP with children and young people who are neurodivergent, especially those who are diagnosed with ADHD. I know there will be readers who will say that they have tried many of the techniques, and 'they don't work'. It will be said by those people who are coping with violent meltdowns, extreme dissociation, and constant destruction. I want to invite people to re-think when they have absorbed more of this book and consider the ideas as part of a process rather than a collection of techniques. If we can follow through our observations of displays of sound and actions and consider the larger picture, we may discover another way. We can remind ourselves that all behaviour is communication.

We have focussed mainly on various forms of play, many of them involving sensory experience, and I would like to finish with a reminder of the importance of storytelling, both the story the child needs to hear as well as the story they need to hear. The following story has been written specifically for children who are neurodivergent; it is a single thread story that refers to NDP activities. There are also some ideas for working with the story.

Please also see the Moose and Mouse story at the end of Chapter One.

Moose and Mouse play Pooh sticks

One day, Moose and Mouse were near their 'little patch of forest' they called home, trying to decide what to do for the day. Moose was quite happy to sit and think for a while. Mouse was feeling very restless and was on top of Moose's head one minute, then rushing down to the ground the next, and now she was collecting stones. 'Can you never stay still?' sighed Moose, 'Even for a few moments?'

Mouse paused for a little while in her personal little game of putting stones next to each other, from little to large, so she had a row of graded stones. 'You forget, my big friend, that all my running around discovers things, I'm the explorer', she said in her determined voice; her 'I know what I am talking about voice!'

'A long, long time ago', she continued, 'Long, long ago, there were Mice who travelled to lots of places to discover new countries and foods and things. Mice are always moving!'

She started singing one of her songs:

'Moving mice, moving mouse
Lots of fun when you leave your house'.

'All right', said Moose, 'Let's go together to the Small River, and I will show you something that I think is new for you'. Excitedly, Mouse scrambled onto Moose's head, and they set off towards the winding water. Soon, they came to a bridge that went across the Small River, and Moose stopped. 'Down you get', he said to Mouse, 'You must find a stick and bring it to the bridge'.

Mouse knew that Moose would explain the purpose of the stick and scurried off to find one. She joined Moose on the bridge, and he said, 'When I knock twice with my hoof, we both drop our sticks into the river and then see when they float under the bridge. Let's try it out'.

They both stood with their sticks. Moose knocked twice, and then they dropped them over the side. They crossed to the other side and waited to see their sticks. 'There they are', squeaked Mouse, 'Both together – look! Let's do it again!' So, Moose and Mouse played Pooh Sticks over and over again. Moose was delighted that Mouse was so happy, running backwards and forwards, fetching and dropping sticks. Something new, that's what she enjoyed!

'Time to go back', said Moose, 'Back to our little patch of forest we call home'.

'It's been a wonderful day', said Mouse, 'Who would have thought that I could find something new, just nearby to home. Thank you Moose'.

Moose was very thoughtful on the journey home; maybe he was beginning to understand Mouse and her moving around.

Activities to explore the story:

1. Play a game of chase, and you are all mice.
2. Slowly walk round the room as Moose.
3. Draw a map showing the small river and the bridge.
4. Discuss the differences between Moose and Mouse.
5. Maybe an adult will take you to a bridge to play Pooh sticks.

So, like Moose, maybe we are beginning to understand neurodivergency and all that 'moving around'. Always time for new discoveries, excitement, and new play and games. Yet we all need to return to our safe place, our rhythm, routine, and predictability. Maybe it is that neurodivergent people need it that bit more.[1]

Note

1 NDP Training: if you are interested in pursuing Neuro-Dramatic-Play please consider studying for our Diploma which can be followed online 'live' or as Self-Guide study. There are also regular Webinars, short courses, and my Substack Newsletter has regular information, therapeutic stories and techniques.

There are more Mouse and Mouse stories on YouTube.

Suggested Reading

Gooding, L. (2023) *Wonderfully Wired Brains: An Introduction to the World of Neurodiversity*. London: Dorling Kindersley.

Holmwood, C. (2023) *Games for Building Secure Relationships in the Early Years*. Buckingham: Hinton House/Loggerhead.

Jennings, S. (1990) *Dramatherapy with Families and Groups*. London: Jessica Kingsley/Hachette.

Jennings, S. (2011) *Healthy Attachments and Neuro-Dramatic-Play*. London: Jessica Kingsley/Hachette.

Jennings, S. (2019a) *Working with Attachment Difficulties in Teenagers*. Buckingham: Hinton House/Loggerhead.

Jennings, S. (2019b) *Working with Attachment Difficulties in School-Age Children*. Buckingham: Hinton House/Loggerhead.

Jennings, S. (2023) *Managing Social Anxiety in Children and Young People*. Abingdon: Routledge.

Magsamen, S. and Ross, I. (2023) *Your Brain on Art: How the Arts Transform Us*. Edinburgh: Canongate Books.

Porges, S. (2021) *Polyvagal Safety: Attachment, Communication, Self-Regulation*. New York: W.W. Norton.

All inquiries: admin@ndpltd.org. www.ndpltd.org

Chapter 4

Using Neuro Dramatic Play (NDP) in schools with children and young people post-Covid-19, developing positive attachments and good mental health

Clive Holmwood

Introduction

For children to be happy and content, they require certain conditions which are essential for them to thrive. It could be argued that the conditions fit into two broad areas: firstly, social and emotional, what happens outside the body, and secondly, biological, what happens inside the body, how their bodies physically process such things as stress and anxiety at a biological level. It is the age-old notion of nature versus nurture (Honeycutt, 2019). I would argue it is a more nuanced approach to thinking that is required post-Covid; it is not simply one versus the other, but how each affects the other and vice versa.

This chapter will consider the issues that have affected babies, children and young people, both pre-school and those of school age, since the world-wide pandemic of 2020, which, due to Covid-19, led to the greatest shut-down of society ever in the modern world. We will consider the importance of children developing into happy and content young people and how the use of Neuro Dramatic Play (NDP) assists in supporting the underlying issues that impact a child's overall health and wellbeing in this post-Covid era.

We must also note the impact that the 21st century, in general, has upon the physical, emotional and mental health of children. Apart from Covid, the impact of social media and the internet (and the cyberbullying and unhealthy online influencers) as well as mobile phones, the climate crisis, wars and worldwide political instability, various financial crises, the rise in costs of heating and food (which leads to parental stress) which can lead to societal and political restricted funding within health and social care. This all presents children and young people in the modern age with a range of potential anxieties that no previous generation has ever had to manage in quite the same way.

There has been a huge rise in mental health issues in the UK and around the world *before* the worldwide pandemic. According to the British National Health Service, in a report published in November 2023, there was 'a rise in rates of probable mental disorders between 2017 and 2020, prevalence continued at similar levels in all age groups between 2022 and 2023'.[1] The same

DOI: 10.4324/9781003498209-6

report suggests that about 20.3% of children aged between 8 and 16 have a probable mental health disorder.[2] Services are overstretched, and CAMHS (Child and Adolescent Mental Health Services in the UK) often only manage to support some of those children diagnosed with more serious mental health issues and those who also meet the NHS thresholds for support. This does not seem to affect younger people alone. Another recent BBC survey has shown that one-quarter of people aged 18–34 never answer the phone.[3] Seventy percent of the same age group prefer texting rather than making or answering a phone call. It seems quite ironic that we have more mobile phones than ever, more effective technology and more ways to communicate, but most young adults don't like to make an actual telephone call.[4] So, if adults are struggling to have direct phone conversations, what will children today be like when they achieve adulthood? In addition, worried and anxious parents who are concerned about losing their jobs and paying the bills may unintentionally have a detrimental impact on their children's physical, psychological and mental health due to their stress in the home environment. How can we manage these 21st-century challenges in both an economical and effective way? Might NDP be one approach that can support those from 0 to 18 to feel happier, more content and have greater overall resilience to weather the future storms that are sure to come in this unpredictable and unstable world?

What is NDP

Neuro dramatic play – NDP was developed by one of the leading dramatherapy and play therapy pioneers, Sue Jennings. She started working as an auxiliary nurse using drama in a psychiatric hospital at the age of 18. Jennings not only set up one of the very first trainings in dramatherapy, she also co-founded the British Association of Dramatherapists.[5] Jennings was very influenced by the work of Peter Slade, whom I consider to be the great grandfather of dramatherapy, and was the first person to coin the phrase as one word – dramatherapy. Slade was an actor and drama teacher who experimented with drama with children, many of whom had a range of physical and mental health problems. From the 1920s onwards, Slade devised his own 'Child Drama', which he later published (Slade, 1954). Slade further developed his ideas in a lecture describing that drama falls into three main categories '(a) conscious and intended therapy, (b) constructive education, and (c) prevention' (1958, p. 5). This echoes, to some extent, some of Jennings' own philosophy in relation to NDP. Sadly, much of Slade's work is no longer taught or considered today. However, this cross-over between child drama as a form of education and dramatherapy is central to our thinking about NDP, which is primarily a therapeutic non-therapy alternative.

One of Jennings' very first books, *Remedial Drama* (1978), showed Jennings' early interest in the uses of drama with children with all kinds of disabilities. She eventually gained a PhD in Anthropology after spending time in the Malaysian Jungle and studying how the 'Senoi Temiars' brought up and looked after their own children (1995). Jennings referred to EPR (Embodiment, Project and Role), a specific part of NDP in the early 1990s in *Play Therapy with Children* (Jennings, 1993) and the original *Handbook of Dramatherapy* (Jennings, 1994). All this led to Jenning's landmark work on NDP *Healthy Attachments and Neuro Dramatic Play* (2011), in which she laid out in significant detail what NDP was.

NDP broadly is a paradigm which brings together brain development, neuroscience, attachment and play and dramatherapy. It integrates a range of arts-based practices, including play, drama, art, music, sound, rhythm and messy play, including sand and water play. It can broadly be defined in three areas: NDP conception to birth (the relationship between the mother and unborn child), EPR – Embodiment Projection and Role from birth to seven years, the developmental stage of the child and Theatre of Resilience (ToR) working with older children and teenagers. The foundation of NDP is about the attachment between the mother and unborn child, the duality of this special relationship as the child develops in the womb, especially from the first trimester onwards when the unborn child begins to sense the world outside of them. Embodiment, Projection and Role (EPR) are considered when working with children from birth to about 7 years. The 'E' refers to Embodiment from birth to about 13 months. This is when the baby is trying to work out who and what they are, what is me and not me, for example. An adult will carefully support the baby to feel safe and comfortable using sensory and messy play. The 'P', Projection from about 13 months to 3 years, refers to the child projecting out from themselves to the world around them and manipulating things, small toys, finger paints, puppets, building blocks etc., music and rhythm, the very early development of story by the age of 3. The 'R' phase, Role, refers to more complex developments of playing characters and telling stories by the age of 7.[6] The third part Theatre of Resilience (ToR), contains much of what is described previously, but there is a greater emphasis on the idea of re-staging, allowing children, especially those 12+ or thereabouts, to revisit some of their earlier childhood experiences through such things as social and therapeutic theatre. This is especially important when used by therapists in a therapy context for children dealing with early childhood trauma. From 8 to 18, there is also greater use of dance, drama storytelling and theatre.

The notions of preventative and therapeutic described by Jennings are also two phrases used by Slade (1954) to describe his philosophy. Showing connections between these two innovators and their work. In a similar way to how Slade used his original child drama in his work, NDP is, first and foremost, therapeutic and not therapy. It is used by many practitioners, including social workers, teachers and teaching assistants and adoptive and birth parents. The primary focus is on using the creative processes as a way of supporting and developing attachments and regulating emotions. NDP is also widely used by registered play, art and dramatherapists within their clinical practice to lead towards elements of understanding and therapeutic healing within a clinical context.

NDP with children – two examples from practice

I have been heavily influenced by Jennings NDP paradigm throughout my professional dramatherapy career of 30 years. I completed the NDP diploma in 2017. As part of this work, I carried out two mini research projects.

Firstly, working in a Junior School, I used the idea of a hero's journey (Campbell, 1993) in relation to NDP (Holmwood, 2021b). The emphasis here was working on the notion of storytelling and play to support children's overall emotional wellbeing. This was not therapy, but therapeutic and the research occurred before the pandemic. I began that chapter by describing the children and 'the obvious nervousness (that) was etched onto their young faces as they stood in front of me pensively in the middle school hall' (Holmwood, 2021b, p. 167). Working with 11 young people over nine weeks, who had all been carefully chosen by school staff, as many of them had challenges relating to their overall self-confidence and self-esteem.

Using 'Sam', a puppet with large eyes and a squeaky mouth, as a central attachment figure, we created a journey together that we were to go on; the group drew an image of a fantastical island that had dangers such as a vortex and poisonous flowers, swamps and good and evil monsters; but it also leads eventually to treasure after a boat trip to get to the island so that we could

Figure 4.1 Sam

Source: From Holmwood, C. (2021) Neuro-Dramatic Play and a hero's journey: a play -based approach in a UK junior school in Jennings, S. Holmwood, C. (Eds) Routledge International Handbook of Play, Therapeutic Play and Play Therapy. London: Routledge. Pg. 173

carry out the adventure. We made and created props and rudimentary costumes out of cardboard, using scissors and glue. One or two children were to take the lead at certain parts of the adventure – everyone – even the shyest, would have a chance to be in charge for a short part of the journey. However, this was after seven weeks of carefully layering each session to build confidence and key skills. The most important part of this process is that we *never* rehearsed the journey, and it wasn't *performed* in front of an audience. That, for some of the children, would have been too much. On week eight, the day of our 'performance', we performed our story to ourselves and one or two witnesses for the very first time, with only a loose structure of what was going to happen, with Sam the puppet (supported by me) leading the way.

What the children had not been told was that at the end of the story, there was literally a treasure chest with golden (chocolate) coins and a stress ball each to take away. In conclusion, I stated, 'The adventure had been a great success. One of the quiet girls who had played the captain on the boat declared afterwards that she had found her voice' (Holmwood, 2021b, p. 175). The puppet 'Sam' had worked as an attachment figure for the whole group. On my return to do a follow-up a few weeks later, the children were silent until I brought Sam back into the room; the room then erupted with laughter and conversation as they reminisced on their performance.

This experience appeared to be incredibly important for this small group of children as they gained confidence, trusted an important attachment figure

Figure 4.2 Annie placing the figures in the puddle of water

Source: From Holmwood, C. (2022) We're going on a bear Hunt, neuro-dramatic play, multi-sensory informed storytelling approaches to working with children under five in Holmwood, C. Jennings, S Jackties, S. (Eds) *Routledge International Handbook of Therapeutic Stories and Storytelling* pg. 116

(Sam/me) as well as each other, and learnt to manage their own anxieties and developed the art of improvisation, having never performed their show to themselves until the day of their 'performance'. In conclusion, one girl said, 'I will not be quiet as I was. Be brave and not scared' (Holmwood, 2021b, p. 176).

A second example from my own practice relates to working on a one-to-one basis with a pre-school-aged child in her own home (Holmwood, 2022a). This, again, was pre-Covid. 'Annie', a happy, content, bright and advanced child for her age of just 20 months, worked with me using Micheal Rosen's *We're Going on a Bear Hunt*, a classic children's tale that is perfect for story-based EPR work. I introduced different elements each week, beginning with a simple telling of the story, then adding the small wooden figures, including parents, the children, the dog and, of course – the scary bear! – for Annie to manipulate the figures.

The addition of a dry and then wet sand tray, alongside my subsequent telling of the stories over several weeks, allowed little Annie to move from embodiment into the projection phase of EPR and even into the beginnings of role with Annie manipulating the figures in the wet sand to eventually tell her own story through movement and action and her own early developing language, when she chose to use it, to show a multi-sensory approach to storytelling. Annie was not a child in need and did not have any special educational needs, but she 'was able to make full use of all the possibilities that were given to her in relation to the experiences we shared' (Holmwood, 2022a, p. 117). This could be clearly seen as preventative, offering a healthy child valuable creative multi-sensory experiences to support their overall development. What was most fascinating was talking to her parents some 18 months after the project; they informed me that, despite the massive time between our work (for little Annie), they still heard her occasionally say, when out and about, 'But I'm not scared', one of the classic lines from Rosin's book that I would repeat each time I told the story. The ideas and concepts had somehow stuck in her head, and she could repeat them and hopefully believe them all that time later.

The impact of Covid-19

The world as we knew it ceased to exist in the UK on 20 March 2020, when the UK government closed schools, colleges, universities, ports and airports, and many non-essential workplaces for an unknown period; no one was allowed to travel. I wrote at the time:

> The skies above my house are clear of all the vapour trails of aeroplanes in the spring sky; almost all air travel has ceased. Streets are eerily quiet, with almost no cars on the road, especially in the evenings when the eerie silence is deafening.
>
> (Holmwood, 2022b, p. 7)

Teaching in my own institution switched instantly to being online, almost instantly, meaning all our connections were virtual and we all had to get used to technology such as Zoom and Teams, which had been there for some years, which few of us had really embraced. Teaching that normally required face-to-face interaction had to be rethought. Ways we had worked for years changed. This was a challenge for healthy and resourceful people. For others, it might exasperate health issues or worries about work, employment and money. We were only allowed out for essential things such as dog walking, for short distances locally each day, still having to keep one meter away from everyone we passed. The one glorious thing I saw was the street art drawn by children at the top of their driveways saying such things as 'God Bless the NHS' (National Health Service in the UK), with rainbows of colour. This, in one sense, was the problem; if they had driveways or gardens, this was at least a blessing but the limit of their world. For children in flats or apartments, then their access to the outside world for the best part of 18 months was severely, if not completely, restricted. Only a tiny minority of children were allowed to go to school, usually the children of 'essential workers' such as health care professionals who worked in the NHS. Many remained at home in sometimes cramped and difficult living conditions with parents who were not working due to the pandemic or their own physical and mental health-related issues.

The impact of Covid on children's education and social development

The world was thrown a curve ball that none of us saw coming, and few of us were prepared for, not even our own governments. It took almost two years, and after a second lockdown (in the UK), before society slowly began to return to normal, but a new normal, where the world could take stock of the psychological as well as physical impact that Covid had had. Mental health issues had been, as we have seen already, on the rise. According to Waite et al. (2021), research carried out early during one month of full lockdown showed a 10% increase in emotional symptoms, a 20% increase in hyperactivity/inattention and a 35% increase in conduct.[7] It also noted that there was an 'increased risk of mental health difficulties, such as those in low-income households and those with SEN/ND, exhibiting elevated symptoms (and caseness) at both assessments' (p. 7). They also noted that 'among preadolescent children there were greater increases in conduct symptoms and emotional, conduct and hyperactivity/inattention among girls (more) than boys' (Waite et al., 2021). The impact in the early months of Covid, therefore, showed what we all feared: the impact on the emotional and social wellbeing of children, noting that girls struggled more in certain circumstances. This is quite apart from the actual physical impact of Covid; according to the Kings Fund (UK), 'Overall'.[8]

According to Lester and Michealson, 'School absences have risen following the COVID-19 pandemic and persistent absenteeism remains high in primary and secondary schools in England compared with pre-pandemic levels' (2024, p. 1). They describe this as a 'perfect storm' coinciding with a rise in anxiety-based school avoidance or Emotionally Based School Avoidance (EBSA). They state it 'does not constitute a psychiatric diagnosis in its own right but often co-occurs with diagnoses of anxiety and/or mood disorders' (2024). They go on to describe the impact it has on 1–5 percent of the school population and that it impacts not only school attendance, learning in the classroom, and impact on children's outcomes at Key Stage 2 but a possible increased possibility of mental health problems.

According to the BBC,[9] a study looking at the effect of the pandemic on babies led by Professors Nicola Botting and Lucy Henry at London's City University[10] is examining the impact of Covid on babies who are now entering primary school. Initial research has suggested there is a major impact on the speech and language of some children. The isolation also led to a lack of face-to-face appointments for early years children with a wide range of health care professionals, which also has the potential to impact their overall health and development. As Professor Botting states,

> We know that the first five years of life are crucial for the development of children's talking and thinking skills, influenced by early experiences . . . One of the most important effects of lockdown could have been on early social interactions between babies, parents and other adults.[11]

I have experienced this anecdotally over the last few years working in schools. Teachers have told me on numerous occasions how some children are beginning school at four or five years old with poor language skills, an inability to use knives and forks and some not even potty trained, which schools have had to assist with.

All of this comes as no surprise as we know a healthy child's development is completely reliant on the attachment between the child and their parental figures and a range of other adults that exert hopefully positive influences over a young child's life (Jennings, 2011). This also includes the importance of children mixing and playing with other children of their own age who are not related to them. Positive brain stimulation is needed to fire the connections and synapsis in the brain of the infant for them to develop a whole host of natural positive responses, including movement and language skills, which leads to developing and managing emotions and more complex relationships with others as they get older (Holmwood, 2023). NDP, EPR and ToR are there to support children and young people to do this using a range of creative processes. Creativity itself is also an essential part of a child's development; creativity and play are the central ways that children, especially in the early years, learn (Owen, 2021).

How can NDP and EPR be used in school post-Covid

In a previous article for the Autism Parenting Magazine (Holmwood, 2021a), I hypothesised the possibility of an anxiety isolation loop (Holmwood, 2021a, p. 46). Although the article was referring to children with autism, we could draw some comparisons here with young children struggling with the after effects of Covid in a school-based environment. I shall return to this shortly. Firstly, a creative arts and NDP approach do not rely on the spoken word being at the centre of the work, in the same way that some young children may be struggling to find the words to express how they are feeling because either, due to Covid, they have not developed sufficient language skills or because emotionally they are unable to express in word form how they are feeling. The younger a child is, the less they can rely on language as their primary form of communication. Play becomes the central way for them to communicate. I also stated, 'Not every child necessarily needs an intervention from an art or play therapist. Neuro-dramatic play (NDP) is a form of developmental play, not a therapy in itself' (Holmwood, 2021a, p. 44). Secondly, I described how children with a diagnosis of autism can, at times, feel quite isolated and might struggle and have poorer attachments (Bowlby, 1988) at home and in school due to the nature of their autism, sometimes not allowing them to make close connections with others, thus leading to potential anxiety as they don't always feel safe as the world around them is unpredictable; children with autism generally want predictability and safety. Even more so since Covid.

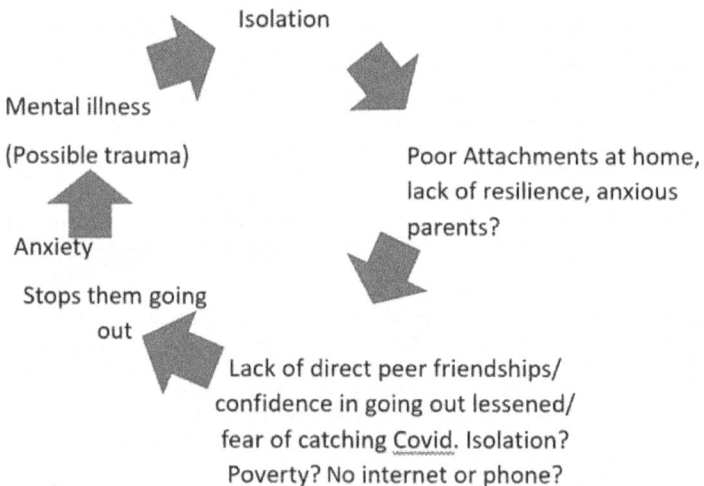

Figure 4.3 Anxiety Loop

Source: From *Autism* magazine, 2021

These characteristics between autistic children and children with attachment difficulties are similar but have different root causes; nonetheless, they may all at times struggle to form relationships with others, and, at times, it is difficult to tell the difference between children who might be autistic and children who may have attachment difficulties (Davidson et al., 2022). It could be argued that one of the chief aims of NDP is the development of attachment through creative approaches:

> The use of creative arts and embodied physical play-based experiences may also allow some children and young people to begin to come to terms with how they might be feeling through approaches that don't rely on verbal communication.
>
> (Holmwood, 2021a, p. 46)

I would therefore argue that this is the case here for children struggling in school post-Covid, regardless of their possible diagnosis.[12] Not only does it offer embodied play, the language of younger children, but EPR offers a structure and prism through which to support children both individually and in groups using a range of activities that have the potential to combat slower development, isolation and potential anxiety. Fostering both peer and family attachments (where family members are involved), which unchecked may lead to more serious issues, such as depression or other serious mental health problems that may require even more specialised intervention. Therefore, staff trained in a NDP approach within a school setting could offer a cost-effective solution to supporting children.[13]

The two examples from my own work earlier (Holmwood, 2021b, 2022a) and my additional work (Holmwood, 2023) offer some possible strategies through which this work could be carried out. In the group approach (Holmwood, 2021b) I described a basic framework over eight weeks in which the children used a developmental framework to work towards a performance/presentation which they performed for themselves. Over the weeks, I developed their cooperation skills, working together, creative skills, developing a story, developing their fine motor skills through art making and creativity by developing essential props and costumes (such as cutting cardboard props with scissors). Finally, they took a leap of faith by performing a semi-improvised show just for themselves and allowing each child to take the lead at a specific stage of the story. Improvising in the playground is something they do all the time; the difference here was working with adults who gently guided the story, that they had developed together, with 'Sam' the puppet (held by me) as the central attachment figure holding the whole piece together. Though this piece of work was pre-Covid the central idea of its potential post-Covid remains the same. Developing emotional, developmental, psychological and physical skills through a semi-improvised creative performance, thus developing their peer and trusted adult attachments. As discussed earlier, this seemed to work for these children, and similar ideas could be developed in schools for children in need now post-Covid.

In a similar vein, my one-to-one piece of work (Holmwood, 2022a, see also Holmwood, 2023) offers a similar idea. Working on a one-to-one basis using a story and layering over several sessions, beginning with the adult telling the story, and using embodied, projective and role-based activities, we layer the experience for the child as their own skills and confidence develop. From just listening to a story to using, for example, sand and water, to them telling or creating their own version of the story. They are unwittingly developing an attachment with a *key* adult, learning new language skills, embodying through touch and physical objects to self-actualisation and having the confidence to develop their own stories. The individual child may then have the skills and confidence to join a group doing a similar project where they can develop their peer attachments even further.

In both the examples explored and discussed earlier in this chapter, the key has been about the adult carefully layering each session or part of the work so that the child or children take a small step each time, and once one minor success has been achieved, they can move on to the next. A skilled practitioner will also know if they need to stay in the same place or take a step back with the child so they can, for example, with flexibility, remain in embodied work for a longer period.

However it is used, and by whomever, it is the careful layering and knowledge of the overall NDP framework that gives the practitioner the key skills they need to support both individuals and groups to develop self-esteem, confidence and positive attachment in the post-Covid era.

Conclusion

Covid-19 has presented the World with a range of complex medical and psychological problems. The effective vaccines that were developed at lightning speed offered many people in the world instant protection from most of the effects of the virus, apart from those suffering from long Covid, many of whom caught it during the early days before the vaccines were available. What the vaccine couldn't do is protect society from both the fear of the virus and the impact that the virus has had upon the two-year period when children and their families were locked away from each other and their school, and face-to-face education, which is a central part to their development. At a time when we had seen rising mental health in young people, prior to Covid, it has, as discussed earlier, created a perfect storm of both post-Covid anxiety and stress partly due to lack of peer attachments coupled with the rise in general mental health conditions in children, or possibly visa verse. Covid has possibly exacerbated some underlying mental health issues and worsened them for some children. Sadly, no vaccine can cure this. I believe EPR has a real place to play in schools in supporting younger children's overall and general mental health as well as beginning to deal with after effects of the developmental gaps caused in young children by Covid. This is because NDP considers both the developmental journey all children need in a creative and distanced way using a variety of creative arts-based activities, focussed on child, peer and adult attachments, in a layered way with an overall holistic approach. This provides practitioners of all backgrounds, including parents, adoptive parents and other family members using this approach with some of the keys to unlock the potential in all the children and young people they work and live with.

Notes

1 https://www.england.nhs.uk/2023/11/one-in-five-children-and-young-people-had-a-probable-mental-disorder-in-2023/
2 https://www.england.nhs.uk/2023/11/one-in-five-children-and-young-people-had-a-probable-mental-disorder-in-2023/
3 https://www.bbc.co.uk/news/articles/crgklk3p70yo. Accessed 26.8.2024
4 https://www.bbc.co.uk/news/articles/crgklk3p70yo
5 Personal conversation with Sue Jennings over several years.
6 I have also looked at this in more detail in Holmwood 2023 where I offer practical activities for these age groups.
7 https://acamh.onlinelibrary.wiley.com/doi/epdf/10.1111/jcv2.12009.   Accessed 22.9.2024
8 https://www.kingsfund.org.uk/insight-and-analysis/long-reads/deaths-covid-19. Accessed 22.9.2024
9 https://www.bbc.com/news/articles/c39kry9j3rno. Accessed 6.10.2024
10 https://www.city.ac.uk/news-and-events/news/2024/may/impact-covid-childrens-language-cognitive-skills. Accessed 6.10.2024
11 https://www.city.ac.uk/news-and-events/news/2024/may/impact-covid-childrens-language-cognitive-skills. Accessed 6.10.2024
12 Of course, there are difficult complexities between attachment disorder and autism in children, but we do not have the space here to discuss these in detail.
13 Again, differentiating between specific diagnosis such has autism or attachment disorder might well be out of the remit of some professionals, but EPR in this context potentially with the support and advice of other health care professionals offers a way forward regardless of diagnosis.

References

Bowlby, J. (1988) *A Secure Base – Clinical Applications of Attachment Theory*. London: Routledge.
Campbell, J. (1993) *The Hero with a Thousand Faces*. London: Fontana Press.
Davidson, C., Moran, H. and Minnis, H. (2022) Autism and attachment disorders – how do we tell the difference? *BJPsych Advances*, 28(6), 371–380. https://doi.org/10.1192/bja.2022.2
Holmwood, C. (2021a) *Autism Parenting Magazine Issue*, 129, 44–47, November.
Holmwood, C. (2021b) Neuro dramatic play and a hero's journey – a play based approach in a UK primary school. In *Routledge International Handbook of Play, Therapeutic Play and Play Therapy*, eds. Jennings, S. and Holmwood, C. London: Routledge, 167–177.

Holmwood, C. (2022a) I'm going on a bear hunt', neuro-dramatic play, multi-sensory informed, storytelling approaches to working with children under five. In *Routledge International Handbook of Stories and Therapeutic Storytelling*, eds. Jennings, S. Holmwood, C. and Jacksties, S. London: Routledge.

Holmwood, C. (2022b) Making a dramatic story out of a crisis – a response to Covid-19: A dramatic perspective. In *The Routledge International Handbook of Stories and Therapeutic Storytelling*, eds. Jennings, S., Holmwood, C. and Jacksties, S. London: Routledge.

Holmwood, C. (2023) *Games for Building Secure Relationships in the Early Years*. UK: Hinton House.

Honeycutt, H. (2019) Nature and nurture as an enduring tension in the history of psychology. In *Oxford Research Encyclopaedia of Psychology*. Oxford University Press, September 30. https://oxfordre.com/psychology/view/10.1093/acrefore/9780190236557.001.0001/acrefore-9780190236557-e-518. Accessed 18.10.2024.

Jennings, S. (1978) *Remedial Drama*. London: A&C Black Theatre Arts Books.

Jennings, S. (1993) *Play Therapy with Children: A Practitioners Guide*. Oxford: Blackwell Scientific.

Jennings, S. (1994) The theatre of healing: Metaphor and in the healing process. In *The Handbook of Dramatherapy*, eds. Jennings, S., Cattanach, A., Mitchell, S., Chesner, A. and Meldrum, B. London: Routledge.

Jennings, S. (1995) *Theatre Ritual & Transformation the Senoi Temiars*. London: Routledge.

Jennings, S. (2011) *Healthy Attachments and Neuro-Dramatic-Play*. London: Jessica Kingsley Publishers.

Lester, K. J. and Michelson, D. (2024) Perfect storm: Emotionally based school avoidance in the post-COVID-19 pandemic context. *BMJ Mental Health*, 27, e300944. Accessed 18.10.2024.

Owen, K. (2021) *Play in the Early Years*. London: Routledge.

Slade, P. (1954) *Child Drama*. London: University of London Press.

Slade, P. (1958, repr. 2003) *Dramatherapy as an Aid to Becoming a Person, Guild of Pastoral Psychology, Guild Lecture No. 103*. London: Guild of Pastoral Psychology.

Waite, P., Pearcey, S., Shum, A., Raw, J. A. L., Patalay, P. and Creswell, C. (2021) How did the mental health symptoms of children and adolescents change over early lockdown during the COVID-19 pandemic in the UK? *JCPP Advances*, 1, e12009. https://doi.org/10.1111/jcv2.12009. Accessed 18.10.2024.

Chapter 5

I fit in by not being myself

Ber Carroll

Profile of the group

Creating relational safety was paramount when I was approached to offer a Wellbeing Programme to a small group of six teenage boys aged 13–14 years of age who were marginalised and found school and friendships challenging. According to Carroll and O'Herlihy (2023) relational safety is essential for authentic expression and emotional wellbeing. They also argue that safety in the relationship is only fully created when true listening, compassion, and understanding are present in order to support the needs of each child or adolescent. The transition into secondary school seemed to have accentuated their behaviours, inducing the escalation in anxiety they were experiencing. These challenges manifested in behaviours that were increasingly viewed as unacceptable by the adults who were looking after them at home and at school. Their behaviours included anger issues, interruptions, defiance, lack of emotional regulation, social anxiety, and lack of empathy. Two of them were assessed as being neurodivergent; one came from a separated family, while the other three had a range of factors which affected their sense of self-worth and self-esteem, such as unsafe relationships and inconsistent care.

Having considered all the preceding, I did not need to ponder long on what approach I would use as my experience as a Play Therapist and Sensory Attachment Practitioner taught me that using Neuro Dramatic Play (Jennings, 2011) would provide a nurturing, safe space, which these teenagers most needed to feel secure. Neuro Dramatic Play considers the nurturing attachment process and provides activities through Sensory Play, Messy Play, Rhythmic Play, Embodiment, Projection, and Role. Neuro Dramatic Play has a profound effect on brain growth, the chemical balance of the body, and the healthy attachment between parents and infants. It influences not only the emotional security but the social development as well. Patterns are established through NDP in the brain that lead to the capacity to regulate and establish tolerance of emotions. *Resilience is built up through NDP and prevents children from being overwhelmed by challenges and changing situations.* It is evident that NDP would support the aspects of growth and development that were required by these adolescents.

DOI: 10.4324/9781003498209-7

Self as soother

Sue Jennings' Nesting Principle reminds us that the adult in care of the child creates a nesting environment in which they can act as their "soother" until such time as they can soothe themselves. As the most important adults in a child's life are their parents or guardians, I met with the parents for two sessions to educate them on NDP and how to apply NDP principles in order to create a nurturing nest in the home, to gain any information about their teenagers that I might need to know and to offer support via email throughout the six weeks and I also met them for a follow-up session when we had finished.

I was very conscious that I, too, would be their soother from the first moment I met with these teenagers, and so I would meet each individual where they are at, which means that while I will have an overall plan to work from, I will be open, ready and willing to move with and adapt to the needs of the group and individuals at any time.

The welcome

Bearing in mind our face-heart connection or Social Engagement System of Porges (Dana, 2020, p. 7) through which we send signals of welcome and signals of warning and through which the other searches for these signals, I welcomed each of them as they entered the room with a smile, a gentle approach of a handshake or high five, soft smiling eye contact and kind tone of voice thus creating a nurturing nest. Even at that, some chose to ignore me as they made for something that caught their eye in the room, and I was under no illusion as to how unimportant I was at that moment! One boy (to whom I will give the pseudonym John), whose body language signified anxiety and fear, entered with head down, hands folded in front of him and stood rooted to the spot a little away from me. When I suggested that he choose a bean bag, he declined and sat at a little table on his own while the others chose a bean bag each. I passed around a sensory basket with squidgy toys and play dough as a means of settling down into our circle of care together for six sessions.

When we understand that the teen who is socially isolating is unconsciously protecting himself from further hurt or rejection, we will be able to support him by turning the barriers of trying to **make** him engage with others into a bridge of understanding, listening, nurturing, and waiting until he is ready to cross that bridge to a less threatening social life. Then and only then can we say, *"I get you"*, and he will know we do.

Our puppet Kari

When we settled, I introduced myself and reassured the teenagers that there was no right or wrong while in this group. I was cognisant of the fact that most teenagers are still bound by the rules of parents, teachers, coaches, and leaders as they long to move toward peer support and ultimate identity and independence and in an effort not to apply more rules, with the help of Kari our teenage puppet we set out what a nurturing nest of care would look like for the coming weeks. As the voice of the teen, Kari expressed how he would like to create a Nurturing Nest of Care for their Physical Care, Emotional Care, Behavioural Care, and Social Care. Sue Jennings correctly states, "Whereas a child or an adult will talk *to* dolls, they will talk *through* a puppet" (Jennings, 2008, p. 6), and the puppet allows a distance to be created for expressing what might not be expressed otherwise, after all, it is the puppet who is saying it!

For his nest of physical care, Kari expressed,

This is what I call physical care where I will feel physically safe in your presence and in the presence of the group. Will you respect my need for space and time? Will your touch be gentle and warm and comforting and only when I am ready for it. Will your ears hear what I am saying and not saying, and will you listen with your heart?

At this point, I invited them to choose a puppet, and for their puppet to respond as they wished and to give examples of times when they felt safe or when this did not happen. It was clear from their responses that physical boundaries and safety were an issue, particularly in the schoolyard and with siblings. I would revisit this over the sessions.

For the Emotional Nurturing Nest of Care, Kari asked that *he would be accepted for who he is and that he would be given the space to explore, explain and express his feelings without judgement, and that the group would try to understand that his feelings are neither right nor wrong and always have a purpose and that he would be helped to live the best version of himself with all our support.* Again, I invited them to use their puppets to give an example of a time when they felt good and a time when they felt challenged, as in, sad, angry, or lonely. I listened and held what I heard in my heart.

Kari *admitted that there were a lot of times when he behaved in ways that got him into trouble, and so in his Behaviour Nurturing Nest of Care, he asked that they would try to understand that when he is behaving in a challenging way what he is really saying is that he is feeling challenged himself and just can't express it in real words.*

In his Social Nest of Care, Kari *expressed a wish that he be included in the games and activities and that, at times, he might not wish to be included and that his wish would be respected.* Their puppets told their stories of exclusion, being called names, and sometimes laughed at.

With the help of Kari and the puppets, we set out what a nurturing nest of care would look like, and by integrating creative interactive NDP activities, the issues that had arisen from this activity would be addressed over the coming weeks

My identity

This **projection** exercise bears in mind the *identity v role confusion* of the teenage years according to the psychosocial development of Erikson. I hoped that we could start by establishing identity through the names which were given to them at birth, to name positive qualities that would help raise their self-esteem, and to encourage a discussion around positive aspects of the individuals and the group. They were each given a small whiteboard for their laps and whiteboard markers of different colours and invited to write their names and draw or write two things about themselves and one affirming fact. They all came up with at least two items that they could identify with, such as sport, art, cars, tractors, animals, and, for some, they needed support to identify an affirming fact about themselves. This activity allowed the teens to speak in a group without feeling judged. It also facilitated self-reflection and promoted self-affirmation. None of them knew the meaning of their names, so I suggested that they ask their parents for the next session. John sat looking on.

I extended this exercise in the second session to make a Group Identity picture using arts and crafts materials, which encouraged the sharing of space, ideas, and acceptance of another's opinions, and they called themselves "The Screamagers". That says it all!

John put his mark on this poster, however small, an indication perhaps of how small he feels in the eyes of the world. It was the beginning of the risky journey of emergence for him through the safety of Neuro Dramatic Play.

Embodiment

A quote from Sue Jennings lays down the importance of embodiment when she states, "The body self is the first step towards the growth of identity", and she continues, "once children have a strong body self, they are able to develop a balanced sense of body image" (Jennings, 2005, p. 36). On the first day, I invited the group to do some embodiment exercises based on a story of Oseo and the Giant, a Native American Story (Jennings, 2021, pp. 20–21), which tells how a small boy is helped to overcome fear and adversity by the caring responses of a mother bird and a squirrel when he journeys through the forest alone. This story helped to demonstrate the nurturing nest of care that we had begun to establish in our group on this first day.

They were invited to move as if stepping quietly through a forest. To stop-look-listen to the sounds they hear, like a slithering snake, to reach high up to a tree for a bird's nest, and to swim across a river with something on their back.

Every challenge is an opportunity

This activity proved to be the most challenging as they elbowed each other, physical space was intruded upon, and the reactions were from irritation to anger. It was a great opportunity to remind them about Kari's Nurturing nest of care and how they need to always consider others. It also offered an opportunity to mentor them on how to express their needs in a tangible way instead of reacting. For example, starting with an "I" message, "I need my space to move around without anyone bumping against me". This is a clear message expressing the needs of the individual without the "you" message of blame. Each week saw an improvement in body/spatial awareness within the group, an understanding of the need for space, and an acknowledgement of having intruded in another's space, with the offering of an apology-progress indeed. True to NDP, *already, patterns were being established through NDP in the brain that led to the capacity to regulate and establish a tolerance of emotions.*

However, John found this too much and retreated to his bean bag. I kept connected with him through Bruce Perry's Prescription of Dosing and Spacing model of offering small manageable connections of comfort, consistently, three to four times an hour. These took the form of a nod, a smile, or a thumbs up (The Neurosequential Model Network Neurosequential.com BDPerry.com Handouts https://www.bdperry.com/handouts).

Educate to regulate

The second week saw a follow-up with the nesting and breathing principle of Sue Jennings (Jennings, 2023, p. 21). Breathing exercises have been scientifically proven to help regulate the nervous system by activating the vagus nerve (Porges, 2011, p. 249). With gentle music playing softly in the background, I invited them to take part in these exercises. Focused breathing on its own can be difficult for some young people with challenges, and the use of straws, bubbles, and windmills proved very helpful in this regard.

Balloons to attune

Balloons were used to attune to their feelings to demonstrate what it might be like to fill ourselves up with emotions and either keep them inside by suppressing them or explode them through angry outbursts. They blew all their anxiety and anger into a balloon, then let the balloons go and let the feeling go with it. This produced laughs and sheer joy as the balloons flew around the room, letting the air out. I remarked that letting our feelings go could produce such an outcome as they would feel lighter and better as a result. They then blew feelings into the balloons, knotted them, and threw them to one another as a way of sharing their feelings with one another and the positive effect that can have on us. I wondered what would happen if we were to suppress our feelings rather than express them in a safe way. "**Explode**" was the resounding reply, and with that, the urge to pop the balloons to mimic that explosion was palpable! Checking in with everyone first that the loud noises were ok, being sensitive to loud noises, John protected himself by covering up on a bean bag and putting his hands over his ears embryonic-like, and in his own time, he popped his balloon much to the cheers of the group.

This could be viewed as the resilience that is built up through NDP and that prevents children from being overwhelmed by challenges and changing situations.

Stories in the sand

"Often the hands will solve a mystery that the intellect has struggled with in vain". Carl Jung (Sreechinth, 2018)

Teenagers who are presenting with challenges in life may have experienced ruptures in relationships, inconsistency, and unpredictability in care, and for that reason, they need to experience structure, sequence, and resolution. This is precisely what stories do. Stories are important because they have a beginning, middle, and end; one thing follows another.

Stories have rhythm, structure, and resolution, and they endorse values and positive attitudes (Jennings, 2021, p. 11).

For four of the sessions, we had story time, and they were invited to take a throw/blanket and wrap themselves up on a bean bag as if it were a nest and to listen to the story. I used sand trays and miniatures to relate the story and to help bring the characters to life. Being able to see the story unfold before their eyes helped keep them interested and focused, which was necessary for the profile of teenagers who were present.

The first story, stated previously, was about Oseo and the Giant. When the story ended, I invited them to come individually to the table and create their own story. One neurodivergent boy jumped up and, with great enthusiasm, created a very short story about a boy who got lost and a bird who carried him home. A story filled with hope, the theme of which continued to be woven into the following sessions. For a few minutes, they all came to the table and had fun with the miniatures as a group, which allowed the quieter ones to take part without feeling exposed.

I advanced the follow-up activities in other sessions by giving each teenager their own sand tray and a large selection of miniatures and nature to choose from to create their own stories. The calming effects of sand was evident as they worked quietly with their individual trays, some moving the sand with their fingers and making patterns and mounds before placing any objects into it. They were also given small containers of water to use. It is an activity that encompasses sensory play, messy play, projection, and role play through the sharing of their story with the group using the miniatures and objects chosen. This signifies the end of Projection Play and a transition to Role play as play is becoming more dramatised through the use of stories. The calmness with which they interacted after the sand stories is indicative of how NDP *influences not only emotional security but social development as well*. It was during the sand activities that John really began to emerge as he used the miniatures, his symbols in his sand tray, to tell his story.

Jennings suggests that we learn about ourselves and others by taking on the role of other

A story written by this writer to address the themes of raising self-awareness, self-worth, and self-esteem and related in the sand inspired the teenagers to construct a boat that they could fit into for a journey to find their own treasure (*Cori-It Takes a Village*). After much deliberation, discussion, and differences of opinions, they decided to turn a table upside down and wrap the fabric around the legs using masking tape to secure it. With a nudge from me to make it a cosy nest, they placed a throw into it, and they took on roles from captain to sailors to Cori, sailing to three different islands marked out with throws on the ground to find their treasure. A metaphor, no doubt, of their own journeys to finding their own treasure, namely their true self. This Dramatic Play, or the R stage, is the culmination of the primary EPR stages.

"Is a joy to be hidden and a disaster not to be found". D.W. Winnicott

During the fifth session, the main activity was mask making with a discussion about how we all wear many different makes to hide what we truly feel. It was revealing to watch as each young person made their own version of their outward self on one side and their true inner self on the inside of the mask. Without prompting from me, they put on their masks and began to Role play how they were feeling. This indicated an initiative born out of a growing confidence and trust in the group. It was with his mask on that John revealed, "I fit in by not being myself". He found a way to reveal his truth and to mirror to us that it is by hiding we protect ourselves from further hurt. He had found safety in the group, and I felt at that moment that our aim to create safety within a nurturing nest had truly been fulfilled for everyone.

Final session: Wrap up with a rap. Rhythm with bongos, tambourines, shakers, bells, body percussion, and voices!

> *The nest is the best*
> *For having a rest*
> *Fun and laughs*
> *For certain, for sure*
> *Popping balloons*
> *Playing in the sand*
> *The nest is the best*
> *The best in the land.*

Where science meets soul

Throughout the sessions, I witnessed the sympathetic nervous system and the parasympathetic dorsal vagus nerve being activated by shutting down and acting out communication. I drew on the science of the Neurosequential Development of the brain of Bruce Perry, using his bottom-up processing to calm the senses, mine first, to regulate before I could proceed to relate and reason. Perry's Prescription model of offering small meaningful doses of engagement by giving time and space when they were needed ensured that the teens felt included and held even at a distance, recalling the primary circle of attachment of Sue Jennings where the mother holds the child in her unconscious (Jennings, 2011, p. 14). This relationship and regulation were aided by Porges' Social Engagement theory of face-heart connection, giving cues of safety for those receiving them. While science is necessary to prove facts, the integration of Neuro Dramatic Play to bring the theories to life is essential.

The approaches used by the theorists mentioned throughout are met with the heart and soul, which is Neuro Dramatic Play. When woven into the fabric of relationships at all ages and stages by meeting individuals where they are at by allowing them to emerge into their truth without pressure to change, NDP provides the opportunity to create relational safety for the true expression of self and, therefore, *NDP* may be used to provide solutions to the challenges of human beings and may offer preventative intervention in place of possible diagnosis and labelling.

References

Carroll, B. and O'Herlihy, D. (2023) *Most Common Challenging Behaviours: Understanding them as Creative Solutions and Finding Possible Interventions*. Points to Ponder. Self-Published.

Dana, D. (2020) *Polyvagal Flipchart: Understanding the Science of Safety* (1st ed.). Norton and Co.

Jennings, S. (2005) *Creative Play with Children at Risk* (1st ed.). Speechmark.

Jennings, S. (2008) *Creative Puppetry with Children and Adults* (1st ed.). London: Speechmark.

Jennings, S. (2011) *Healthy Attachments Neuro-Dramatic-Play*. London: Routledge.

Jennings, S. (2021) *Dancing into Life: A Practical NDP Course Book of Theory, Techniques, Ideas and Stories* (1st ed.). London: Routledge.

Jennings, S. (2023) *Managing Social Anxiety in Children and Young People*. Oxon: Routledge.

Perry, B. *The Neurosequential Model Network Neurosequential.com, BDPerry.com Handouts*. https://www.bdperry.com/handouts

Porges, S. (2011) *The Polyvagal Theory: Neurophysiological Foundations of Emotions Attachment Communication Self-Regulation* (1st ed.). Norton.

Sreechinth, C. (2018) *Musings of Carl Jung*. USA: UB Tech.

Chapter 6

The expanded EPR framework and Theatre of Resilience for young adults – from theatre to the coming-of-age ritual in response to social trauma

Shiu Hei Larry Ng

Background: waiting for a revised developmental horizon for young adult care

The experience and characterization of young adulthood are notably responsive to socio-political-economic contexts (Arnett, 2015; Blatterer, 2007). In today's globalized socio-political-economic landscape, young adults confront intricate challenges and crises shaped by diverse impacts across developed and developing countries (Danziger and Ratner, 2010; Hong and Chung, 2022). These factors significantly influence the developmental pathways of young adults and give rise to distinctive mental health needs (Kito and Ueno, 2016; Mahmoud et al., 2012).

Regrettably, to date, the distinctive needs of young adults have been disregarded within most social welfare systems, particularly when compared with other populations such as children, elders, minority groups, or patients diagnosed with specific conditions, while this population also often refrain from seeking mental health services, partly due to the inadequacy in addressing their specific needs (Cadigan et al., 2019; Singh and Tuomainen, 2015). Simultaneously, these needs remain inadequately addressed within prevailing academic discourses, which are still largely constrained by paradigms originating from fields like developmental psychology and social sciences, established over half a century ago (Arnett, 2018; Côté, 2014; Nelson, 2021; Robinson, 2015; Tello-Navarro et al., 2024). Meanwhile, critiques from 'progressive' thoughts, including postmodern, poststructuralist, postcolonial theories, critical psychology, etc., challenge conventional theories of human development for their perceived linear distortions and totalizing tendencies (Bronfenbrenner et al., 1986; Burman, 2016; Morss, 2013; von Tetzchner, 2023). These critiques prompt not just a few researchers and practitioners in mental health and helping professions to eschew developmental perspectives entirely.

Correspondingly, many contemporary theories in psychotherapy exhibit reluctance to revise established developmental frameworks or rebuild new ones, preferring to disengage from allegiance to any specific developmental

DOI: 10.4324/9781003498209-8

theory. In clinical practice, these dynamics pose challenges – either the developmental dimension is further marginalized or even totally ignored, or outdated developmental frameworks may be indiscriminately integrated under the guise of eclecticism during application. In response to the mental health concerns of young adults, a demographic insufficiently addressed in prevailing developmental frameworks, such approaches become incapable of effectively meeting the specific needs of this population due to a lack of understanding and theoretical differentiation of this developmental stage.

Specifically, within the realm of dramatherapy, the major theories, predominantly based on humanistic or postmodern traditions (e.g., Johnson and Emunah, 2020; Gaines and Butler, 2016; Landy, 2008; Jones, 2007), often lack a clear foundation in specific developmental theories or any inherent theory regarding life stages/course. Consequently, these theories tend to lack specificity in developmental aspects and how drama/theatre relates to human development, leading practitioners to often employ external developmental theories from the psychodynamic tradition or statistical and experimental psychology in an eclectic manner. This amalgamation raises concerns about the theoretical validity of merging theories from occasionally or implicitly incompatible paradigms with conflicting principles. Moreover, on a practical level, it introduces challenges regarding the selection of dramatic/theatrical interventions guided by these major theories in dramatherapy, which may result in interventions lacking developmental specificity or appearing developmentally arbitrary.

Among the major theories in dramatherapy, Dr. Sue Jennings' approach and its revising and expanding model, articulated since the 90s (Jennings, 1992, 1997), stand out as rare examples that are *developmentally grounded and specific*. For the past decade, its original prototype, the Embodiment-Projection-Role (EPR) developmental model, which theorizes the parallel process of child development and the evolution of play and dramatic form as structures of both experience and imagination from birth to age 7, has been enriched by Dr. Jennings' new theory of Neuro-Dramatic-Play (NDP) (Jennings, 2011). NDP focuses on another crucial axis in all stages of human development, particularly emphasizing its base on nurturing, which includes containment, care, and attachment as essential aspects, highlighting play as constitutive to health and security. NDP represents not merely an expansion but fundamentally a transformation of EPR.

This breakthrough and transformation also revitalizes another significant aspect of Dr. Jennings' comprehensive framework, previously named 'Theatre of Healing' (ToH) (Jennings, 1994, 1995), which emphasizes the linkage between ritual and theatre, underscoring the significance of ritual for transformation. This concept is now revised into 'Theatre of Life (ToL)' for preventive purposes and 'Theatre of Resilience (ToR)' for therapeutic interventions (Jennings, 2011), highlighting the relationship between different forms of theatre (and arts) and health/well-being. While often receiving less attention than the EPR model, ToH/ToR/ToL holds considerable potential for further enrichment and sophistication, providing detailed developmental stages from age 8 onwards. Furthermore, Dr. Jennings' approach is *not only developmental but also integrative*, synthesizing perspectives from multiple disciplines such as theatre art, psychology, anthropology, and other social sciences. Thus, this renewed framework, comprising NDP, EPR, and ToH/ToR/ToL, offers a promising direction for research and practice that can be continuously expanded and revised to address the specific characteristics and needs of later developmental stages beyond childhood and adolescence, because these later stages, including young adulthood (the focus of this chapter), are notably and directly influenced by ever-changing socio-political-economic conditions.

This chapter aims to demonstrate the particular significance and relevance of Dr. Jennings' framework to young adults in addressing their specific needs.

The shifted understanding/expectation on 'adulthood' and 'young adulthood'

'Adulthood' for human beings is never merely a biological concept; it is socio-politically constructed and highly responsive to societal changes. The transformation from a manufacturing economy to a knowledge economy, alongside significant social-cultural shifts like the technological, sexual, women's, and youth movements (Arnett et al., 2014), has notably prolonged the transition from adolescence into adulthood remarkably (Arnett et al., 2014; Côté, 2014; Furstenberg, 2008). Consequently, some scholars have proposed adding "emerging adulthood" (approximately 18–25 or 18–29) as a distinct stage of human development (Arnett et al., 2014; Robinson, 2015). Moreover, the landscape of adulthood, largely centered around work, has become significantly complicated under the liquidized, fragmented, and precarious conditions of the economy and employment created by the extreme evolution of capitalism into the form of globalized neoliberalism. This complexity fosters a pervasive and constant sense of *insecurity* and *disorientation*. Such complications further differentiate the stages within adulthood (Arnett, 2015; Robinson, 2015), surpassing the classical division of life stages, like the three-stage division of adulthood into early/young adulthood, middle adulthood, and late adulthood (Erikson, 1978). Nowadays, despite the lack of universal consensus among scholars and professionals, "young adulthood" is often narrowed down to describe a period largely overlapping with "emerging adulthood" and/or covering the early period when people leave school (usually tertiary education) and enter society (Furlong, 2009).

While many discussions about this period of life centered around Arnett's emerging adulthood theory (Tello-Navarro et al., 2024), this theory was formulated prior to the global financial crisis and many other international political chaos/conflicts in the last 15 years. Therefore, it sometimes exhibits a positive or optimistic tone, particularly reflected in "possibilities/optimism" as one of the five distinct features of this developmental stage. However, the current global scenario is marked by greater complexity and adversity. Many emerging adults and young adults, instead of actively exploring life possibilities in a romantic sense, are passively forced to struggle among and jump around different fragmented options predetermined by a much larger structure beyond their control, to the extent that numerous individuals cannot even imagine any alternatives achievable by their own agency. This passivity is not solely due to the economic system. The increasing centralization of power and top-down domination of the political regime in both democratic and non-democratic countries worldwide, under the excuse of collective benefit and national security, charged with politically constructed and manipulated discourses of crisis and emergency, also instill a strong sense of frustration and passivity in the new generation of emerging and young adults, manifested in feelings of *powerlessness* and *hopelessness*.

Crisis experienced by young adults: fragmentation, disorientation, detachment

The experiences of the author as a dramatherapist (as well as a theatre practitioner and university instructor) working with young adults in Hong Kong resonate with these observations. The situation in Hong Kong can be viewed as a condensed case of hybridity, wherein various major international forces intersect. It is a highly developed cosmopolitan city characterized by extreme capitalism, with a colonial history and undergoing radical political changes in the last decades brought about by a non-democratic top-down regime that is rising internationally regarding its economic influences. The young adults of this generation in Hong Kong were born around the time of the handover from the UK to China. They experienced the SARS outbreak during their childhood and the global financial crisis during adolescence. Additionally, they lived through three significant political protests in 2012, 2014, and 2019, all marked by high participation from teenagers and young adults, in response to the increasing top-down control from a completely non-democratic government. Furthermore, they endured the enactment of the national security law with absolute power in 2020, under which no protests challenging the government pressure are possible, and three years of the COVID pandemic. This generation has also been profoundly influenced by the rise of social media, internet culture, and other digital revolutions, such as A.I. technology in recent years.

Still, one can argue that, for most residents, Hong Kong remains a well-off area, far from explicit emergencies and material shortages compared to other places such as Myanmar, Iran, Israel/Palestine, Sudan, Ukraine, etc. However, as the author observes, young adults in Hong Kong seem to be generally overwhelmed by manifold social trauma, characterized by a strong sense of *powerlessness* and *hopelessness* (as evidenced by the significant increase in emigration in recent years), and largely torn apart by the *fragmentation* and *uncertainty* under capitalism, as reflected in the pervasive mood of *disorientation* and *detachment* in many aspects of life, echoing research findings like Ng et al. (2024). Given that Hong Kong embodies a compressed hybrid of numerous global forces, certain prominent characteristics of these young adults, as observed in clinical settings, may also hold relevance for care practices also in other places. However, the proportion and combination of these features may vary depending on the local context.

In summarizing the author's clinical experiences, the challenges encountered by emerging and young adults in Hong Kong manifest in several distinct features. First, they grapple with a series of *contradictions*. For instance, this generation of youngsters still experiences the pressure of a highly competitive society with a huge population in a small city, while many of them perceive little reward in terms of satisfaction/meaningfulness or guaranteed security even if they manage to overcome most of the competition. Additionally, they are presented with a seemingly diverse array of pathways to societal integration, as portrayed by societal narratives and online platforms, yet recognize that these options are largely homogenized within the framework of the globalized capitalist economy.

Moreover, confronted with this apparent abundance of choices, discerning meaningful connections between them proves challenging for these individuals. Instead, they perceive these options as *fragmented* items or *hybrid* aggregates lacking coherence in meaning, just like many commodities displayed in the shops of a shopping mall. While they may demonstrate a heightened tolerance or familiarity with such hybridity or fragmentation, it comes at the cost of a general sense of *detachment* or a default inclination to avoid commitment, akin to the rarity of commitment to any short video clips on Instagram, YouTube, or TikTok.

Such *contradictions*, *fragmented/hybrid multiplicity*, and *general detachment* appear to render many emerging and young adults vulnerable to feelings of disorientation and a lack of motivation. Those who do exhibit impulses to take action are often motivated by *fear/anxiety* rather than passion or a sense of purpose. Ironically and unfortunately, during the three big social protests, many youngsters participated intensively with passion and a sense of mission, not just fear and anger, like an eruption of agency from a state of prolonged dormancy (Cheung, 2017), but the social movements ended up being completely suppressed by top-down absolute power. This generally reinforces the feeling that all efforts are futile, especially in front of both totalitarianism and capitalism, as they have experienced. Deep down, it is an existential crisis regarding meanings (To and Sung, 2017) with a transpersonal dimension concerning values.

Even worse, despite the prevailing mood of disorientation, they are not afforded the opportunity to pause, reflect, or explore at the pace of a highly competitive society, starting from their early education, which also deeply influences the parenting they receive. This pace, coupled with the fragmented hybridity of many aspects, contributes to *remarkable chaos in their developmental trajectories*. It is common to encounter young adults who are highly functioning or even excellent in certain academic or professional domains but remain severely underdeveloped in other aspects of life, developmentally speaking. Such a chaotic state engenders many perplexing frustrations in their lives, making it difficult for them to discern what is going wrong or what is lacking.

The need for an aesthetic, imaginative, and playful integration for young adults

In addressing the prevailing *fragmentation*, *disorientation*, and *detachment* experienced by contemporary young adults, the core issue, according to the author, lies in *reclaiming integration*. This aspect is deemed essential for both therapeutic interventions and preventive measures. Simply enhancing psychological flexibility (Johnson, 2009) or broadening the choices of coping strategies (Clayton, 1994; Jefferies, 2019) is insufficient, as part of the problem is related to impacts from the overabundance of choices and being excessively flexible in a detached manner.

However, the attainment of such integration *cannot* be solely achieved through cognitive or rational means. Even within contemporary academia, fragmentation persists across different disciplines, often devoid of interconnection or collaborative discourse. Interdisciplinary endeavors remain scarce, and conflicts persist between the realms of science and humanities. Societally, communities are dissipating, and the public domain is rife with political polarization, impeding integration in social spheres. Moreover, within the realm of employment, societal fragmentation and isolation are exacerbated by neoliberal capitalism. Furthermore, in interpersonal communication, social media and internet platforms have proven inadequate in fostering integration, instead exacerbating fragmentation and isolation, particularly amidst the inundation of information overload.

What the expanded EPR framework can offer for an aesthetic integration?

As inspired and guided by Dr. Jennings' EPR framework enriched by NDP and extending into ToR (Jennings, 2011), the author envisions one hope *to facilitate such integration aesthetically, imaginatively, and playfully*. On the one hand, this approach illustrates the possibility of integration developmentally in the dialectical evolution of EPR, grounded in nurturing attachment actualized via NDP. On the other hand, Dr. Jennings' early theory of Theatre of Healing (1994) demonstrates the possibility of integration enabled by *the synthesis of theatre and ritual*, historically recognized as a major method for reconciling conflicts and chaos in human experiences across civilizations.

In essence, according to the author's understanding, EPR is *not only developmental but also dialectical*. It starts with the infant developing its corporeal existence of being in its body and being bodily in the world (E stage), prior to a clear differentiation between self and not-self. Through messy play as a transitional step, the infant begins to discern the traces it leaves in the world, leading to the differentiation between self and others/objects and the exploration of various plays involving traces and objects, and then also plays involving making projection to the mental construction of objects (P stage), seemingly opposite to the direct operation of the E stage. Subsequently, with transitional media such as stories, puppets, masks, and mime, this opposition is overcome by the synthesis of E and P when the child develops various abilities to imagine oneself as another, including imitating the other, playing as the other, reversing perspective between self and other, and shifting among different perspectives of roles, etc. Role mediates between self and other, while the system of roles enables mental freedom among different possibilities of action (R stage). In such *dialectical integration*, the differentiation between the components of E, P, and R remain, but interconnected, and the free transition from one to another becomes possible.

Upon establishing this synthetic foundation, the child, equipped with fundamental EPR competencies and components, progresses into an advanced developmental phase (ToR/ToL). Here, diverse developmental pathways, *with different emphasis on either E, P, R, or their combinations*, become possible for further exploration and development. The development of various styles across different art modalities and theatre forms reflects and contributes to this advanced developmental phase from age 8 onward. For example, all the forms outlined in Bailey's (1999) helpful schema, known as the 'Drama Therapy Pie', could be regarded as variations of theatrical structures potentially developed during this phase. Additionally, more sophisticated social-cultural practices, including rituals, are integral to this developmental stage. Through Dr. Jennings' approach, the intrinsic connection between these social-cultural practices and the arts is underscored with a developmental perspective. These developments are key to facilitating *aesthetic integration* for young adults suffering from disorientation, fragmentation, and detachment.

Therefore, when working with young adults far beyond the age 8 and much more complex developmentally, the EPR framework is predominantly employed within its ToR/ToL phase. This involves a theoretically guided assessment to evaluate the clients' current developmental progress, pathways, and configurations in terms of E, P, and R as principles and typology of combination, i.e., building a personal EPR profile. Additionally, the earlier EPR sequence for the period from birth to age 7 can still serve as a useful reference model to identify any absent, distorted, or disrupted elements in the foundational developmental phase, which calls for developmental repair that requires a particularly strong nurturing base facilitated by NDP.

Some tactical principles in using the EPR approach for young adults

Drawing from practical experiences, several key principles emerge in the application of the EPR framework to assist emerging and young adults, taking into consideration their distinct characteristics. Firstly, owing to the prevalence of formal education and the nature of modern education, possibly compounded by the prevailing political ethos of bystanderism and the media and internet's culture of audienceship, this demographic often exhibits detachment from their bodies while heavily relying on intellectualization, or at least adopting an observational stance of objectification. According to the EPR model, they tend to demonstrate a general weakness and unfamiliarity with E, juxtaposed with an overdevelopment in one mode within P, namely, propositional language around objects or locutionary speech act (Austin, 1975). They may not respond effectively when prompted to engage in activities related to E or R, as defense mechanisms often kick in when they become conscious of participating in such activities. Furthermore, they are commonly unfamiliar with play and often internalize some negative associations of this word.

Instead, strategically, it is often helpful to focus more on P and frame it as a "task", "exercise", or "exploration" before introducing the term "play" more naturally in later phases. The initial redevelopment goal is to diversify modalities of play with objects or external media within P and then facilitate their imaginative projection onto these play objects, be they drawing, construction, lyrics, or story. Self-expression and self-awareness are gradually facilitated during this process of projective play, serving as *a re-entrance into the whole EPR spiral of growth*. Furthermore, after focusing on P, it is often easier for them to move onto R instead of E, which may appear too 'mysterious' or 'abstract' to young adults. Once they feel comfortable and playful with R, then it becomes easier for them to enter E from R as a stylistic extension or transposition of R.

The major-minor combination of EPR components as a tactic is also generally helpful. This involves, for instance, integrating activities from both P and R, with P being the primary focus of consciousness, despite the involvement of numerous elements of R that may remain consciously peripheral

Table 6.1 Different intermediary play organized according to types of transitional function

E-P transition	• Messy play • Trace play
P-R transition	• Storytelling (with changing perspectives) • Puppet play • Theatre in the box • Mask Play • Mime (based on Lecoq physical theatre pedagogy)
R-E transition	• Non-figurative, expressive movement for the inner world of a character • Musical style drama with dance • Opera • Poetic and ritual physicalization of the dynamics of a drama (e.g., Artaud Theatre of Cruelty for ritual trance) • Greek tragedy's chorus work • Lecoq's clown work (from mask to authentic contact with pure presence)
R-P transition	• Brechtian narrating about the character • Brechtian narrating from the character • Brechtian demonstrative acting of (social) *gestus*
E-R transition	• Acting exercises from rhythm and sensory impulse to create character (e.g., Grotowski's physical acting and mysterious play, the reverse metaphor exercise from Decroux's Corporeal Mime, etc.)
P-E transition	• Singing from lyrics to melody • Dancing inspired by a picture • Dancing with an object with a specific structure and/or texture

or even unconscious. Such combined activities effectively prepare a seamless and gradual transition between stages. Examples of this include storytelling with significant moments of in-role action or speech or role-playing with musical elements gradually integrated with dance.

Corresponding to this strategy, transitional or intermediary types of play between stages are especially important when working with young adults. As they are in the phase of ToR, the developmental trajectories are diverse for different individuals, and they no longer adhere to the EPR sequence in the early child phase. This implies that transitions can occur in many other orders between E, P, and R. Therefore, it is helpful if practitioners pay attention to various possible types of intermediary play beyond those seen in the transitions from E to P and from P to R in the earlier EPR sequence.

As examples, the following table outlines some possibilities that the author usually uses:

A Case Example of a Young Adults Dramatherapy Group across Four Seasons

To exemplify some of the principles and strategies discussed thus far, this section presents a case study of a one-year volunteer project aimed at supporting stressed young adults aged 23 to 26 through group dramatherapy for both preventive and therapeutic purposes. These participants, who have graduated less than four years prior, are in a transitional phase of entering the workforce. While they do not have specific diagnoses, they self-perceive themselves as stressed and exhibit certain characteristics indicative of suboptimal and disturbing mental health conditions. Additionally, many of them have varying degrees of involvement in at least one of the three recent social protests.

This group underwent sessions spread across four seasons through-out the year, with two individual sessions scheduled for each partici-pant between each segment and after the final segment. The primary objective was to facilitate *aesthetic integration* and *communal integra-tion*, allowing participants to experience *imagination and play as avenues for self-expression, self-awareness, and self-understanding, as well as con-nection and communication with others.*

The EPR approach in the ToR phase informs the design and adjust-ments made throughout all four seasons. One significant aspect of exploration involves revisiting Dr. Jennings' earlier concept of the Thea-tre of Healing, which underscores *the integration of theater and ritual* with *a transpersonal dimension.* This concept is further enriched by NDP to foster *nurturing and healthy attachment,* offering *a response to the existential crisis* commonly experienced by young adults, particularly in the present era.

Of particular focus is *the ritual of coming-of-age,* chosen deliberately due to the absence of such rituals in developed cities like Hong Kong. All group members articulated that the university's graduation ceremony lacked any significance as a coming-of-age ritual, citing contemporary universities' resemblance to commercial entities and the perception of undergraduate education primarily as a preparatory phase for entering the workforce. Therefore, the group creates their own coming-of-age ritual in the last season.

Another remark is the flexibility of the second season in response to the group theme. In this group, the collective theme was about relationships and intimacy, while in another group under the same project, the group theme was about shadow, taboo, and shame.

Season one: self-expression and self-awareness via different modalities of arts

The first season of this young adult group, consisting of eight 3-hour weekly sessions, aims to facilitate and cultivate an ethos and praxis of utilizing various modalities of art for self-expression and self-awareness. Projective plays (P) and role-plays (R) feature prominently, while embodiment plays (E) are comparatively less emphasized on a conscious level. This preference arises from the recognition that many participants, typical of numerous young adults in Hong Kong, may lack familiarity with direct bodily engagement and could potentially feel disoriented during activities primarily focused on E unless these are approached as 'warm-up games' rather than core exploratory endeavors.

Furthermore, P is typically introduced prior to or integrated with R, with elements of E often subtly interwoven or organically extended from these activities. This strategic integration aims to captivate participants' attention through the imagination of story and drama, thereby providing a 'good reason' and impetus to move their bodies and sense the feelings flowing therein. Besides this strategic design based on EPR, the use of sensory play, rhythmic play, and interpersonal play under the NDP principles appears on the level of facilitation instead of the content of this design. In this season, self-expression and self-awareness (via arts) are taken as the initial step of self-connecting, which grounds all the rest in the following three seasons.

Season two: self-understanding via relationship and intimacy (romance and family)

The second season, consisting of eight 3-hour weekly sessions, centered more around R through fictional roles and scenes as the participants get used to stepping into others' shoes in dramatic enactment. The overarching aim shifted towards deepening self-understanding in relationships or in relation to others while expanding their repertoire of interpersonal interactions through playful or even seemingly 'crazy' fictional role plays. Particularly in the latter portion of this phase, thematic exploration increasingly delved into aspects of intimacy within both romantic and familial contexts. Usually, in between or after the fictional role plays, participants, out of character, have opportunities to reflect upon the roles or engage in dialogue with the characters in order to process the experiences of enactment as possibilities of life. Despite the focus on R as the principal component, the sessions in this phase continued to integrate P and E as supplementary activities, serving to either prepare participants for or conclude the main body of R.

In this season, the therapist pays special attention to the participants' coping patterns and communication styles, as well as the potential consequences in their lives. Habitual, emerging, and underdeveloped patterns (as alternative options) are identified through various role plays set in diverse scenes. The therapist designs these scenes as opportunities to challenge habitual patterns, support emerging ones, and redevelop underdeveloped ones. Additionally, the resisting forces that hinder or disturb the experimentation and redevelopment of alternatives are identified, offering clues for the therapist to trace deeper complexes in the participants' psyches or the unfinished business that still influences the present. Often, the same role in a scene is portrayed multiple times by different participants, enabling mutual learning and revealing that certain qualities or strategies can be either helpful or harmful depending on the context, emphasizing the importance of flexibility and creativity.

In later sessions, the therapist assists the participants in consciously identifying their habitual patterns and recognizing the diversity of alternatives they have already experimented with and created in different scene plays. They are also guided to explore the similarities between their habitual patterns and those of significant others in the course of their upbringing.

In the final session, participants share with each other five adjectives describing their initial impressions of each member and another five adjectives about how they currently perceive others, having spent two seasons playing together. Finally, each participant is invited to identify one quality they wish to learn from each member, recognizing its potential to enhance their own lives.

Season three: personal themes of challenge/exploration at present stage of life

The third season, consisting of eight three-hour weekly sessions, aims to facilitate participants in identifying their personal themes of challenges or exploratory themes for their current life stage as perceived by them via an oblique approach, which allows the unconscious psyche to contribute. Each participant is guided to create a fictional story that remains open-ended over the course of the sessions through various story-making and storytelling exercises, following the thread of the major characters they have created. Thus, P dominates in this season, with E and R serving as supplementary elements.

Other modalities of P, besides storytelling, are employed in later sessions as an intermodal extension of the imagination. For instance, participants are invited to envision the stories they have created as a book or a movie and to design a book cover, movie poster, and trailer for the movie. Furthermore, following Dr. Sue Jennings' idea of Theatre of Resilience for people (from the age of 8 onwards) to develop a diverse richness of the structures of experience, expression, and imagination, certain movements or episodes of the story are presented through different theatrical forms and styles, employing techniques such as theatre in the box or taking on non-actor roles in theatre, such as different designers.

In later sessions, each of them, in the role of the 'author', is also interviewed by other participants acting as journalists, discussing their inspirations or ideas behind the stories they have created and considering possible developments for future episodes. This intermediary role of 'author', situated between the fictional and the real, aids participants in reflecting on their stories through dramatic scenarios such as press conferences or radio interviews. In the final session, they are also guided to act in either the role of 'author', 'a main character', or themselves, to talk to either the 'author', 'a main character', or themselves. Furthermore, they take on the role of 'a reader' or 'an audience' who by chance reads or watches this story, presented in either a novel, a movie, or a show, and share in this role about what he/she sees, feels, and thinks during or after reading or watching this story. Lastly, participants, as themselves, are asked to imagine if the story, or a certain part or moment of the story, were a metaphor. They are prompted to consider what it could represent and how they feel about it. In conclusion, they are asked to write down questions and wishes about their lives on colored papers, which also serve as the starting point for the next and final season.

Season four: embracing adulthood via the creation of personal coming-of-age rituals

The final season, consisting of eight three-hour weekly sessions, targets guiding the participants to create their own coming-of-age ritual for integration and empowerment. Considering that ritual or ceremony may be unfamiliar to contemporary youths or young adults, the progression of these sessions systematically equips participants with the requisite components for ritual creation. This progression is structured primarily according to the EPR sequence, as it serves not only as a vehicle for ritual formation but also as a mechanism for developmental repair and integration.

Within the EPR sequence, a significant emphasis is placed on projective play (P), as it emerges as the preferred medium through which young adults feel most secure and contains essential components necessary for the establishment of a ritual framework. Key components include *mythology* (representing the transpersonal dimension), *symbols* (serving as conduits for transpersonal messages and inspirations), *ritual space*, and *the connection to inner mysteries*.

Correspondingly, the eight sessions are delineated into five distinct stages:

1) The initial session seeks to re-engage participants in the self-exploration process, transitioning them from embodiment (E) to projective play (P)

through messy play (with water and flour), a process from sensory chaos to form construction, culminating in *the creation of a mythological world* (from flour dough) in the role of 'god creator'.

2) The second and third sessions concentrate on *the creation of symbols* in relation to this mythological world, realized through visual arts (drawing, construction, and installation).

3) The fourth session is dedicated to *creating a symbolic space*, utilizing materials with special textures, such as colored wooden blocks, stones, and dry plants, in combination with the artworks (or parts of them) created in previous sessions. Participants are encouraged to envision *the symbolic space as a stage, altar, and landscape of the psyche* and to imagine the events unfolding within it.

4) With a sense of symbolic space from session four, sessions five and six deepen the exploration of the created mythological world in further detail, delving into *the inner world of symbolic characters to provide a container for emerging inner mysteries.*

5) The final two sessions concentrate on integrating the preceding elements through *designing and enacting two coming-of-age rituals*: one for a youth character within the created mythological world (session 7) and the other for the participants themselves (session 8). This final session involves setting up individualized ritual spaces with different symbolic decorations, where participants undergo the ritual under the imaginary gaze of a puppet representing the 'god of coming-of-age', crafted by each participant themselves. The session concludes with participants opening a gift box crafted in a prior session and symbolically receiving an imaginary gift, signifying and celebrating their transition into adulthood.

What follows is the detailed outlines of each session in the concluding season, *delineating the activities categorized according to the EPR framework*. This demonstration illustrates the potential application of Dr. Jennings' EPR framework, augmented by NDP, within the ToR phase. It serves as *a response to the existential challenges faced by young adults in Hong Kong*, characterized by feelings of *fragmentation, disorientation,* and *detachment* stemming from various *traumatic experiences linked to societal events and socio-political-economic structures.*

Concluding remarks

Young adulthood is largely socio-political-economic constructed, and the life experiences and mental health of young adults are highly responsive to societal changes, political institutions, and economic systems. Clinical experiences and practical understanding from working with young adults are not only valuable for therapy practices and preventive care services but also crucial for socio-political critique and sociological reflections. From the author's

Table 6.2 Session plan/record for the final season

(*In the column of EPR type, capital letters mean major type, while lower-case letter refer to minor type, according to *the major-minor strategy* discussed earlier)

Activities	EPR Type
Stage One: Mythology	
Session 1: The Creator, World Creation, and Myth	
• Mirror exercises for connection and updating each other's life during the break.	E-P
• Creating still images/gestures representing moments during the break by sculpting group members' bodies.	P-e
• Sharing metaphors describing what the world is like for each of them lately.	P
• Imagining a transitional space for digesting complex experiences within or in front of such a world.	P-re
• Water play.	E
• Flour play, adding more and more flour into the water.	E
• Gradually molding clay-like flour.	E-p
• Imagining oneself as a World Creator/God, crafting a world with clay-like flour dough.	P-re
• Creating "human beings/people" in this world.	P-r
• Creating a myth and storytelling about this world and its inhabitants.	P
• Sharing.	--
Stage Two: Symbols	
Session 2: Symbols of the Myth World	
• Free drawing with water on special cloth.	E-p
• Designing logos for each other and discussing design ideas.	P
• Designing a personal logo (symbol) to be the magic entrance into the mythological world they created in Session 1.	P
• Moving the body to draw the logo in space, exploring different interpretations.	E-P
• Creating a dice with six symbols on every face, including the personal logo and five additional symbols representing different aspects of the world.	P
• Building an installation with the dice and natural materials (stones, leaves, flowers, and wood branches).	P
• Contemplating the installation, then asking questions about life and playing with the dice to imagine different "responses" by different symbols facing up each round.	P-r
• Free writing a poem inspired by the installation or the experience of divining via dice.	P
• Sharing.	--

(Continued)

Table 6.2 (Continued)

Activities	EPR Type
Session 3: Collage of Symbols	
• Body massage.	E
• Touch exercises.	E
• Making sounds and movements in response to the sounds of a partner.	E
• Creating a collage drawing of the six symbols from the world.	P
• Narrating scenes from the world, with echo voices from group members like a chorus.	P-e
• Placing the dice on the collage drawing.	P
• Crafting small clay figures with different gestures representing the dice's symbols.	P-e
• Integrating the clay models into the collage drawing.	P-e
• Sharing.	--
Stage Three: Symbolic Space	
Session 4: Stage, Altar, and a Map/Landscape of the Psyche	
• Playing with the colored wooden blocks with different shapes.	P
• Collectively using these wooden blocks to make different installations/sculptures to represent different types of emotions.	P
• Collectively sculpting "space" with these wooden blocks.	P
• Collectively creating a collective altar/platform/stage for exploration.	P
• Creating their own "space" with those colorful wooden blocks plus other art materials.	P
• Imagining created spaces as a stage, exploring potential dramas happening there.	P
• Imagining created spaces as an altar, exploring potential rituals happening there.	P
• Imagining created spaces as inner landscapes/maps of their own psyche.	P
• Sharing.	--
Stage Four: Connection to Inner Mysteries	
Session 5: The Frame and Inner Dialogue	
• Creating a ritualistic atmosphere via ensemble music playing.	E
• Making a "frame" for the drawing symbolizing the world each of them created in Session 3 as an extended creation.	P
• Exhibition and appreciation of each other's work, sharing feelings and associations.	P
• Looking at the created mythological world again through the extended artwork and identifying a character in this world.	P-r
• Engaging in the dialogue with the character and themselves through "role-reversal" in psychodramatic techniques.	R
• Sharing.	--

(Continued)

Table 6.2 (Continued)

Activities	EPR Type
Session 6: Inner Dialogue (continued)	
• Christmas ritual setting and improvisation with objects.	P
• Playing with the objects and miniatures, followed by storytelling improvisation.	P
• Selecting miniatures to represent characters from previous worlds and placing them on the artworks from previous sessions.	P-r
• Dialogue and interaction between the miniature character and three things/characters in the world/artwork, in which the miniature character is played by the author themselves, with other characters played by other group members, who only repeat the lines the author designed and assigned.	R-p
• Condensing experiences into keywords.	P
Stage Five: Creating Coming-of-Age Rituals	
Session 7: The World Creator and Preparation for Coming-of-Age Ceremony	
• Revisiting the framed drawing again and checking where the attention and feeling go.	P
• Playing once again the role of the "World Creator" and observing the mythological world anew.	P-R
• Narration/Monologue from the World Creator's perspective about children and teenagers in the world, and particularly, one of them.	R
• Narration/Monologue from the World Creator's perspective about teenagers in that world and particularly one of them.	R-P
• Narration/Monologue from the World Creator's perspective about mid-age adults in that world and particularly one of them.	R-P
• Embodiment (gesture) and enactment (monologue) of one to-be-adult teenager in that world and then the Creator that sees him/her.	R-E
• Designing a coming-of-age ceremony for that specific to-be-adult youth.	P
• Imagining a dream that a to-be-adult youth makes just after the ceremony and a special gift from the god for the completion of the ceremony and being an adult.	P
• Making a gift box for the gift that the participants themselves would receive after their own coming-to-age ceremony.	P
• Sharing work-in-progress.	P
Session 8: Personal Coming-of-Age Ceremony	
• Dancing together in live music.	E
• Shifting between collective dance and individual dance with elements from the collective dance and other participants' dance in live music.	E
• Playing with some materials and then constructing individually a big puppet representing a god of coming-of-age for oneself.	P

(Continued)

Table 6.2 (Continued)

Activities	EPR Type
• Putting the god puppet on one wall in the room and then individually decorating a ceremony space around it with different objects and materials for their own coming-to-age ceremony.	P
• Placing the created gift box from the last session in this ritual space.	P
• Contemplative dialogue with the god puppet in one's own ritual space.	R
• Playing with the ritual objects they set up and then gradually transforming into movement and dance, supported by abstract music.	R-P-E
• Settling down again for a moment of stillness in silence.	E
• Opening the gift box to imagine the present therein for celebrating their new stage of life.	R-P
• Placing the present nearby and going into a position, like sleeping with eyes closed.	R
• Imagining the first dream they make after the coming-to-age ceremony.	P-r
• Writing a poem, a memo, or a letter to themselves after waking up.	P
• Free sharing about the gift, the dream, or anything else.	P
• Ritual of closure with physical connection and verbal metaphor for their future as an adult.	E-P-R

clinical experience, it becomes evident that the mental health challenges faced by young adults transcend mere psychological and individual realms, extending beyond mere 'adaptation', with a passive and uncritical tone. These challenges have a transpersonal dimension regarding meanings, necessitating an integrative approach that is not just rational and cognitive but playful, imaginative, and aesthetic. Dr. Jennings' expanded EPR approach provides a developmentally specific and systematic framework that guides care practitioners and educators to flexibly support young adults in redeveloping through play, theatre, and ritual via a diversity of pathways.

References

Arnett, J. J., Žukauskienė, R. and Sugimura, K. (2014) The new life stage of emerging adulthood at ages 18–29 years: Implications for mental health. *The Lancet Psychiatry*, 1(7), 569–576.

Arnett, J. J. (Ed.) (2015) *The Oxford Handbook of Emerging Adulthood.* Oxford University Press.

Arnett, J. J. (2018) Conceptual foundations of emerging adulthood. In *Emerging Adulthood and Higher Education*. Routledge, 11–24.

Austin, J. L. (1975) *How to Do Things with Words.* Harvard University Press.

Bailey, S. (1999) *What Is Drama Therapy?* www.dramatherapycentral.com/What-is-drama-therapy/

Blatterer, H. (2007) Adulthood: The contemporary redefinition of a social category. *Sociological Research Online*, 12(4), 1–11. https://doi.org/10.5153/sro.1563

Bronfenbrenner, U., Kessel, F., Kessen, W. and White, S. (1986) Toward a critical social history of developmental psychology: A propaedeutic discussion. *American Psychologist*, 41(11), 1218.

Burman, E. (2016) *Deconstructing Developmental Psychology*. Routledge.

Cadigan, J. M., Lee, C. M. and Larimer, M. E. (2019) Young adult mental health: A prospective examination of service utilization, perceived unmet service needs, attitudes, and barriers to service use. *Prevention Science*, 20, 366–376.

Cheung, C. K. (2017) *Emerging Adulthood in Hong Kong: Social Forces and Civic Engagement*. Routledge.

Clayton, M. (1994) Role theory and its application in clinical practice. *Psychodrama Since Moreno: Innovations in Theory and Practice*, 121–144.

Côté, J. E. (2014) The dangerous myth of emerging adulthood: An evidence-based critique of a flawed developmental theory. *Applied Developmental Science*, 18(4), 177–188.

Danziger, S. and Ratner, D. (2010) Labor market outcomes and the transition to adulthood. *The Future of Children*, 133–158.

Erikson, E. H. (1978) *Adulthood*. W. W. Norton & Co.

Furlong, A. (2009) *Handbook of Youth and Young Adulthood: New Perspectives and Agendas*. London: Routledge.

Furstenberg, F. F. (2008) The intersections of social class and the transition to adulthood. *New Directions for Child and Adolescent Development*, 2008(119), 1–10.

Gaines, A. M. and Butler, J. D. (2016) The history, trends and future of North American drama therapy. In *Routledge International Handbooks of Dramatherapy*, eds. Jennings, S. and Holmwood, C. Routledge, 52–64.

Hong, G. and Chung, H. J. (2022) Assessing the impact of the great recession on the transition to adulthood. *Sociological Methods & Research*. https://doi.org/10.1177/00491241221113871

Jefferies, J. (2019) Role theory and role analysis. In *One-to-One Psychodrama Psychotherapy: Applications and Technique*, ed. A. Chesner. London: Routledge.

Jennings, S. (1992) *Dramatherapy with Families, Groups and Individuals: Waiting in the Wings*. Jessica Kingsley Publishers.

Jennings, S. (1994) The theatre of healing: Metaphor and metaphysics in the healing process. In *The Handbook of Dramatherapy*, 93–113. London: Routledge.

Jennings, S. (Ed.) (1995) *Dramatherapy with Children and Adolescents*. London: Routledge.

Jennings, S. (1997) *Introduction to Dramatherapy: Theatre and Healing, Ariadne's Ball of Thread*. Jessica Kingsley.

Jennings, S. (2011) *Healthy Attachments and Neuro-Dramatic-Play*. Jessica Kingsley Publishers.

Johnson, D. R. (2009) Developmental transformations: Towards the body as presence. *Current Approaches in Drama Therapy*, 2, 65–88.

Johnson, D. R. and Emunah, R. (Eds.) (2020) *Current Approaches in Drama Therapy*. Charles C. Thomas Publisher.

Jones, P. (2007) *Drama as Therapy: Theory, Practice and Research*. Taylor & Francis.

Kito, A. and Ueno, T. (2016) Mental health and individual experience of unemployed young adults in Japan. *Industrial Health*, 54(1), 20–31.

Landy, R. J. (2008) *The Couch and the Stage: Integrating Words and Action in Psychotherapy*. Jason Aronson.

Mahmoud, J. S. R., Staten, R. T., Hall, L. A. and Lennie, T. A. (2012) The relationship among young adult college students' depression, anxiety, stress, demographics, life satisfaction, and coping styles. *Issues in Mental Health Nursing*, 33(3), 149–156.

Morss, J. R. (2013) *Growing Critical: Alternatives to Developmental Psychology*. Routledge.

Nelson, L. J. (2021) The theory of emerging adulthood 20 years later: A look at where it has taken us, what we know now, and where we need to go. *Emerging Adulthood*, 9(3), 179–188.

Ng, P. Y. N., Yang, S. and Chiu, R. (2024) Features of emerging adulthood, perceived stress and life satisfaction in Hong Kong emerging adults. *Current Psychology*, 1–13.

Robinson, O. (2015) Emerging Adulthood, Early Adulthood, and Quarter-Life Crisis: Updating Erikson for the Twenty-First Century. In *Emerging Adulthood in a European Context*. Routledge, 17–30.

Singh, S. P. and Tuomainen, H. (2015) Transition from child to adult mental health services: Needs, barriers, experiences and new models of care. *World Psychiatry*, 14(3), 358.

Tello-Navarro, F., Bastias, L. S. and Hernandez-Gonzalez, O. (2024) Evolution and research trends about emerging adulthood: A bibliometric analysis. *Emerging Adulthood*. https://doi.org/10.1177/21676968231222431

To, S. M. and Sung, W. L. (2017) Presence of meaning, sources of meaning, and subjective well-being in emerging adulthood: A sample of Hong Kong community college students. *Emerging Adulthood*, 5(1), 69–74.

von Tetzchner, S. (2023) Critical developmental psychology. In *Typical and Atypical Child and Adolescent Development* (vol. 1). Routledge, 70–71.

NDP in therapy

Chapter 7

Into the unknown – a young hero's journey from Ukraine

Alison Chown

Place attachment – the people and place bond

As a non-directive child-centered play therapist working in outdoor spaces, I am interested in the idea of attachment to place, sometimes described as a people and place bond. Noted as a concept that is easy to describe but harder to define, in simple terms, we can think of it as when the physical environment has symbolic meaning and evokes emotions in us or as the emotional bond we have with a particular place, where we feel connected to it and have positive feelings arising from it or the components of it. This then gives us a sense of safety, security and containment, such as we felt in the presence of our attuned primary carer. Most of us will have places we like to spend time in and places we seldom visit. I have always liked open spaces: hilltops, beaches and stretches of green space. Deeply forested woodland evokes memories from childhood of dark fairy tales, of witches and wolves and of being unable to see the way forward. Open spaces, particularly the beach, can lift my spirit, make my soul soar and wrap around me like a soft blanket.

As therapists, we are well-schooled in attachment theory and the importance of positive relationships with the people in our lives to give feelings of safety and security, but we also need to consider the idea of attachment to place, both for ourselves and our clients. However, our understanding of the significance of space and place is a complex issue beyond the scope of this chapter, but discussed more fully in Tuan (1977), Scannell and Gifford (2010) and Manzo and Devine-Wright (2021).

Our attachment to places grows out of the exploration of our surrounding environments as we develop. Where we play, go to school and hang out with friends all have a meaning to us and contribute to our identity and sense of security. We may talk of 'our roots' as being in a particular place.

> Place comes into existence when people give meaning to a part of the larger undifferentiated space in which they live. Whilst abstract knowledge about a place can be developed in a relatively short space of time, the 'feel'

DOI: 10.4324/9781003498209-10

of a place takes longer to acquire, growing out of . . . routine activities and everyday experiences, as well as more significant life events.

(Jack, 2010, p. 75)

Place, and how we see it and feel about it, is an important aspect of our development. Just as our key attachment figures provide us with a sense of security that allows for exploration and supports our curiosity, feelings about the places we inhabit are also significant in the development of our identity and sense of belonging. As secure attachments to people enable us to gradually extend our horizons and move further away from them, our attachment to significant places and the sense of security this gives allows us to venture forth and develop feelings of mastery, embarking perhaps on our own hero's journey. In relation to the emotional ties which we develop with places, Tuan (1977) notes that:

The profound attachment to the homeland appears to be a worldwide phenomenon. It is not limited to any particular culture and economy. . . . The city or land is viewed as mother, and it nourishes; place is an archive of fond memories and splendid achievement that inspire the present; place is permanent.

(1977, p. 154)

Where we come from and where we live are crucial aspects of who we are, so when we are uprooted in times of crisis, a key attachment is lost. As with losing a human attachment, this can seriously impact our identity and feelings of security and safety. For immigrants and refugees, the strength of feeling for a place and their attachment to it is intensified by the loss of that place (Scannell and Gifford, 2010).

Displacement and cultural considerations

Across the world, in mid-2023, a total of 110 million people were forcibly displaced, with over half of all refugees and others in need of international protection coming from just three countries – the Syrian Arabic Republic, Afghanistan and Ukraine. At the end of 2022, some six months earlier, this figure stood at 108.4 million, 40% of whom were children under 18 (UNHCR, 2024). Save the Children (2024) defines a refugee as a person who is seeking safe haven after being forced to flee violence, persecution and war, whilst other definitions would also include environmental disaster. Of the 110 million displaced persons, 36.4 million of these are of refugee status, with half of these being children. They predominantly live in refugee camps with little or no access to education and healthcare, almost entirely dependent on aid and without freedom of movement.

Following the invasion of Ukraine in February 2022, Europe saw the biggest and fastest displacement of people since World War II (Save the Children, 2024). By July 2022, some 104,000 people had arrived from Ukraine through the UK government's visa scheme and by September, 20,000 school places had been offered to children arriving from Ukraine (DfE, 2023). These children were uprooted from familiar surroundings during heavy fighting and bombing, leaving family members behind, many of them serving in the Ukrainian armed forces. Huge numbers fled to Poland and then to the UK. Arriving here under a nationality-specific immigration route, Ukrainians were placed with host families who supported them to settle into their new surroundings and tried to help them make sense of a new life dependent by and large on the kindness and generosity of strangers.

Cultural considerations

When we are forced to move from our own culture to another, we undergo a process of cultural adaptation and change – acculturation – where we adopt, acquire or adjust to the new environment. During prolonged contact, we may make cultural modifications by adopting or borrowing aspects of another culture or merging the two. Where one culture attempts to eliminate another, we may be forced to acquire their basic attitudes, mores and habits to survive, whereas if we are in a less hostile situation, two cultures may become blended in a more harmonious way. For those refugees coming from Ukraine, we might perceive the difference in cultures to not be as defined as it might have been had they been fleeing from Afghanistan or Syria, where many are in refugee camps for prolonged periods or make perilous journeys by boat. However, the trauma of war and the uprooting from one's known life would have similar impacts on psychological, physical and social well-being. What remains important in either circumstance is to keep a connection with one's own country and culture in order to know who we are.

Culture (or cultural differences) may pose a challenge to play therapists, even within the context of an accepting, non-judgmental and non-directive stance, since cultural bias may be an influence present for the therapist, the client and their parents (Thomas, 2016). For parents, there may be some mistrust generated from culturally differing understandings of the need for and the purpose of therapy. Our own experience of family structures and dynamics may colour our judgment of alternative structures or norms. We need to be aware of these challenges and also respectful of the other contexts that the child has existed within that will have impacted their behaviors and development. Parents may not see the issues highlighted in the referral as matters of concern, may not be familiar with the idea of behaviorally based mental health concerns or see such concerns as indicative of severe, incurable psychiatric illness and therefore highly stigmatizing (Thomas, 2016, p. 53). As play therapists, we can never fully know our clients' cultural experiences and perceptions, despite our wish to. However, if we engage from a place of cultural humility, an awareness of the limitations of our knowledge and reflection on our own potential cultural biases, we are best placed to understand the child and their world as they see it with their own eyes and enter their own internal framework (Ray et al., 2022).

Case study of V

For those Ukrainian children who gained a school place, some like my client, whom I shall call V,[1] would have accessed additional support, including play therapy sessions. My client was a 10-year-old, Russian-speaking Ukrainian male referred for play therapy by his school, who were concerned about his aggressive behaviour towards his peers. He was described as 'defiant' and very physical, with social times being particularly challenging. There was also some thought that he might be experiencing learning issues beyond those arising from language difficulties and that he understood more than he appeared to. He had been in the UK for only a couple of months or so but had traveled with his parents and younger sister, aged 3. His brother had also come over and was attending university in England and living with the hosts some distance away. One set of his grandparents was also here, with the others remaining in Ukraine. Since his father spoke little English, fuller details were harder to glean and I was mindful that reliving the circumstances of their leaving and subsequent journey to the UK may have been too painful to recount, particularly since one set of grandparents remained in Ukraine. What we did elicit was that the family had fled their hometown after their shop and home had been destroyed and they had initially spent a week sheltering underground. They then spent time in a small village in the mountains before fleeing to Poland, where they stayed for a short time before making the journey to England. They were currently living with a host family but hoped to get their own accommodation as soon as possible and V's father was looking for work. Although this background information was 'sketchy', I was reminded of one of Landreth's Rules of Thumb – "How the therapist feels about a child is more important than what the therapist knows about the child" (2002, p. 99).

Since his school was on the other side of the town, his father would bring him to the school I was working in after I had seen my existing client group. Sessions would last for 45 minutes, and his father would then collect him. During my brief exchange with his father to explain the arrangements, he indicated that they used Google Translate on a phone with the host family and after discussion with the Headteacher, it was agreed that we could use an iPad for this if needed.

The playroom in which I worked was large and light, with a door opening onto a secure tarmac play area in which there was a wooden playhouse and a shed where outdoor toys were stored, including trikes and trailers for 5–7-year-olds. On the back of the playhouse was a series of angled connecting 'gutters' for water play or for rolling objects down. There were also two crates of very large Lego-type bricks, some plastic stepping stones and two bridges. There was a small area of grass in one corner with some weeds and old logs, and around the edges of the tarmac and in some cracked areas, many more weeds and tufts of grass.

I was acutely aware that V was attending play therapy sessions without any real understanding of what they might be, although I did manage to make it clear that we would have 12 sessions together in total. In response to my inquiry about how school was for him, he said, "I like here, in UK". I have to admit to a degree of apprehension in the first session since neither of us spoke each other's language, but somehow, we muddled through with some short verbal exchanges and various signs and gestures. For a short while, he went around the room exploring the resources before settling on the sand tray, where he used a digger to fill the back of a tipper lorry to move sand to a corner of the tray and pile it up. The tailgate of the tipper lorry was missing and sand kept falling through the gap. V wanted to find something to fix this and, eventually, after trying several different solutions, used a small flap of card, which he taped to the bar at the top of the gap. This lasted for only a short time, but he continued to use the lorry without the door and before abandoning it. Verbal reflections were tricky, even simple ones, as I was unclear about how much he understood. School staff had suggested this would be more than was obvious, but I found myself relying more on my own feelings and 'gut' sensations as well as closely observing V's energy, body language and facial expressions. I was aware, too, of how important my own non-verbal language would be, particularly since V might also be relying on these for clues and would likely pick up any incongruity I showed. (Oaklander, 1988) In paying close attention to these things however, I needed to ensure V didn't interpret this as being under close scrutiny and that I was fully present to witness the content of his play.

Jennings (2011, p. 15), in her introduction to Neuro Dramatic Play, describes three 'primary' circles of containment, care and attachment and notes, "As a metaphor, these circles are like a primary 'theatre in the round' between two performers, mother and the unborn or newborn child". This replicated the first few sessions with V, who was stepping into the unknown with yet another stranger. The room and fenced outdoor area provided containment and I provided 'care' through my attunement and unconditional acceptance of him. This then allowed for an attachment to develop in the form of a therapeutic alliance. In my own writing (Chown, 2014), I suggest a fourth circle, that of exploration, extending the play, stories and dramatic action, the 'theatre in the round' that follows as our curiosity takes us further from our key attachment figures. V's exploration was his hero's journey, the processing of his experiences of leaving his home and entering a new land, overcoming obstacles (or barriers) to defeat the monster of darkness. His own and his host family were his mentors, and during our sessions, he found his ally in the therapist, a loyal and reliable companion, witness and co-creator willing to take a risk alongside the hero.

Later in that first session, V found some ping pong balls, which he took outside and dropped down the guttering, laughing as they hit the ground and bounced away. He went inside, emptied the large chalk sticks from their bucket and used this to try to catch the balls. After around ten minutes, he went back inside to the sand tray and moved more sand about before finishing by painting a picture of his house. There was much movement (or travel) in this session, movement of the sand and the rolling ping pong balls and his own movement around the room and between the room and the tarmac area, a theme that would be repeated in the coming sessions and a metaphor for his own movement through many places.

He arrived late for his second session and painted a picture of his house again, but this time, there was a smaller 'house' in the garden, which he said, "is fire". Reflecting that there was a smaller house, and it was burning, I was met with a shake of his head and an indication that he wanted to use the iPad. He set up a Cyrillic keyboard and used this to tell me about the small house in his picture that was used to both chill and cook meat on a fire, perhaps a form of barbecue. It would have been easy to use this translation method to have a more typical series of interactions, but neither of us seemed interested in doing so, except for the odd phrase here and there and in any case, it would have been very intrusive, akin to having a third person present. Due to his late arrival, this session was shorter than usual and he expressed surprise and a little annoyance when I gave him his ten-minute warning and said he was "liking painting", an indicator that he might make good use of the sessions.

In the third session, he again filled the tipper truck with sand and moved it about the sand tray, piling up and adding more to it before moving it to another place. Then he took a police car, ambulance, firetruck and a plane, driving them across the floor, crashing them and then finally laying them out at the corners of a big square on the floor, with each one being placed against either the wall or a table leg. He had previously referred to the plane as Russian, and this seemed a clear statement about his experiences in Ukraine and that, out of the chaos, he could command some order. Bearing witness to this was key, commentary and reflection much less so, and I felt no words were needed. He was more subdued with less energy, and I felt there was an understanding between us that this had been his world, his external and internal landscape, boundaried by the chaos of invasion, and he wanted me to see it. We shared an unspoken knowing. To have made any meaningful verbal reflection, I would have needed to translate via the iPad, which at this point would have been entirely inappropriate and broken the 'bond' of the moment. As McCarthy notes:

> My witnessing was not done from afar and I was not busy analyzing or interpreting or pathologizing what was being depicted. I was however, seeing the story, sensing its' import and allowing myself to be moved by it along with the boy.
>
> (2012, p. 31)

As child-centered, non-directive play therapists, we understand that play is the child's language and, therefore, words are not needed since the symbolism of the play is enough. (Oaklander, 1988). Within the therapeutic relationship, we are attuned to and present for our clients – we are living in the moment with them and using our connection with them to hear and see their stories. We trust in the process unfolding before us and trust that our clients will know what they have to do. We bear witness to their experiences without judgement or interpretation.

In the second half of his session, V went to the large sandbox and asked for water to use in it. He constructed a barrier inside which he poured the water to form a lake, channeling and diverting the water around the barrier. Barriers (or obstacles), which became a recurring theme, appeared later in the session when he went into the outside area, found a trike in the shed and rode it around the track. He instructed me to place barriers on the route. He then circumnavigated these by going off the track, laughing as he did so. To travel to the UK, his family would have had to overcome many obstacles, both physical and psychological. On the hero's journey, the guardian poses a barrier to the quest, blocking the way, representing our own internal struggles. Finding a way past or through them gives us feelings of mastery, develops our sense of skillful self and feeds our growing autonomy.

Towards the end of the session, V indicated he wanted me to gather some of the big building blocks while he continued to cycle around, narrowly missing me when I crossed the track, which seemed to greatly amuse him. He built two towers, which he appeared to be indicating was a city or town, twin aspects perhaps of his 'before and after' life or an indication of conflict between two opposing internal psychological states, Erikson's (1968) industry versus inferiority arising from the challenges of adapting to a new home life and school.

He continued this play across the next two sessions, arriving, dropping his rucksack in the corner and heading more or less straight for the outdoor space and the trike. I was always amused at the sight of this tall, well-built 10-year-old riding on a small trike with his knees almost under his chin. He repeatedly rode around the track, avoiding any obstacles he had instructed me to put in place and veering off at odd moments to avoid something unseen. It was in these sessions that he started to tidy the yard, clearing rubbish and other debris he found in a far corner of the area and pulling up weeds and grass. Perhaps he was clearing away the 'debris' of his journey before embarking on the next stage, ensuring the place was clean enough for a fresh start. Perhaps he is clearing out aspects of his 'old' self to prepare for new challenges ahead. His father had indicated that he liked to help with jobs both inside and outside the house and he certainly showed himself to be skillful and organized in this task. He also marked out a car park near the boundary fence, told me the playhouse was 'shops' and built a small structure, which he indicated was a house, as if he was mapping out the small world of his hometown to both remind himself and to show me.

His English seemed slow to improve, but I sensed the school was right in that he understood more than he appeared to. He attempted some basic statements, generally to instruct me or try to clarify what he wanted to do. Mostly, we relied on a few words, Google Translate if desperate and lots of signs, gestures and facial expressions. If I offered any props, such as emotions cards, these were quickly rejected. I did use commentary on his activities and some simple reflections, and although I felt there was more understanding there than it might at first appear, he seldom responded.

These earlier sessions had shown me where V had come from: the chaos, intrusions and restrictions of war and uprooting from all that was familiar, leading to the start of his hero's journey to a new land. However, although his attachment to his known place had been disturbed and dislocated, he seemed to have a significant amount of resilience. Jennings in introducing the concept of NDP, discusses her earlier Embodiment, Projection and Role (EPR) paradigm and notes that competence in EPR is essential to healthy development and "charts the progression of dramatic play from birth to seven" (2011, p. 17). It enables the child to engage in play that is sensory, rhythmic and dramatic, play that is creative in the use of clay and other art materials and established what she calls the creative dramatized body. V had a very strong sense of his physicality – his body self – being secure and strong in his movements and engaging enthusiastically and competently in much physical play. When he arrived for each session, he seemed to know what he needed to do and went straight to do it. Despite my efforts, I never met his mother or sister or saw the family together, but my sense was that he had a strong bond with his father and positive early attachment experiences. Since he had traveled from Ukraine with his family, this would also have been a factor in supporting his level of resilience. Jennings (2011) positions both NDP and EPR under Theatre of Body, leading to Theatre of Life, both of which are preventative. She sees Theatre of Resilience, stage two of dramatic development as therapeutic, involving repetition and rehearsal and sharing endeavors with others, allowing for the creative artist inside us to have a stage. V was engaged in rhythmic, repetitive play, riding the trike round and round, cleaning and clearing and building structures. I was present both as a witness to his story and an actor in it under his direction.

He then missed two sessions, one on either side of the Christmas break, but following his return, the clearing continued, to which he added cleaning and, later, a new theme emerged of building or reconstruction. He wanted to clean the tarmac area before doing any more building. He found a small brush in the playhouse, found a trike with a trailer attached and a small wooden trolley. He pointed to an area of weeds along the fence, 'inviting' me to pull them up and put them in the trolley. He went to another area and began doing the same, putting his weeds in the trike trailer. Both were then emptied onto the grass in the corner. Then we swept the whole area. During the week, it had rained and the drain in the corner of the yard, which was already covered in mud, became clogged with debris from the guttering. He started to remove this with his hands and went to lift the drain cover to delve more deeply. I was concerned that this was more than a tad unhygienic and indicated that he should wash his hands and look for something to use. He found a small trowel from the sandbox to continue with. He scooped everything into the small wooden trolley and again dumped it in the corner. Following this, he went to the sink, filled a small pot with water and started to clean the area with the brush, sweeping the water towards the drain in the middle of the area. He was very focused, energetic and industrious, sweeping away the unwanted.

In the subsequent sessions, he would start by riding the trike around the track and negotiating any obstacles he had asked me to construct so that when he veered off course, he also had to miss me – only narrowly on several occasions, finding my 'nervous' reactions very entertaining. It became a game we both found highly amusing and it strengthened the therapeutic relationship we had built. I love what I call the 'I know you know I know' aspect of the therapeutic relationship, where there is unspoken acknowledgment that we can trust each other to keep within the limits but where experimentation with both power and control can be had. After this, he went to the storage shed, rummaged around right at the back and found some tubing and connectors. He went inside and attached the tubing to the tap so that water poured out across the tarmac. He indicated to me and to the brush, and my part in the plan was clear – I was to brush the water towards the central drain while he hosed various areas down. I was his co-creator, his ally.

In the penultimate session, construction/reconstruction became central, and it seemed as if he felt the ground was now clean and clear enough to allow for the next scene in his dramatic play. My task was to gather the large building blocks, load them into the trike trailer and wooden trolley and take them to the middle of the area where the stepping stones and bridges were. I then had to build a wall while he rode the trike around and gathered bricks in the trailer, dropping them off at my wall. I had to build it as high as possible until it became wobbly and started to collapse. Then my task became gatherer of the blocks or pieces, the one who contained the mess, while he continued to ride around and around the track. In discussing NDP and messy play Jennings (2011) notes that this type of rhythmic play and movement is essential for grounding and stability and the trike and track had been a key feature of Vs' sessions. As he watched the collapse of what had been created, he could soothe himself with this familiar activity.

In the final session, he asked me to help him build four walls, leaving a gap for the doorway and then told me it was 'the shop', the shop they had owned. He knew how to offset the bricks to make the walls more secure than mine had been and the shop sat within a right angle he had made by joining the two bridges, forming a container for the play and the chaos it might represent and perhaps symbolic of the coming together of his past and present lives. In front of the building, he drew lines, wrote the word STOP and used cones to restrict access to the shop. Here, he could experience a sense of power and control that would have been very absent during the destruction of his home.

After he had finished building, he ran up and across the two bridges, leaped from them with high energy and once again climbed onto the trike and set off around the track. Finally, when I gave him his ten-minute warning, he asked me to help him deconstruct the shop, gather all the blocks and put them back

Figure 7.1 A rectangle of low block walls with a doorway inside a right-angled pair of small bridges set on a tarmac play area.

Source: Photograph – Author's own

in the crates one last time. We went inside, looked together at his paintings, which he did not want to keep and, for one final time, he put the red truck in the sand tray, picked up his bag, said "Goodbye" and we went down the corridor to meet his father. This play, this theatre in the round of his hero's journey, had been his catharsis.

The closing

The hero's journey is a three-stage affair. First comes the departure or separation from the current existence, followed by the initiation and challenge that is issued. Leaving his home in Ukraine and fleeing to the UK, starting a new and possibly temporary life with a new school system to adapt to, all posed significant challenges. The blocks along the track he rode around were symbolic of all of these. The final stage is that of return to the homeland. Although a physical return to Ukraine was not likely in the near future, if at all, V could return to it through his play but with a new order and a sense of empowerment.

In trying to gain a coherent understanding of place attachment, Scannell and Gifford (2010) developed their Tripartite Model, a conceptual framework based on three variables, Person, Place and Process, the sub-section of the latter being affect, cognition and behaviour. Affect provides for functional needs such as safety and security and echoes our need for positive experiences and emotions. Cognition answers the question 'Why is this place important?' and concerns knowledge, meanings and memories, both positive and negative. Behavior (or play) can bring together both cognition and affect and can be described as the physical manifestation of the connection. As language limited verbal communication to basics, I found this framework helpful in gaining insight into aspects of V's play, such as the depth of attachment he felt to his home and the trauma of his leaving.

From a discussion with his Ukrainian Support Assistant (SA) at school, I learned that the education system in Ukraine was more rigid than in the UK. V's command of English remained limited, and adapting to the demands of the school system posed a significant challenge for him. We can speculate that his aggression might well be a result of the war, but we cannot be sure as this would be based on our own cultural assumptions. Starting a new school at an age when everyone is already in friendship groups is hard enough, but when you don't speak the language, frustration can set in and a physical response is understood when a verbal one cannot be posed. Experiencing a less rigid system may take some adjustment and not understanding where the boundaries are can lead to accidental overstepping. His SA also noted that V often refused to complete a task, even with support, so there may well have been some learning needs that would require assessment. However, if you can't compete with your peers academically or verbally, in order to maintain some sense of self, competing physically may be your only option. V liked to play rugby, so, in time, this may well provide a positive channel for his energy and competitive spirit. Understanding his perspective in order to ensure the right support is offered requires the school staff to view the situation through an unbiased cultural lens that allows them to understand V's world as he experiences it and to try to stand in his shoes for a while. In a busy school, time for reflection is often hard to find, but with his teachers as mentors and his SA as an ally he has the capacity to embark on a second hero's journey.

Note

1 For reasons of anonymity, I have chosen to present my client as V for Vittaliy, meaning 'full of life' for the energy of his play and his openness to the experience of play therapy.

References

Chown, A. (2014) *Play Therapy in the Outdoors: Taking Play Therapy Out of the Playroom and into Natural Environments*. London: JKP.

DfE. (2023) *Keeping Children Safe*. https://www.gov.uk/government/publications/keeping-children-safe-in-education--2

The Education Hub. (2023) *One Year on From Russia Invading*. School Places. https://educationhub.blog.gov.uk/2023/02/one-year-russia-invading-ukraine-school-places/

Erikson, E. (1968) *Identity: Youth and Crisis*. New York: Norton.

Jack, G. (2010) Place matters: The significance of place attachments for children's well-being. *British Journal of Social Work*, 40, 755–771. https://doi.org/10.1093/bjsw/ben142; https://academic.oup.com/bjsw/article/40/3/755/1661955

Jennings, S. (2011) *Healthy Attachments and Neuro-Dramatic-Play*. London. Jessica Kingsley Publishers.

Landreth, G. (2002) *Play Therapy: The Art of the Relationship*. New York: Brunner-Routledge.

Manzo, L. and Devine-Wright, P. (2021) *Place Attachment: Advances in Theory, Methods and Applications*. Abingdon: Routledge.

McCarthy, D. (2012) *The Manual of Dynamic Play Therapy*. London: JKP.

Oaklander, V. (1988) *Windows on Our Children*. New York: The Gestalt Journal Press.

Ray, D., Ogawa, Y. and Cheng, Y. (2022) *Multicultural Play Therapy: Making the Most of Cultural Opportunities with Children*. New York: Routledge.

Save the Children. (2024) *Refugee Crisis: Facts About Refugees*. https://www.savethechildren.org/us/what-we-do/emergency-response/refugee-children-crisis

Scannell, L. and Gifford, R. (2010) Defining place attachment: A tripartite organizing framework. *Journal of Environmental Psychology*, 3(1), 1–10. https://www.academia.edu/4606679/Defining_place_attachment_A_tripartite_organizing_framework

Thomas, G. (2016) Bridging the cultural divide. In *Challenges in the Theory and Practice of Play Therapy*, eds. LeVay, D. and Cucschieri, E. London: Routledge, 52–70.

Tuan, Y. (1977) *Space and Place: The Perspective of Experience*. University of Minnesota Press.

The UNHCR. (2024) Refugee Agency. *Refugee Data Finder*. https://www.unhcr.org/refugee-statistics

Chapter 8

The use and themes of water in NDP-informed Art Therapy

Bridget Rees

Introduction

This chapter explores the use and themes of water in therapy. It describes how different clients coming to Art Therapy have used water as an important part of their therapy process. Vignettes from the therapy work illustrate how an understanding of the Neuro-Dramatic-Play® (NDP) and Embodiment-Projection-Role (EPR) paradigms informed the therapist to support the clients with their use of and relationship with water, both in and outside of the therapy sessions. One case described is with a child, the other with an adult, in the therapist's independent practice. They both show that playing with and using the theme of water can be helpful, healing and enjoyed by people of any age.

Why water?

From its arrival on earth to the vast areas it traverses before emptying into the sea, water holds all the knowledge and experience it has acquired. As phenomenal as it may seem, water carries its whole history, just as we carry ours (Emoto, 2005).

Water is fundamental to our being and our wellbeing. Where there is water, there is life! Life first existed as single-cell organisms in water before making the transition to land – we all come from the primal waters. Approximately 70% of the earth's surface is covered in water and our bodies are also made up of around 70% water. Across cultures and religions, water is used in rituals for cleansing, healing and blessing and is often linked with spiritual transformation. Some ancient mythologies and texts describe a cosmic ocean that envelopes the world from which the earth began, along with stories of global floods. In its different states (solid, liquid, gas), water takes many forms and transitions endlessly between these. We have ice crystals, icebergs, morning mists, roaring waterfalls, muddy puddles, blood plasma and tears, to name but a few. Water is within us and around us and 'is the great internal/external connection' (Jennings, 2021, p. 10). Ultimately, water will become a

DOI: 10.4324/9781003498209-11

part of our bodies, our plants and our environment. Importantly, from NDP and attachment perspectives, babies live in the watery environment of the womb for the first nine months, sharing heartbeats with the mother. It is here that attachment begins to form (Jennings, 2010, 2012, 2021).

Water is often used as a metaphor for emotions: a flood of tears, a wave of relief, emotional spillage or drought, to name but a few. Jung (in Jung et al., 1969, p. 9i) maintained that 'water is the commonest symbol for the unconscious'. The connection is drawn from water's ability to dissolve and transform. Just like water, we have the ability to transform our emotional and psychological states, affected by influences from our environment.

Whilst water is not a living organism as such, it can be considered to have vitality, with the ability to transform its state time and time again. In its liquid state, it has been observed that water molecules found in rivers, streams and other naturally flowing waterways are affected by vortex-like movements, giving it a different sort of structure and vitality in these places compared with still water (Schauberger, 1998 in Andersson, 2002; Pollack, 2017). It has even been hypothesised, by observing photographs of ice crystals, that water can change its molecular structure in response to human thoughts and words (Emoto, 2004, 2005). This raises the question – could the molecular structure and vitality of water within us be affected by our actions, even our thoughts and intentions, therefore affecting our wellbeing? This is not to be explored further here but raises an interesting hypothesis. The implications of this add another layer to the simple fact that playing with water can be fun, enlivening, regulating and soothing. Playing with water has an effect on us.

Changing states

We know that deeply disturbing, distressing or frightening (traumatic) experiences affect us physically, emotionally and psychologically (Schaer, 2005). These experiences are held in our memory systems in both explicit (conscious, brain-held) and implicit (unconscious, body-held) ways (Dew and Cabeza, 2011; Squire and Dede, 2015). Contemporary Art Therapy practices and trainings are trauma-informed and acknowledge the role of neuroscience and neurobiology in understanding how trauma affects the brain and body and, therefore, how trauma affects relationships and behaviours. Current thinking is that we must employ the body and brain to regulate our nervous systems and integrate brain-body approaches in the treatment of trauma (Porges and Dana, 2018; Siegel, 2000; Siegel and Bryson, 2012; Van der Kolk, 2014). This understanding has given rise to Polyvagal Theory, which suggests that different types of nervous systems help us to recognise when we feel safe or are under threat (Porges, 2011, 2017). The theory holds that even when a threat has passed, our bodies can remain in a state of perceived danger and we still experience stress and anxiety. We can be left with trauma being held in the body as well as in our memories (Van der Kolk, 2014). An integrated approach in therapy will help to re-integrate our different nervous systems and get them working with each other again for better overall health, wellbeing and functioning (Porges and Dana, 2018).

Siegel and Bryson (2012, p. 11) liken integration to 'being in the river of well-being', peacefully going down the river in a canoe. On either side of the river are two banks – one is 'chaos' – the other 'rigidity' (Siegel and Bryson, 2012). If we go too close to chaos, we feel out of control, so we want to move back into the calm flow of the river. But if we go too far towards rigidity, that's where we impose control and are not able to adapt, compromise or negotiate. Being in the flow of well-being is being in a state of integration, when the different parts of our brain are working well together to help us move back and forth between these two banks. Using the analogy of the different states of material water, we could also think of liquid water being the flow of regulation, with ice being the frozen state of rigidity and steam being the randomness of chaos. We have the capacity to be along the continuum of these different states at different times; the optimum of these is flow.

We can think of our brains as having vertical and horizontal systems. The vertical parts develop in order as we grow: amygdala, hippocampus, prefrontal cortex (survival, emotional, relational and thinking parts). The horizontal hemispheres organise our functioning: left (logical, linguistic and literal) and right (emotional, non-verbal and experiential). A whole-brain approach to parenting and therapy allows for the movement between these two banks of the river and the flow between vertical and horizontal brain activity (Siegel and Bryson, 2012).

Developmental stages

Different stages of child development since birth and what is needed to support each of the developmental stages have been described by many theorists, including Bowlby (1988); Erikson (1958, 1964); Jennings (2010); Kagin and Lusebrink (1978); Lusebrink (1990, 2010); Piaget (1952); Sheridan (1973) and Vygotsky (1978). The overarching themes are similar, but there are slight differences in the ages and the titles given to the stages.

For the purposes of this chapter, I will refer solely to the Embodiment-Projection-Role (EPR) stages as defined by Jennings (1990, 2010).

The stages of development have their origins in observing children, and whilst no stage can be missed out, there are individual differences in the rate at which children progress through the stages. With children, these stages occur sequentially in this order to more complex processing. If all is well, older children and adults are able to move through these stages in any order and combination, on a continuum, integrating the different ways in which body and brain interact to experience the world.

Table 8.1 EPR as defined by Sue Jennings

Stage of development	Age	What is being developed	Play activities to support
Embodiment (sensory)	birth to 13 months	A sense of a body/self through experience using the whole body and senses.	Rhythmic, water, sensory and messy play, movement, dance
Projection (perceptual)	13 months to 3 years	A realisation that there is a world beyond our own body – which we can have an effect on by handling and manipulating materials and objects.	Rummaging, sorting, building with bricks and Lego, mark making, drawing, painting
Role (cognitive)	3.5 years to 6 years	A sense of how people 'should' behave – learning about the other (empathy). Thinking and reflecting.	Active storytelling, dressing up, role play, puppets, fairy stories

Integrating stages and states

Art therapy that addresses trauma, including complex trauma (which has its origin in adverse experiences in early childhood), will likely be more effective if using a bottom-up approach that integrates the EPR stages. Moving first through Embodiment (sensory), then Projection (perceptual) and Role (cognitive) stages helps clients first to feel what they need to feel without words and then start to have an awareness before moving on to a cognitive understanding of what they have experienced. According to Steele and Malchiodi (2012), traumatic memory must be externalised in 'symbolic' and 'sensory' forms before it can be expressed through language and successfully integrated.

Like an infant under 13 months, when working at the Embodiment stage, a client may use rhythmic repetition of movements or sounds without understanding why they are doing it. They may not have the words to name what is going on. The therapist is to be mindful of allowing this to happen and not intrude with questions that would interrupt the process by expecting the client to use cognition or the stage is lost. For example, using sounds like 'mmm, aaahh' or simple statements like 'keep going, take your time' are useful (Elbrecht, 2018). At the Projection stage, we can ask questions that relate to the client's perception, such as 'How does that feel in your body?' The therapist could make suggestions of movements or mark-making, using that to enhance this awareness. The more cognitive stage of Role allows for meaning to be made of the experience and will often come with dialogue between the client and therapist – the telling of the story. I often see this near the end of a therapy session if a client is already able to do this or it may take several sessions or a much longer length of time if the client is neither psychologically nor developmentally ready.

Understanding the need for integration and working with the body's systems has meant that contemporary Art Therapy practices are developing frameworks around the more embodied aspects of art making. Malchiodi (2020) advocates for a four-part model of arts-based healing practices that allow for *movement, sound, storytelling and silence*. Silence is an important factor of being able to look inside oneself through interoception – the sense of the body's internal state. Interoception is a key factor in sensorimotor approaches to Art Therapy, such as Bilateral Body Mapping and the use of the Clay Field (Elbrecht, 2012, 2018, 2021). In these sensorimotor approaches, clients are invited to close their eyes, using both left and right hands together (bilateral) and working in silence, although some people would not be able to tolerate this or it might not be developmentally appropriate (for example, a young child will need to know another person is there). The bilateral nature of these techniques helps to connect the horizontal aspects of the brain (Elbrecht, 2018) and the repeated, rhythmic nature aids sensory soothing and emotional calming (Bronson, 2000; Gerhardt, 2006; Jennings, 2010, 2012; Jennings et al., 2021) as well as releases embedded emotions (Elbrecht, 2018).

Traditional Art Therapy has been perceived as relying on the making of an image, onto which the client's thoughts and feelings are projected (Case and Dalley, 1992; Dalley, 1984; Schaverien, 1991). However, embodied techniques move away from the creation of an image as central to the process and instead are movement or process-led, although images can come when the embodied processing has been done. Reflecting on the process or image with the therapist then uses the more cognitive part of the brain, which helps to integrate the embodied aspects that have just been processed – for example, 'I have just experienced strong emotions felt in my body, I now understand what was happening'.

Themes of water in Art Therapy

At the start of therapy (and a theme that's returned to repeatedly), we work on grounding aspects to help clients establish a sense of safety. In Art Therapy, this can be done by inviting clients to draw, make or visualise a place where they have felt safest or happiest. Whether working with children or adults, a theme that occurs time and again (in my experience) is being in nature. And the most common place that I have witnessed people describe and depict is that of a beach or being by the sea. Often, children might remember a happy time with their family, playing together, digging in the sand and splashing about in the waves. Adults will recall their childhood memories, as well as recognise the here-and-now qualities of the sense of space, fresh air and different sensations. The back and forth of the waves provide a rhythmic and soothing sound; we have a big expanse of blue (or near blue or other colours!) in the sky and sea before us; we experience the sensory aspects of smelling the sea air, tasting the salt on our lips, feeling the wet and dry sand with our hands and feet. A visit to the beach is quite an integrated experience from a sensory perspective.

Water and sand, therefore, lend themselves to being wonderfully therapeutic materials to work with to connect with the felt sense of safety (it is recognised that this is not for everybody, however).

Water Play and NDP

One of the main principles of NDP is that attachment is developed between mother and infant in the womb in a 'playful pregnancy' (Jennings, 2012, p. 3). This is through rhythmic motion, singing and swaying, and the baby feeling and hearing the mother's heartbeat. The womb is considered the primary safe space and is where the 'infant begins to develop sensory awareness in a wet and slippery environment' (Jennings, 2012, p. 5). Playing with water (on its own or with flour, cornflour, paint, etc.) reminds us of this primal experience, as well as the playfulness as children we had when splashing about in the bath, the sea, rivers or jumping in puddles.

Jennings et al. (2021, p. 10) emphasises Water Play as being 'fundamental to Early Child Development and is the precursor to more varied sensory play'. It enhances both fine and gross motor skills and fosters mathematical thinking, scientific exploration and problem-solving abilities. Water Play can enhance social-emotional development when playing with others, can build a child's confidence and independence and can stimulate a child's imagination, creativity and storytelling skills. Water is nature's most engaging sensory toy for children.

In the case of difficulties such as bed-wetting, Jennings (Jennings et al., 2021) suggests that 'by encouraging water play many children stop wetting the bed. By controlling water outside of their bodies, they are then able to control water inside their bodies'. As well as helping with issues of bed-wetting, I have seen playing with water in therapy beneficial for:

- Increasing confidence in water (i.e., in swimming pools);
- Building tolerance to handling wet/slimy materials (where sensory avoiding);
- Down-regulating over-stimulated nervous systems (calming and soothing);

- Up-regulating under-stimulated nervous systems (enlivening and invigourating);
- Increasing positive attachments between children and caregivers (playing together);
- Unconscious material is externalised and processed (play naturally unfolding for the benefit of the client, without imposing conscious direction).

The following vignettes describe two case scenarios in which water has been used to integrate the areas of Embodiment-Projection-Role. A brief discussion follows each.

Case Scenario 1 – Child

Background

Poppy (pseudonym) was six years old when she was referred to therapy by her GP. Since the age of 18 months, when she became unwell with a high temperature, she did not eat or drink (which included drinking water) and declined to take any medication for the duration of her illness. This could last for a couple of weeks. Following the most recent sickness bug, she did not talk, open her mouth (to brush her teeth) or swallow her saliva. She was hospitalised in order to give her treatment and avoid dehydration, leading to the use of a tube and drip. Her mother described this as traumatising for both her and her daughter.

Art Therapy sessions

Poppy attended Art Therapy with her mother (who will be referred to as Mum) as we followed the Dyadic model of Art Therapy (Hendry and Taylor Buck, 2017; Taylor Buck et al., 2012, 2014). We agreed on this from the start so that Poppy would feel safe, and this model was established through assessment with Mum first and with consultation with Poppy. From the first session, Poppy was mostly non-verbal, occasionally whispering something to Mum to pass on to me. The sessions were very much child-led, and Poppy was invited to create what she wanted. She engaged with the materials in the room with great enthusiasm and confidence and paid attention to what Mum and I were saying, responding non-verbally and creatively (e.g., with nods or making something).

In the first few sessions, I noticed that the materials Poppy used were dry – using pens and playing with sand and toys. There was an absence of water, even if water was probably required; for example, if Poppy was painting or using glue, these materials were not diluted, nor were brushes washed in water. One of the first things she engaged in was to decorate a mask. A plain white cardboard mask was coloured around the nose and mouth with pink, blue, green and purple pen. Later, shades of blue, pink and purple sequins were stuck on the forehead with undiluted PVA glue.

A couple of sessions later, Poppy played with some dolls. They were pretending to take a bath, drink and do a wee. All pretending though – no actual water, although it was always available. Session 8 saw Poppy mixing PVA glue with blue paint. I wondered if this was a step towards water. Also in session 8, Poppy began humming to herself whilst absorbed in her play and she absentmindedly put the end of a paintbrush in her mouth. She was not yet talking in the sessions.

Mum had some sessions 1:1 with me so we could reflect on the joint sessions, as well as providing a space for her to be able to explore her feelings and do her own processing. She expressed, both verbally and non-verbally (using paint mixed with water – repeated blue circles inside pink and purple circles) her desire for Poppy to be more free with the use of water in therapy and to be able to take it in her body as an essential part of her wellbeing. The next session, Poppy used small sponges to print repeated circles using blue paint mixed with a little water, together with some pink circles and squares. These motifs seemed to resemble Mum's painting, which Poppy had not seen.

Also, in the parent sessions, we explored medical treatment planning and consent – Mum and Dad were to discuss with Poppy (when she was well) the kinds of things that might happen to her body, what the medical treatments were and how they could help and what Poppy might be OK with and what she would decline.

In session 11 with Poppy, and with a prior discussion between Mum and me, Mum explored her own experience of hospital treatment, namely having her tonsils out when she was a child. Poppy was very interested in this and listened to the story, which Mum told with the help of Play-Doh to make the infected tonsils and a head with an open mouth to represent from where they were removed. Mum wondered aloud which colour Play-Doh she should make the tonsils. Poppy spontaneously exclaimed 'pink!' and, without hesitation or acknowledgement of verbalisation, Mum selected the appropriately coloured Play-Doh and they proceeded to make the tonsils together. They were large balls of pink/purple Play-Doh, covered with small white dots of Play-Doh to represent the infection (Figure 8.1). In that same session, Poppy then went on to play with water in two small plastic cups, the kind that are given in hospital when offered oral medication. She also brought to the table a little toy clam that opens and closes its shell and, when open, pokes its tongue out.

After that session, Mum let me know that Poppy was delighted that she had spoken and that Poppy had sung and made 'baby noises' in the car on the way home and as soon as she got home, she told her father (Dad) all about it and was very proud of herself.

In session 15, Poppy played for the first time with toy food, as well as mixing flour and water in bowls and cups. I asked if I could let her know

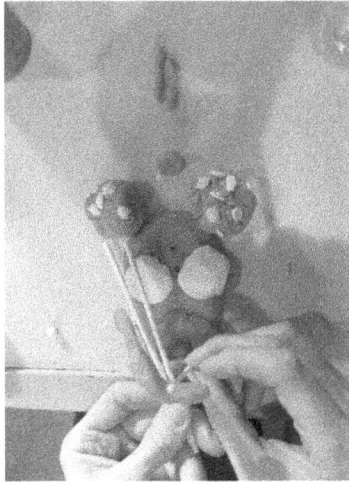

Figure 8.1 A face and tonsils made from Play-Doh

something about bodies, using flour and water, and she agreed. I used a funnel and a tube connected to the small end and said it represented our tummy and the tubes to take the waste out. When the mixture was thick, it would not pass down the tube. This might make our tummy hurt if we couldn't wee or poo. By adding water, the mixture passed through the funnel and tube. We used a bowl to catch what came out the other end. Poppy then took over and had fun playing with the idea of wee and poo.

Poppy didn't come to the next session as she was ill and had a high temperature. Thankfully, it didn't progress to anything serious and she returned to therapy the following week. It was in this returning session (number 16) that she very carefully made what she called a 'nest': a cardboard container with shredded paper in which she placed a variety of shells, pebbles and a pinecone. A couple of sessions later, there was lots of water and sensory play! Pasta and water were mixed together in two bowls. A mixture was created with water, glue, glitter and paint. Water and paint splashed all over the table and were blotted with paper towels. Poppy also used animal puppets on her hands and feet and was getting them to chat away with each other.

At Session 22, Poppy agreed to have some 1:1 time with me whilst Mum sat in the waiting area. She asked for Mum's watch, partly to check the time we had established we would have without Mum and partly (I assumed) as a Transitional Object (Winnicott, 1971, 2005). During this time, Poppy played with a baby doll, gave it water as a drink and 'fed' it flour and water mix. Baby did a 'wee' in a potty and Poppy seemed delighted with her play. She showed Mum when she returned to the therapy room.

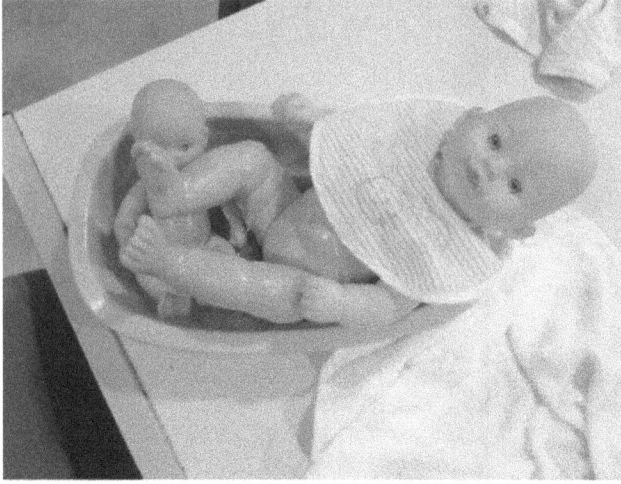

Figure 8.2 Two baby dolls in a toy bath on a table.

Two sessions later, at session 24, Poppy played with two baby dolls, one large, one small, in a toy bath, splashing and singing (Figure 8.2). Items on the table were getting wet, and near the end of the session, Poppy took a red feather that had got wet on the table, wiped it around her face and sang and danced around the room, continuing the wiping with the wet feather. Poppy dried her face with a paper roll, holding it over her face like a mask, singing and dancing around the room.

Poppy didn't attend the next session as she was ill. Mum emailed the day before she was due to attend the next session, stating that Poppy was in hospital. She had woken with a high temperature, was finding breathing difficult, was vomiting every hour and was extremely dehydrated with acid in her kidneys. In hospital, Poppy was given antibiotics and fluids through a drip, together with anti-sickness medicine. Mum was being clear with Poppy about what was happening and Poppy consented to treatment by nodding.

Mum continued to email me from the hospital. The next day, Poppy was not swallowing her saliva and she was keeping her mouth firmly closed. I suggested that parents use puppets to encourage Poppy to 'speak' using her hands *as if* her mouth was opening. Parents employed this playful approach, and in the night, Poppy woke and asked for water. She took a tiny amount.

Poppy was discharged from hospital five days later. Her temperature had been brought down and whatever infection there was had been reduced. She was still not eating, drinking or talking and her lips were stuck together. The image of the last therapy session we'd had together was in my mind – the baby dolls in the bath and how free and playful Poppy had been. I suggested water play in the bath at home.

I was relieved to hear from Mum that Dad had 'worked wonders'. Dad had gently, through play in the bath, managed to encourage Poppy to move. She opened her mouth, released her saliva and brushed her teeth whilst in the water. From then on, she was talking again.

Mum had described that, although playing *with* water was helpful, it was her need to be *in* water that was so essential for her. We had another few sessions to close and the feedback afterwards was that Poppy was feeling a lot safer and was now able to do things like Covid tests and have the Flu spray, which she declined to do previously.

Summary of Case Scenario 1

Poppy would attend hospital when she was very unwell but attended Art Therapy only when she was well. She could think about the traumatic hospital environment whilst being in the safer environment of the Art Therapy room with Mum, having fun making and playing. The humming and putting of the paintbrush in her mouth in session 8 demonstrated that she was less anxious and progressed to the first verbalisation and playing with water in session 11. This could parallel the developmental stages of first sucking, then babbling – mum had described Poppy's 'baby noises' in the car – the Embodiment stage. As the therapy sessions progressed, Poppy's play with water increased, as did her verbalisations. Projection and Role stages were employed in the telling of the story about Mum having her tonsils out, which included talking about feelings. Although in the therapy sessions, Poppy engaged mainly in projective play, it helped to inform an embodied approach at home, which was key to her unlocking her rigidity. Playing together in the bath at home had helped Poppy to move away from the 'bank of rigidity' and get back into the 'calm flow of the river'.

Case Scenario 2 – Adult

Background

Anna (pseudonym) was in her sixties when she self-referred to Art Therapy, as she wanted to experience the more playful side of herself again. After experiencing repeated trauma as a child and an adult, she found herself stuck both emotionally and physically. She was suffering from chronic fatigue, lack of sleep, physical pain, difficulty concentrating and an inability to switch off from circular thoughts. Anna had identified that being at a beach was her safe place, but she was out of touch with the reality of being there. She had previously enjoyed outdoor swimming in the sea, rivers and lakes. Anna had, in the past, been engaged in art practice using painting and photography, but these days found it difficult to muster the energy and concentration for these.

Art Therapy sessions

Despite wanting to create art and be playful, Anna would often say that she 'couldn't' when invited to do so in the therapy sessions. She would be overwhelmed by tiredness or find that she couldn't get off the track of speaking about a particular topic. Anna was keen to persevere, and so at times when Anna so desperately wanted to be creative but couldn't, I offered her warm water in a bowl or sand in the sandtray, just to put her hands in without having to do anything else. The shift from being only in her head to being more in her body was instantaneous every time. As Anna began to play with the material with her fingers, her breathing changed from shallow to deeper, with some big exhales as I saw her body become more relaxed. She also played with water at the sink, using bowls, jugs and sieves.

Anna's play at these times might remain with just water or move from water to sand or vice versa, feeling through what she needed to feel. When Anna was ready, the play moved on to projective play using objects and figures in the sandtray. On occasions, Anna made representations of water, such as the sea, a lake or river. We did guided visualisations in which I talked through Anna imagining herself at a beach, sometimes going in the sea. We would check in first, whether she was up for a [virtual] swim that day or not, as it was often enough to just look at the water.

As the sessions went on, Anna was ready to try something new. I suggested using shaving foam and paint directly on the table, using a bilateral approach. The tabletop in the therapy room is a smooth Formica, which is great for moving hands and materials across its surface. Anna smeared the shaving foam and paint across the table with both hands, pushing down with her palms, making circular movements at the start, as if giving a massage. Pushing forwards and out synchronised with exhales, whilst the pulling down was on the inhales. Sometimes she had her eyes closed. Anna's breathing became slower and deeper, and she began to connect more with the sensory aspects of what she was doing, which she said afterwards allowed her to slow her thoughts down or even temporarily not have them as a priority. This process enabled her to become more body-focussed. Anna said she enjoyed the 'naughty' aspect of this process – being allowed to make a mess on the table, which was 'fun' and 'childlike'.

After a little while of slowing down and becoming more relaxed, Anna started to play with the materials in a different way by writing words and drawing in the shaving foam and paint mixture with her fingers. This process was repeated in several subsequent therapy sessions – feeling and playing (Embodiment), followed by drawing and writing (Projection). Anna was aware that the Embodiment stage was like swimming a breaststroke. She was determined to get back to swimming and started to use the local pool once a week after her therapy sessions, even if only for a very short time. This built up to some occasional swimming in wilder places, where Anna could feel more alive and at home.

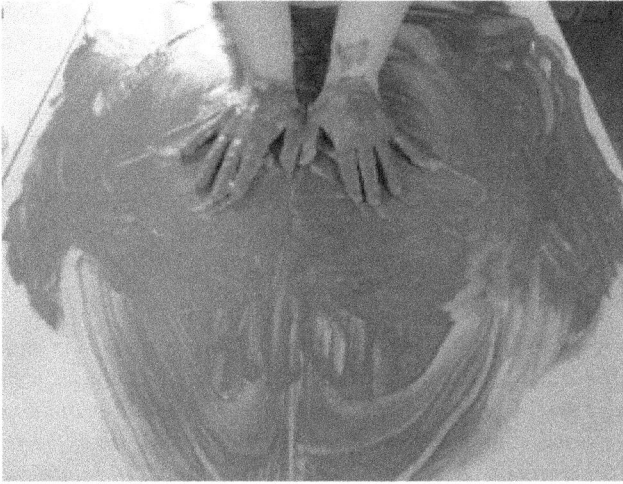

Figure 8.3 Two hands pressing down on a tabletop, rubbing paint over the table-top. The hands are covered in paint.

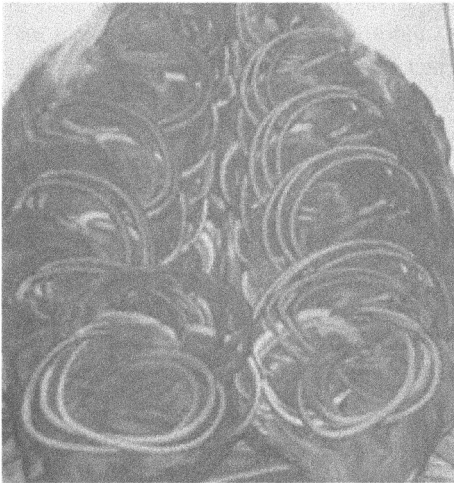

Figure 8.4 Paint smeared on a tabletop with swirling patterns, same on the left and right side, looking a bit like a human brain.

In one of the later sessions, using the sensorimotor approach with shaving foam and paint, Anna noticed that the marks that were left in the materials resembled a 'brain' and it was like she had been massaging her brain (Figures 8.3 and 8.4).

As we prepared to finish therapy, Anna made plans to join one or two art groups and courses. She had also joined a wild swimming network. At the last session, Anna brought in to show me the new swimming bag she had bought and was very much looking forward to using it. She gave me this feedback on swimming and the use of the sensory materials in her therapy sessions:

I feel at home in water. It is where I belong – in, on and by water. The sea is where all life began. And it is where I want to return after my death.

Swimming gives me freedom, buoyancy, floating, weightlessness. When I swim, the transition from land to water (being in another element) has a calming effect. I get in and the rhythm of my whole being changes. My breathing slows down, my emotional state slows. With swimming, I have to be in the moment, in the present, to stay afloat. And with outdoor swimming, I am in the landscape, too. Sea swimming makes me feel safe, held and connected to the wide blue expanse of water and sky. It makes me feel free.

The water takes away any stress and worries and it replaces it with joy. I always feel better after a swim, wherever it is, indoors or outdoors. Outdoor, cold-water swimming is invigourating and gives me a feeling of euphoria. It makes me feel alive and happy. A swimmer knows water through sensation, through feeling the water. Swimming gives me a deep feeling of joy, happiness, laughter and childlike wonder. The main feelings I have about swimming and water are freedom, aliveness, happiness and belonging.

I absolutely love being in blue (blue space) above and below (sky and water). I love the feeling of open space, open horizon, expansion, endless possibilities. I love lying on my back in the sea, feeling held and safe and looking up at the sky. It's magical. The sea helps me to reconnect to my own 'wild'. Swimming, surfing and water sports take us out of our heads and into the sensory world of our bodies, allowing us to find our own sense of aliveness.

Summary of Case Scenario 2

At the start of therapy, Anna was experiencing such a disconnect from her body that it took a lot of effort to pause talking and just hold her hands in a bowl of water. The water was warm for comfort and was similar to body temperature. This process helped Anna to reconnect with her embodied sense of self. The sensorimotor work with shaving foam and paint had a focus on the out-breath, which helped to relax Anna's nervous system. She was using the movements as if she were swimming, which helped her to prepare for actual swimming, which would give her a sense of joy and safety as she reconnected with her body. Helping Anna to return to swimming was a great outcome of the therapy.

Conclusion

Both case scenarios demonstrate the use of techniques in the therapy that integrate the more embodied aspects of art making. The bottom-up approach of moving through the stages of EPR through moving, feeling, using the senses, making, then reflecting or story-telling ensures a body-brain approach that helps the client process the non-verbal aspects of their body-held trauma. In both cases, the clients played with water during the therapy sessions and it was important for them to experience their bodies in water outside of the therapy sessions. This helped them to become more playful, relaxed and back in their flow. From an NDP perspective, we are mindful that this is where we all started – with our bodies in a watery environment for the first nine months.

Water Play at the Embodiment stage encourages us to become aware of our body and can involve splashing, pouring and squirting, often in repeated rhythmic ways. There is no end product – it is process, movement and sensory-led. In therapy, this can help people to regulate their nervous systems and allow the body to do what it needs to do without conscious intervention. The Projection stage sees themes of water being drawn, painted and made and often helps people to connect with their happy time or safe place. Although it hasn't been the focus of this chapter, the Role stage can also incorporate themes of water. For example, we might see someone pretending to be a river, moving their body as if flowing or rushing and making sounds to accompany the movement. Or we might tell a story with a water theme.

Just like water itself can have different states and transform, we can use water or themes of water in Art Therapy to help clients transform their neurobiological and emotional states. We can feel the water, feel our body, feel our feelings and then express these using language to integrate the experience. People of any age and stage can benefit from connecting with water, whether it is through play, art making, storytelling or simply being in the water.

References

Andersson, O. (2002) *Living Water: Viktor Schauberger and the Secrets of Natural Energy* (2nd ed.). Gateway.

Bowlby, J. (1988) *A Secure Base: Clinical Applications of Attachment Theory*. London: Routledge.

Bronson, M. (2000) *Self-Regulation in Early Childhood*. New York, NY: Guilford Press.

Case, C. and Dalley, T. (1992) *The Handbook of Art Therapy*. London: Routledge.

Dalley, T. (1984) *Art as Therapy: An Introduction to The Use of Art as Therapeutic Technique*. Tavistock/Routledge.

Dew, I. T. Z. and Cabeza, R. (2011) The porous boundaries between explicit and implicit memory: Behavioral and neural evidence. *Annals of the New York Academy of Sciences*, 1224(1), 174–190. https://doi.org/10.1111/j.1749-6632.2010.05946.x

Elbrecht, C. (2012) *Trauma Healing at the Clay Field: A Sensorimotor Approach to Art Therapy*. London and Philadelphia: Jessica Kingsley Publishers.

Elbrecht, C. (2018) *Healing Trauma with Guided Drawing: A Sensorimotor Art Therapy Approach to Bilateral Body Mapping*. Berkeley, CA: North Atlantic Books.

Elbrecht, C. (2021) *Healing Trauma in Children with Clay Field Therapy: How Sensorimotor Art Therapy Supports the Embodiment of Developmental Milestones*. Berkeley, CA: North Atlantic Books.

Emoto, M. (2004) *The Hidden Messages in Water*. Beyond Words.

Emoto, M. (2005) *The Secret Life of Water*. Beyond Words.

Erikson, E. H. (1958) *Young Man Luther: A Study in Psychoanalysis and History*. New York: Norton.

Erikson, E. H. (1964) *Childhood and Society* (2nd ed.). W. W. Norton.

Gerhardt, S. (2006) *Why Love Matters: How Affection Shapes a Baby's Brain*. London: Routledge.

Hendry, A. and Taylor Buck, E. (2017) Dyadic parent-child art psychotherapy with children who have been exposed to complex trauma. In *Creative Therapies for Complex Trauma: Helping Children and Families in Foster Care, Kinship Care or Adoption*, eds. Hendry, A. and Hasler, J. London: Jessica Kingsley Publishers.

Jennings, S. (1990) *Dramatherapy with Families and Groups*. London: Jessica Kingsley Publishers.

Jennings, S. (2010) *Healthy Attachments and Neuro-Dramatic-Play*. London: Jessica Kingsley Publishers.

Jennings, S. (2012) *Neuro-Dramatic-Play Part One. A Play-Book for Adults of Theory and Practice*. Penang, Malaysia: Pheonix Printers SDN NHD.

Jennings, S. et al. (2021) *Dancing into Life*. Wells: Close Publications. Available as e-Book.

Jung, C. G., Adler, G. and Hull, R. F. C. (1969) *The Collected Works of C. G. Jung, Vol. 9, Part 1: The Archetypes and the Collective Unconscious* (Bollingen Series, No. 20, 2nd ed.). Princeton University Press.

Kagin, S. L. and Lusebrink, V. B. (1978) The expressive therapies continuum. *Art Psychotherapy*, 5(4), 171–180. https://doi.org/10.1016/0090-9092(78)90031-590031-5)

Lusebrink, V. B. (1990) *Imagery and Visual Expression in Therapy*. New York: Plenum Press.

Lusebrink, V. B. (2010) Assessment and therapeutic application of the expressive therapies continuum: Implications for brain structures and functions. *Art Therapy: Journal of the American Art Therapy Association*, 27(4), 168–177. https://doi.org/10.1080/07421656.2010.10129380

Malchiodi, C. (2020) *Trauma and Expressive Arts Therapy: Brain, Body and Imagination in the Healing Process*. New York: Guildford Press.

Piaget, J. (1952) *The Origins of Intelligence in Children* (M. Cook, Trans.). New York: International Universities Press (Original work published 1936).

Pollack, G. H. (2017) *The Fourth Phase of Water, Beyond Solid, Liquid, and Vapor*. Seattle: Ebner and Sons Publishers.

Porges, S. W. (2011) *The Polyvagal Theory: Neurophysiological Foundations of Emotions, Attachment, Communication, and Self-Regulation*. New York: WW Norton and Co.

Porges, S. W. (2017) *The Pocket Guide to the Polyvagal Theory: The Transformative Power of Feeling Safe*. New York: WW Norton and Co.

Porges, S. W. and Dana, D. (2018) *Clinical Applications of the Polyvagal Theory: The Emergence of Polyvagal-Informed Therapies*. New York: WW Norton and Co.

Schaer, R. (2005) *The Trauma Spectrum: Hidden Wounds and Human Resilience*. New York: W. W. Norton.

Schaverien, J. (1991) *The Revealing Image: Analytical Art Psychotherapy in Theory and Practice*. London and New York: Routledge.

Sheridan, M. (1973) *From Birth to Five Years: Children's Developmental Progress*. Taylor & Francis Ltd.

Siegel, D. J. (2000) *The Developing Mind: How Relationships and the Brain Interact to Shape Who We Are* (3rd ed.). New York: Guilford Press.

Siegel, D. J. and Bryson, T. P. (2012) *The Whole-Brain Child: 12 Proven Strategies to Nurture Your Child's Developing Mind*. Great Britain: Robinson.

Steele, W. and Malchiodi, C. (2012) *Trauma-Informed Practices with Children and Adolescents*. New York: Routledge.

Squire, L. R. and Dede, A. J. O. (2015) Conscious and unconscious memory systems. *Cold Spring Harbor Perspectives in Medicine*, 5(1). https://doi.org/10.1101/cshperspect.a021667

Taylor Buck, E., Dent-Brown, K. and Parry, G. (2012) Exploring a dyadic approach to art psychotherapy with children and young people: A survey of British art psychotherapists. *International Journal of Art Therapy*, 18(1), 20–28.

Taylor Buck, E., Dent-Brown, K., Parry, G. and Boote, J. (2014) Dyadic art psychotherapy: Key principles, practices and competences. *Arts in Psychotherapy*, 41(2), 163–173.

Van der Kolk, B. A. (2014) *The Body Keeps the Score: Brain, Mind, and Body in the Healing of Trauma*. New York: Viking.

Vygotsky, L. S. (1978) *Mind in Society: The Development of Higher Psychological Processes*. Cambridge, MA: Harvard University Press.

Winnicott, D. (1971) *Therapeutic Consultations in Child Psychiatry*. London: Hogarth Institute of Psycho-Analysis.

Winnicott, D. (2005) *Playing and Reality* (Classic ed.). Abingdon: Routledge.

Chapter 9

Hunter's journey back to his nest

Application utilising the NDP and EPR in parent and child nature-based play therapy

Catriona O'Neill-Hayes

A therapeutic touchstone story to set the scene provides insight into the lived world of a boy named Hunter. Like the archer that draws the arrow back, neuro-dramatic play provides Hunter with the opportunity to gently return to his in-utero and early birth experiences. Resembling the bow providing security as it safely holds the arrow before it can launch forward, Hunter is nested and nurtured in his experiences in parent and child sessions. Through the occurrence of embodiment, projection, and role (Jennings, 1990). Hunter brings us on a journey into his world as he explores and delights in parent and child nature-based play therapy. Like the archer who firmly holds its bow and arrow, Hunter's deep connection with nature and his early attachment figure embraces a holding like no other, which gently enables him to developmentally spring forth to meet his true authentic self.

The tenets of attachment theory recognise that infants have an innate survival need to attach to another person and that the initial hours and days after birth are crucial for this bonding process to occur between infant and parent (Hallin et al., 2011). Hunter was born by emergency caesarean section at 40 weeks, having experienced a relatively rare phenomenon 'a true knot cord'. Such an event can occur when the umbilical cord loops around itself and tightens during pregnancy, which can deprive the developing foetus of nutrients and oxygen, potentially having long-term neurological consequences (Lichtman et al., 2020). During this critical period of early attachment and bonding, Hunter was abruptly separated from his mother, which impacted their ability to bond. Hunter's mother developed postpartum depression following his traumatic birth, which further disrupted the attachment process.

When we promote a healthy bond in infants, the benefits are immense. The brain region linked to attachment is also responsible for regulating empathy, fear, intuition, emotional and behavioural responses, adaptability, and morality (Meyer, 2011). Hunter, now aged 9 years old, presented with a diagnosis of autism spectrum disorder (ASD) and significant sensory processing difficulties. Hunter was also presenting with motor learning difficulties, struggling with transitions, and having difficulty managing his emotions.

DOI: 10.4324/9781003498209-12

Hunter's mother voiced that she would like for him to gain more accept-ance in relation to his ASD diagnosis and for him to become emotionally regulated. The author welcomes the concept of the position held by autistic individuals and their parents and carers in relation to 'difference' rather than 'disorder', and how they conceptualise the features associated with ASD dif-ferences to be acknowledged, understood, celebrated, and accommodated (Claiborne Park, 1982; Grandin, 1995; Greene, 2006; Ring et al., 2018). In considering Hunter's early attachment process and its impact on parent and child and understanding that children function within the context of connec-tions with their caregivers, it was deemed appropriate to engage Hunter and his mother in dyadic nature-based play therapy sessions, with consideration for the interweaving of Neuro-Dramatic-Play (NDP) (Jennings, 2011) and the Embodiment-Projection-Role developmental Paradigm (EPR) (Jennings, 1990). The brain's capacity to transform itself in response to experience due to neuroplasticity enables relational ruptures to be revisited and repaired (Siegel, 2012). It was envisaged that the circle of attachment recreated in dyadic nature-based play therapy sessions utilising the NDP and EPR devel-opmental paradigms would promote playful relationships, considering sen-sory experiences, rhythmic games, and 'dramatised' interactions (Jennings, 2011). Nature play therapy considers the relationship with nature as the main axis in a process that involves the use of creative methods to explore the relationship in a metaphorical and symbolic way (Berger, 2017).

As stated by Winnicott (1964):

Having reached the child, we try to look at his world with him, and to help him sort out his feelings about it, to face the painful things and discover the good things. Then we try to consolidate the positive things in the child and in his world and help him make the most of his life.

(pp. 46–57)

In the initial assessment phase of the process, the information gathered informed and guided the therapist in preparation for the touchstone story intervention. The touchstone is a focused, directive, narrative intervention based on Rogerian principles (Prendiville and Howard, 2014). It encom-passes the therapist presenting a synopsis of significant elements in the child's life story while in the presence of their parent or supportive ally, using toys to provide psychological distance. It also acts as an aid in building the thera-peutic relationship and in the establishment of safety and trust (Prendiville and Howard, 2014). Hunter embodied this process by proceeding to make a symbol of his beloved companion and dog, Riley.

The developmental paradigm of EPR follows the evolution of dramatic play from birth to seven years (Jennings, 2011). Right from the beginning, and with caution, Hunter engaged in embodiment play as he placed his hands into the thick mud. As soon as Hunter's hands felt too dirty, he would go and cleanse them. This cleansing is possibly an awareness following his birth, as he was taken away from his mother's arms and wiped clean. There was a sense he was titrating this experience of staying messy for longer, and with every session, he would leave it that little bit longer to wash his hands. The sensations of Hunter's 'messy' birth experience were recreated in the process to enable him to ask his mother for help to wipe away the mess, just like the helpless newborn baby would receive with such attunement and compassion.

In one of his early sessions, there was a sense that Hunter was recreating a time when he was in the womb, and he felt safe and contained. Hunter would verbally share, "It feels nice in here", and as he moved from the safety of the tent (womb) into the attached tunnel (birth canal) he moved feet first with a huge sense of overwhelm and anxiety. Hunter appeared to be re-experiencing his birthing experience, yet this time, his mother was there to provide him with his circle of care, which forms attachment with mother and child (Emerson, 1989; Jennings, 2011).

Hunter was nurtured and rocked and held by his mother as she fed and soothed him. The rhythm of the rocking and humming from Hunter's mother provided him with an internalised sense of repetition and predictability. Resembling the bow providing security as it safely holds the arrow before it can launch forward, Hunter is nested and nurtured in his experiences in parent and child sessions. This is fitting, as Ovtscharoff and Braun (2001) state, "The dyadic interaction between the newborn and its mother which serves as a regulator of the developing individual's homeostasis" (p. 33).

In Hunter's development of his body and self to establish a healthy brain-body connection, he would run and jump through the forest trail. We are hardwired for empathetic attunement to each other at a neurological level. The mirror neurons in our brains help support this process (Rizzolatti et al., 1980; Cozolino, 2006). As Hunter was mirrored in his movements along the forest floor, he delighted in this.

As sessions progressed, the recreation of the circle of containment as we came together at the river was evident. Such containment is established pre-birth within the womb; it serves as the source of life and the first circle full of safe waters (Jennings, 2011). Hunter was invited to dip his feet in the waters, and as he tiptoed across the river in this exploratory stage of the process, his mother expressed her joy and expressed how "he would never do that". Hunter relayed, "Mum can hold me back sometimes", as he mastered crossing the river. In his testing for the protection stage and in establishing trust within the process, Hunter would question everything. Hunter would push boundaries, and when the ACT model was provided, this aided an honouring of the process, and within the limits of protection, anything that Hunter said was accepted (Axline, 1947).

The ACT model is used to facilitate the process of communicating under-standing and acceptance of the child's intentions, to clearly define the limit, and offer alternative behaviours and actions (Landreth, 2002):

A = Acknowledge the child's feelings, wishes, and wants
C = Communicate the limit
T = Target acceptable alternatives (Landreth, 2002).

An example of how this was included:

A = Hunter, I can see you are feeling angry at Mum, and it is ok to feel Angry.
C = But your Mum is not for hitting.
T = Let's pound the clay instead.

The therapist role-modelled this, and this is a strategy that Hunter's mother implemented at home and which she referred to as a "game changer". Dur-ing the dependency and therapeutic stage, Hunter felt safe enough to express his fears about swimming with his head underwater, his need to have a rela-tional connection, and his struggle to accept his Autism diagnosis. During this stage, Hunter initiated a game of hide and seek in which he expressed his annoyance at his mother when she found him. Hide and seek is a crucial neu-ral exercise for exploring trust versus mistrust within relationships. The hider can feel uncertain as they are unable to detect safety cues from the seeker's face and voice. As the seeker comes closer, tension rises until the parent calls out, "I found you", which results in a startling effect for both players and then following the initial discovery, safety and connection are re-established through both players expressing warm facial expressions and gentle voice (Porges, 2011; Norris and Lender, 2020). For Hunter, he was rejecting being found by his mother. A curiosity inferred that Hunter was struggling to meet and find his true self.

Hunter was validated in his frustrations when he spoke about his mother "being stupid" and whenever something didn't go as he wished. For exam-ple, when he tried to untie the knots in the ferns along the narrow path, he expressed, "I just want to get out of my body; it's all your fault". This may illustrate Hunter's perspective of his birth trauma as he projects what he per-ceives to be the bad aspects of himself onto his mother as his primary object, which demonstrates the significance of the mother holding her experience of the birth trauma both in body and mind (Klein, 1955; Van der Kolk, 2014). Hunter was verbally expressing how out of control and fearful he felt when he was entangled in a knot during his birthing process. This provided an opportunity for Hunter to repair this early rupture in their relationship as his mother validated his feelings. For Emerson (1989), the empathetic connection with the child by the parent, in a deeply compassionate and understanding

Figure 9.1 The Nesting Tree

way, helps heal the woundedness. As the process developed, Hunter continued to be encircled in his mother's arms, and his awareness in relation to his
mother increased. Hunter found a tree that had a hole in the hollow, and he
referred to this as his nest (Figure 9.1).

Hunter's mother, in her role as a Mummy bird, would fly away and return
to Hunter's nest with a candy string as a worm to feed baby bird Hunter, who
accepted her nurture.

In this exploratory stage of the process, Hunter expressed, "I don't like it
when someone says autism is special".

As time progressed, Hunter continued to play the game of hide and seek,
and, over time, he was more accepting of being found by his mother. As
Hunter's neuroception of safety had developed, he was willing to try something he had never tried before. As Hunter climbed a steep hill, he asked his
mother to go to the end of the hill and open out her arms. Just like the game
of hide and seek, the tension rises as Hunter prepares himself for what he is
about to do. Hunter runs down the steep slope, and when he reaches the end,
he receives a full embrace from his mother. Words cannot describe the feelings of exhilaration and delight in this moment, which feels like when a baby

is birthed. Hunter played this embodied experience over and over as a neural exercise to create that felt sense of safety and trust within their relationship and connection within his body.

In Hunter's projection stage of development within his process, he was invited, along with his mother, to make a woodland creature to represent Autism. His mother named hers "forest with the great hearing ear" as she reflected on Hunter's wonderful ability to hear. Hunter made his clay creature, stating, "It is a person, and he is cleaned and has a cute name called Dot".

Hunter had relayed how James McClain, who is the Irish football captain, had a diagnosis of Autism and he said, "There is hope for me yet".

During the process, Hunter's mother was receiving weekly calls on how to support him at home with bedtime routine and how to co-regulate through positive touch, singing songs, hand clapping games, and mirroring activities, therefore validating his worries while setting limits and providing ample opportunity for movement. Hunter's mother shared that Hunter appeared a lot more content because of the co-regulation he was receiving and that he was able to tolerate his baby brother eating. He had also made a new friend, joined a football club, and was sleeping much better.

When it was determined that Hunter appeared resourced and regulated, a therapeutic story called *All my Stripes*, a story for Autistic children about a zebra who learns to understand he is different from his classmates, was introduced into his session. This story explored the feelings associated with feeling different, and it also highlighted all the zebra's stripes (strengths and contributions) as well as relaying that autistic people have different brains all their lives. Research demonstrates that storytelling has a profound impact on the brain with the release of dopamine, and it can engage many parts of the brain, such as the motor, sensory, and frontal parts of the cortex (Jennings, 2017). As Hunter sat on the wooden log alongside his mother, the story enabled him to feed back (mirror neurons) his pleasurable feeling of listening to and contributing to the story as he and his mother spoke about all his special stripes. Hunter's mother expressed to him, "I am so glad that you were born". Hunter appeared to be accepting of this as he cuddled into his mother.

The role stage of Hunter's process involved Hunter exploring the perspective of another. He did this when he initially role-played how he would feel when he felt someone was looking at him and explained in detail how he got a type of pins and needles sensation in his body. When Hunter went into the role of observing another, he saw a whole different perspective, and he indeed realised that the observer was curious.

Close to the termination stage of the process, Hunter verbally expressed, "Do you know it's kind of good how my brain works". "Do you know kids with autism can see better, taste better, and even smell better cos we have the best air freshener in our car". Hunter had built up a tolerance for sensory play, as he stated while playing in the mud, "No point washing my hands until I'm done, cos I'll just have to wash them again". This demonstrated Hunter's innate ability to arrive at a new solution following co-regulation work, which expanded his window of tolerance to mess. Hunter appeared to feel grounded, flexible, open, and curious (Siegel, 2012).

As Hunter looked at the cobweb hanging from a tree, he stated, "Look, it's a spider web", and then proceeded to say, "It's not a web any more", which reflected Hunter's feeling of being more accepting and balanced in body, spirit, and mind.

Hunter had not just developed a relational secure attachment with his mother, he also recognised he had gained an attachment to a place as he stated, "I still have this place that I can come back to", referring to mother nature, which provided a deep connection for Hunter and his early attachment figure as they embraced a holding like no other, allowing him to spring forth to meet his true authentic self developmentally.

Reference list

Axline, M. (1947) *Play Therapy*. Cambridge, MA: Houghton Mifflin.

Berger, R. (2017) *Environmental Expressive Therapies Nature Assisted Theory and Practice*. London: Routledge.

Claiborne Park, C. (1982) *The Siege: A Family Journey into the World of an Autistic Child*. Boston, MA: Back Bay Books.

Cozolino, L. (2006) *The Neuroscience of Human Relationships. Attachments and the Developing Social Brain*. New York: W.W. Norton and Company Ltd.

Emerson, W. (1989) Psychotherapy with infants & children. *Journal of Pre-and Peri-Natal Psychology*, 3(3), 190–217. https://doi.org/10.1007/978-3-030-41716-1_35

Grandin, T. (1995) *Thinking in Pictures and Other Reports from My Life with Autism*. New York: Vintage Books.

Greene, C. (2006) 'I should have listened to my mother': A mother's account of her journey towards understanding her young child with autism. *Good Autism Practice*, 7(1), 13–17.

Hallin, A., Bengtsson, H., Frostell, A. S. and Stjernqvist, K. (2011) The effect of extremely preterm birth on attachment organisation in late adolescence. *Child: Care, Health and Development*, 38(2), 196–203. https://doi.org/10.1111/j.1365-2214.2011.01236.x

Jennings, S. (1990) *Dramattherapy with Families, Groups and Individuals*. London: Jessica Kingsley.

Jennings, S. (2011) *Healthy Attachments and Neuro Dramatic Play*. London: Jessica Kingsley.

Jennings, S. (2017) *Creative Storytelling with Children at Risk* (2nd ed.). New York: Routledge.

Klein, M. (1955) On identification. In *New Directions in Psychanalysis*, eds. Heimann, P., Klein, M. and Money-Kryle, R. London: Karnac, 176–235.

Landreth, G. (2002) *Play Therapy: The Art of the Relationship*. New York: Routledge.

Lichtman, Y., Wainstock, T., Walfisch, A. and Sheiner, E. (2020) The significance of true knot of the umbilical cord in long-term offspring neurological health. *Journal of Clinical Medicine*, 10(1), 123. https://doi.org/10.3390/jcm10010123

Meyer, D. (2011) *Neuroplasticity as an Explanation for the Attachment Process in the Therapeutic Relationship.* http://counselingoutfitters.com/vistas/vistas11/Article_52.pdf

Norris, V. and Lender, D. (2020) *Theraplay the Practitioners Guide.* London: Jessica Kingsley Publishers.

Ovtscharoff, W. Jr. and Braun, K. (2001) Maternal separation and social isolation modulates the postnatal development of synaptic composition in the infralimbic cortex of Octodon degus. *Neuroscience*, 104, 33–40.

Porges, S. (2011) *The Polyvagal Theory: Neurophysiological Foundations of Emotions, Attachment, Communication, Self-Regulation.* New York: WW Norton & Company.

Prendiville, E. and Howard, J. (2014) *Play Therapy Today Contemporary Practice with Individuals, Groups, and Carers.* New York: Routledge.

Ring, E., Daly, P. and Wall, E. (2018) *Autism from the Inside Out. A Handbook for Parents, Early Childhood, Primary, Post Primary and Special School Settings.* Bristol: Peter Lang Publishing Group.

Rizzolatti, G., Buchtel, H. A., Camarda, R. and Scandolara, C. (1980) Neurons with complex visual properties in the superior colliculus of the macaque monkey. *Experimental Brain Research*, 38, 37–42. https://doi.org/10.1007/BF00237928

Siegel, D. J. (2012) *The Developing Mind: How Relationships and the Brain Interact to Shape Who We Are* (2nd ed.). New York, NY: Guilford Press.

Van der Kolk, B. (2014) *The Body Keeps the Score: Brain, Mind, and Body in the Healing of Trauma.* London: Penguin.

Winnicott, D. W. (1964) *The Child, the Family, and the Outside World.* London: Penguin.

Section 4

NDP and international perspectives

Chapter 10

Unlocking healing through neuro-dramatic-play in Malaysia

A journey of empowerment

Jaff Choong Gian Yong

Introduction

In the heart of every child lies a world of imagination waiting to be explored, a realm where play reigns supreme and possibilities are endless. Yet, for many children living in orphanages, this world is often overshadowed by the harsh realities of their circumstances. As a counseling psychologist working closely with orphanages in Rembau, PJ, and KL, I have witnessed firsthand the transformative power of play in healing the wounds of trauma and nurturing the souls of these children.

In this chapter, my intention is clear: to create awareness of the profound importance of play in the lives of children in orphanages. These children, who are frequently disregarded and ostracized, ought to have every chance to enjoy childhood and get over their prior traumas. Through Neuro-Dramatic-Play (NDP), a therapeutic method that harnesses the therapeutic potential of play, I aim to shed light on how play can be a catalyst for growth, healing, and empowerment.

All children need to be able to play, no matter what their situation. Play is not merely a frivolous pastime; it is a fundamental aspect of childhood development (Ndlovu et al., 2023; Wu, 2023). Through play, children discover things about the world, themselves, and their place within it. They acquire critical social, emotional, and cognitive abilities via play. And maybe most significantly, they begin to heal from the trauma's scars and make sense of their experiences via play (Achmad et al., 2022).

In my work with orphanages, I have encountered countless children grappling with trust issues, attachment difficulties, low self-esteem, and overwhelming anger. Many of these children were pushed to mature significantly later than they should have been because they were denied access to regular developmental processes, which are crucial to their health. Play is a vital medium for many children, enabling them to reconnect with their sense of wonder, rediscover their childhoods, and build deep connections with others.

One of the key paradigms of NDP is the concept of Nurture and Nesting, which focuses on creating a safe and secure environment for the child

DOI: 10.4324/9781003498209-14

(Jennings, 2011). Through activities that emphasize comfort, safety, and connection, children are able to establish a sense of security and trust, laying the foundation for healthy attachments. This paradigm is especially crucial for children in orphanages, many of whom have experienced profound loss and abandonment.

The second developmental paradigm in NDP, Embodiment-Projection-Role, takes this process a step further by allowing children to explore different roles and identities in a safe and supportive environment (Jennings, 2011). Children can explore new aspects of themselves, change into different characters, and communicate their innermost thoughts and feelings through role-playing, storytelling, and creative expression. Through the development of their feeling of agency and empowerment, children are better equipped to deal with the challenges of adulthood with resilience and confidence thanks to this paradigm.

Finally, the third developmental paradigm in NDP, the Theatre of Body, the Theatre of Life, and the Theatre of Resilience, empowers children to embrace their bodies, their lives, and their inherent resilience (Jennings, 2011). Children learn to become resilient and confident through movement, expression, and self-reflection. This paradigm is particularly transformative for teenagers facing the daunting prospect of leaving the orphanage at the age of 18, as it instills in them the confidence and resilience they need to navigate the transition to adulthood.

NDP could transform the lives of children staying in orphanages by offering them the tools they need to overcome their traumas. By encouraging play and promoting the use of NDP in orphanage settings, we can ensure that every child can play, heal, and develop.

Neuro-dramatic-play

The origin of NDP traces its roots to Prof. Dr. Sue Jennings' pioneering work in the field, drawing from her extensive expertise, elaborating on the concept of attachment and its profound relationship with NDP, emphasizing that the process of attachment begins as early as six months before birth (Jennings, 2011). NDP is an attachment-based play methodology designed to foster sensory development, rhythm, embodied experiences, and social interaction among participants (Jennings, 2011).

While NDP is not classified as traditional therapy, its multifaceted nature encompasses various therapeutic elements, making it a potent tool in the therapeutic process. NDP stands as a unique therapeutic approach that diverges from traditional methods, offering a dynamic framework for healing and growth. It transcends the confines of conventional therapy, embodying a holistic ethos that prioritizes internal playfulness, cognitive stimulation, and artistic expression.

Central to NDP is the cultivation of internal playfulness, harnessing the innate capacity for imagination and creativity within each individual. Through the exercise of the brain, NDP engages cognitive processes, stimulating neural pathways and promoting cognitive flexibility. Drawing upon art materials from the environment, NDP fosters a sensory-rich experience, tapping into the sensory modalities to facilitate emotional expression and exploration. As a practitioner, I have personally witnessed the transformative power of NDP in facilitating therapeutic breakthroughs and fostering holistic well-being.

Central to NDP are various forms of play, including messy play, rhythmic play, water play, and dramatic play, all geared towards holistic development (Jennings, 2011). There are three paradigms of NDP: the first paradigm of the NDP focused on Nurture and Nesting (NaN) focuses on creating a safe and secure environment for children. The second paradigm, Embodiment-Projection-Role (EPR), underscored the interconnectedness of physicality, imagination, and role-playing in NDP (Jennings, 2011). Finally, the third paradigm, the Theatre of Resilience (ToR), emphasizes NDP's potential in building resilience and coping mechanisms in individuals (Jennings, 2011).

The question of whether NDP should be directive or non-directive sparks debate within therapeutic circles, with proponents advocating for both approaches. The decision ultimately breaks down to the needs and preferences of the client, emphasizing the need for individualized care and respect for autonomy. In my practice, I prioritize a client-centered approach, allowing the client to lead the way and honoring their unique journey. Creating a safe space is paramount before delving into the therapeutic process, recognizing that security and attachment serve as crucial coping mechanisms for orphans who have experienced profound loss and trauma. The process unfolds organically, incorporating elements of messy play, rhythmic play, and dramatic play to facilitate emotional expression and regulation.

At the heart of NDP lies its ability to engage the right hemisphere of the brain, unlocking the door to creativity and metaphorical thinking (Jennings, 2011). By harnessing the power of the right hemisphere, NDP encourages clients to tap into their innate creativity, fostering a sense of exploration and discovery (Jennings, 2011). Metaphors and symbols become potent tools for expression, allowing clients to communicate complex emotions and experiences in a non-verbal manner (Jennings, 2011). Through the rich tapestry of metaphorical language and symbolic representation, clients can navigate the depths of their psyche with greater ease and clarity, paving the way for profound insights and transformative growth. As a practitioner, I remain committed to harnessing the therapeutic potential of NDP, guiding clients on a journey of self-discovery and empowerment.

Children in the children's home

In the quiet corners of orphanages, where the laughter of children should echo, there lies a profound silence – a silence born from the weight of loss, abandonment, and unspoken pain. Within these walls dwell children who have known more sorrow than most, whose innocent hearts bear the scars of shattered families and fractured dreams. As a therapist working closely with orphanages, I have borne witness to the untold stories of these children – stories of resilience but also stories of profound trauma and suffering.

Each child who finds themselves in an orphanage has a unique past and a story of tragedy and grief. Some have been abandoned by parents unable to provide for them, while others have lost both parents in horrific accidents. Nevertheless, others have been abandoned by parents who are working alone and are having financial difficulties. For these children, orphanages become both sanctuary and prison – a place of refuge, yet also a stark reminder of their fractured pasts.

Amid this tumult, some children find temporary solace in the arms of adoptive parents, only to be cast back into the cold embrace of the orphanage once more. The rejection of their adoptive families adds to the pain previously experienced by these youngsters, who already struggle with the trauma of abandonment. Left adrift in a sea of uncertainty, they struggle to make sense of their shattered dreams and fractured identities.

The orphanages themselves, often non-governmental organizations grappling with financial constraints, become battlegrounds of survival for these children. In a desperate bid to secure funding, orphanages open their doors to visitors, transforming the children into unwitting performers in a tragic charade of charity. Forced to entertain and appease their benefactors, the children learn to wear masks of false cheerfulness, concealing the pain and trauma that lurks beneath the surface.

Beneath their brave façade, the children carry the heavy burden of trauma – a burden that manifests in myriad ways. Insecurity, trust issues, and overwhelming anger are the constant companions of these children, their silent tormentors shaping every aspect of their lives. Trust, once shattered, becomes a fragile commodity, hoarded away like precious treasure in the depths of their souls. Even as they smile and engage with visitors, they remain distant, wary of opening their hearts to the pain of rejection once more.

For many of these children, attachment becomes a twisted dance of longing and fear – a delicate balance between craving closeness and recoiling from the specter of abandonment. Anxious attachment, dismissive-avoidant attachment, and fearful-avoidant attachment become their silent companions, shaping their relationships and coloring their perceptions of the world. Some children get so consumed by their own pain that they withdraw from others. Others cling desperately to any semblance of affection, their hearts aching with the fear of being forgotten and abandoned once more.

There are times when this sea of misery is illuminated by flashes of intense clarity and hope that shine through the shadows like beams of light. There was a particular child that came to mind, a two-year-old who had a habit of biting anyone who approached him too closely. At first glance, his behavior seemed like a mere act of defiance, a bid for attention wrapped in the guise of aggression. However, additional investigation revealed that his actions were driven more by a desperation for human connection than by hostility. This cry was full of doubt and fear mixed with a sense of optimism.

The road to recovery for these children is filled with obstacles and challenges; it requires not only empathy and tolerance but also a deep understanding of the complex relationships between attachment and trauma. Through NDP, we seek to offer a safe space where these children can discuss their inner lives, communicate their pain and grief, and rediscover their sense of self and worth. Through play, they learn to rewrite the narratives of their past, to embrace their vulnerabilities, and forge new pathways toward healing and wholeness.

Yet, healing is not a linear process, nor is it without its setbacks and struggles. For every step forward, there are moments of doubt and despair – moments when the weight of their pain threatens to overwhelm them once more. But despite everything, hope endures; it is a glimmer of light that shines through the cracks in their broken hearts and shows them the path to a brighter tomorrow.

Being a caregiver or advocate for these children means witnessing their loss and suffering, providing a space for them to communicate their sorrow, and supporting them as they go through the healing process. This is both our greatest difficulty and our greatest honor. Even if the path ahead may be difficult and drawn out, it is one that is worthwhile because these orphaned youngsters hold within them the hope of a better future, one that will be shaped by their resiliency and steadfast spirit rather than by the flames of their suffering.

The journey of empowerment

In the work, flexibility is key! From creating a Safe Place to Facing Challenges, each step must balance the "freedom" for creativity or playfulness and the "discipline" to maintain the necessary boundaries. Sessions, ideally held weekly for two hours in a consistent location, adapt to each child's pace of growth. Avoiding excessive length or brevity, we tailor treatment to nurture progress without overwhelming or underwhelming the children.

Creating SafePlace

Creating a nurturing and trusting environment for children is fundamental in the first paradigm of nurture and nesting in the developmental paradigm of

NDP (Jennings, 2011). The concept of a "SafePlace" is pivotal in this paradigm, acting as a sanctuary where children can feel secure and develop trust. This SafePlace is not merely about creating a physical space filled with toys and materials; it also encompasses the creation of a psychological space that fosters a sense of acceptance and non-judgment, enabling children to truly be themselves.

Understanding the dual nature of "space" is essential. Physical space, while important for providing tangible resources such as toys, is insufficient on its own for nurturing a child's sense of safety. The psychological space, on the other hand, is more abstract and arguably more critical. Children can express themselves freely there without worrying about criticism or punishment. This space allows them to explore their identities, emotions, and thoughts in a supportive setting.

Reflecting on my experiences, I recall the advice given by Professor Jennings, who emphasized the importance of allowing children to engage in activities of their choice, including messy play. Initially, my discomfort with the disorder made this challenging. However, I soon realized that facilitating such play was crucial for opening communication channels and building strong relationships with the children. This type of play, which may seem chaotic, is a vital tool for children to express and manage their emotions and interactions.

I always said: "When rapport is there, trust is there, then hope follows" (Yong, 2021). The sequential nature of relationship building begins with creating a comfortable rapport with the children, fostering trust, and, eventually, instilling hope. Our role as therapists or caregivers extends beyond mere observation; it involves active participation and engagement in the children's world. As if in their own stage play, children should feel they are both the directors and the actors, with the freedom to dictate the course of their play. Our job is to be present, to play along, and occasionally reflect on their behaviors, emotions, thoughts, and experiences, ensuring that most of the time, we are simply there, playing with them according to their whims.

Additionally, it is critical to acknowledge and value the uniqueness of each child's participation level. When new children join, some may immediately explore and interact with the available toys and materials, while others may hesitate or refrain from participating. Such behavior is perfectly acceptable. It is essential to allow them the space to engage at their own pace, reaffirming the safe and accepting nature of the environment we strive to maintain.

Creating a Safe Place in both physical and psychological dimensions is thus not just about ensuring safety and trust; it is about embracing the child's choice, fostering open communication, and building relationships that are anchored in mutual respect and understanding. This method builds the groundwork for the child's future growth and development in addition to promoting their present well-being.

Assessing needs and goals

As we endeavor to create a safe space for children, it is vital to simultaneously assess their individual needs to tailor our therapeutic goals effectively. Generally, children's needs can be categorized into two groups: the need for authority and the need for affection (Zheng et al., 2015). The want for power is a desire for control, whereas the need for love translates into a need for sensitivity and affection (Zheng et al., 2015). Identifying and understanding these needs is crucial as it guides the direction and methods of therapy tailored to each child.

To facilitate this understanding, it is essential to maintain thorough records of each child's behavior and needs during play sessions. This process involves close communication with the caregivers or wardens of the orphanages. For instance, having the warden complete a Strengths and Difficulties Questionnaire (SDQ) before starting the play sessions can provide valuable baseline data on each child's emotional and social competencies and challenges. This initial assessment aids in setting realistic and specific therapeutic goals.

Furthermore, it is critical to have frank conversations about expectations with the children while making sure they feel heard and understood and avoiding making unfulfillable promises. Such conversations help build trust and clarify the objectives of the therapy, making the sessions more meaningful.

Following each session, it is beneficial to utilize tools like the Session Rating Scale (SRS). The SRS helps in evaluating various aspects of the therapy session, including the effectiveness of the relationship built, the relevance of the goals and topics discussed, the approaches or methods used, and the overall session experience. This scale is particularly advantageous for new therapists as it provides a structured way to reflect on and assess the effectiveness of each session. By focusing on these ratings, therapists can continually adjust their strategies to meet the evolving needs of the children better.

Such meticulous assessment and reflection ensure that the therapy remains dynamic and responsive to the children's needs. This not only enhances the therapeutic outcome but also supports the development of a stronger, more effective therapeutic relationship. Each session, therefore, contributes to a deeper understanding of the children's needs, helping therapists to refine their approach and interventions accordingly. This ongoing cycle of assessment, interaction, and adjustment is fundamental in ensuring that the therapy remains aligned with the individual needs of each child, fostering an environment of growth and healing within the safety of the designated space.

The therapeutic sessions

Emotional Regulation – This stands as a cornerstone within the NDP module and is particularly crucial when working with children residing in orphanages. Within this stage, the embodiment phase of the second developmental paradigm, EPR (Embodiment, Projection Role), plays a pivotal role. Here, sensory play, messy play, water play, rhythmic play, dance, and movement become essential tools for children to explore and express their emotions. Through these embodied experiences, children can tangibly engage with their feelings, facilitating a deeper understanding and management of their emotional states. Additionally, various interactive activities are employed to invite children to delve into their emotions further. They are encouraged to express themselves through drawing and dramatic enactment, weaving their emotional narratives through art and performance. Engaging in emotion-based storytelling, playing the emotional stone, and participating in the card game further provide avenues for self-expression and emotional exploration. By integrating these diverse approaches, children are empowered to navigate the complexities of their emotions in a safe and supportive environment, fostering greater emotional resilience and well-being.

In Neuro-Dramatic-Play (NDP), the paradigm of Embodiment, Projection, and Role (EPR) serves as a powerful vehicle for emotional regulation and expression (Jennings, 2011). Through activities such as messy play, sensory play, and rhythmic play within the embodiment stage, children are provided with a safe and secure environment to explore and express their feelings. In the projection phase, drawing and expressive arts become mediums through which children can project their unconscious emotions onto external forms. Finally, in the role-play or dramatic play stage, children consciously embody their emotions, examining their body changes and vocal expressions. This holistic process allows children to become aware of and acknowledge their emotions, paving the way for healing and growth. By engaging in this procedure, children are prepared to gain power and face challenges, equipped with the self-awareness and emotional resilience needed to navigate their inner worlds and emerge stronger.

Gaining Power – Within the NDP pinnacle of growth, marking the moment when children discover their innate ability to help themselves in new and empowering ways. Through role-play, children develop a heightened awareness of their physical changes, engaging in what is known as the theatre of the body. This stage allows for reflection on both the roles they portray and their own bodies, fostering deeper self-understanding. As children transition into the theatre of life, they harness their newfound power to confront life's challenges as if equipped with superpowers. A key indicator of their progress in gaining power lies in their projection work, where they transform their inner thoughts and emotions into outward expressions. It is important to allow children to progress at their own pace, as they will signal when they have achieved this stage. Once they have mastered the art of transformation, the focus shifts to strengthening and prolonging their newfound resilience, preparing them for the challenges life may present.

Facing Challenges and Reclaiming Future – After gaining the power of change, the focus shifts to preparing children for future challenges, particularly as they transition out of orphanages. Strengthening resilience becomes paramount in equipping children with the tools they need to navigate life's uncertainties. The theatre of life offers a platform for children to explore different perspectives and cultivate resilience. Activities such as creating symbolic trees of life, hope, or appreciation empower children to reclaim their futures and confront challenges head-on. By engaging in these activities, children develop a sense of agency and empowerment, enabling them to face the future with confidence and resilience.

Furthermore, the theatre of resilience within NDP serves as a transformative space for children to further bolster their resilience. Through dramatizations of classic literary works such as Shakespeare's "Midsummer Night's Dream" and Wu Cheng'en's "Journey to the West," children immerse themselves in narratives of strength and triumph over adversity. Characters like Puck and Sun Wukong embody resilience and power, offering therapeutic insights for children grappling with life's chaos. By embodying these characters and exploring their journeys, children gain new perspectives on their own struggles, fostering resilience and empowerment in the face of life's challenges.

Termination

Termination marks a crucial milestone in the therapeutic journey, signaling the culmination of growth and progress while paving the way for newfound independence and resilience. As a practitioner working with children in orphanages, I recognize the significance of a proper termination process in fostering autonomy and preventing the re-experience of feelings of inadequacy. Throughout the therapeutic process, I laid the groundwork for termination by instilling a sense of empowerment and self-confidence in the children. One creative strategy I employed is the "pizza" metaphor, introduced during the phase of gaining power. Each child participated in drawing slices of pizza, symbolizing their preparation for the eventual end of therapy. As the children decided how many slices to draw, they gained agency and ownership over their progress. Upon completion of therapy, the metaphorical consumption of the pizza represents the celebration of their growth toward independence.

Termination represents not only an end but also a new beginning – a testament to the resilience and growth of the children in orphanages. Through careful preparation and ongoing support, we empower these children to embrace their independence while providing a safety net to ensure their continued success. Termination is not the end of the journey but rather a stepping stone toward a brighter, more empowered future.

Table 10.1 Sample of Planned Sessions

Session	Objective	Activities	Materials to prepare
0	Preparation	1. Approach the person in charge 2. Meet up with the warden and communicate with them about their needs and goals	1. Informed consent
1	Creating SafePlace	**Nurture and Nesting** 1. Introduction 2. Icebreaking a. Throwing ball b. Paper plane **Embodiment – Sensory Play** 1. Messy play – corn flour with water	1. Ball 2. A4 Papers 3. Color pencils
2		**Nurture and Nesting** 1. Throwing the ball to create a story 2. Creating SafePlace – imagination and play with the fabrics **Embodiment – Rhythmic Play** 1. Handclapping and table clapping 2. Use drum to design rhythm **Bedtime story**	1. Ball 2. Fabrics 3. Musical instruments 4. Color pencils 5. A4 Papers
3	Assessing Needs and Goals + Emotional Expression	**Embodiment – Sand Play** **Projection – Sand Play** **Story Telling** **Bedtime story**	1. Sand tray 2. Toys and miniatures
4		**Embodiment – Clay** **Projection – Clay** **Story Telling** **Bedtime story**	1. Clay 2. Cover for the floor 3. Tempera paint for clay
5	Emotional Regulation	**Projection – Mask Making** **Role – Theatre of Body** 1. Play with the Mask **Story Telling** **Bedtime story**	1. Paper plate 2. Scissors 3. Glue 4. Color pencils 5. Papers 6. Fabrics 7. Musical Instruments

(Continued)

Table 10.1 (Continued)

Session	Objective	Activities	Materials to prepare
6		**Embodiment** 1. Play with the recycled materials **Projection** 1. Build their dream home, ideal room for themselves **Role – Theatre of Body and Theatre of Life** 1. Combine their houses and rooms 2. Form the community Weather Massage Game	1. Recycle materials 2. Scissors 3. Glue 4. Color pencils 5. Mahjung papers 6. Musical instruments 7. Fabrics
7		**Story Telling: Monster** **Projection** 1. Drew the monster in mind **Role – Theatre of Body and Theatre of Life** 1. Play the sounds of the monster 2. Acted as monster 3. "Defeat" the monster	1. Color pencils 2. Papers 3. Fabrics 4. Musical Instruments
8		**Story Telling: Yes-No** **Projection** 1. Six Part Story **Bedtime story**	1. Color pencils 2. Papers 3. Fabrics 4. Musical Instruments
9	Facing Challenges and Reclaiming Future	**Story Telling: Journey to the West (Monkey King)** **Projection** 1. Draw the monkey king 2. Discuss the story **Role – Theatre of Life** 1. Act out the story	1. Color pencils 2. Papers 3. Fabrics 4. Musical Instruments 5. Mahjung papers
10		**Story Telling: Journey to the West (Monkey King) Part 2** **Role – Theatre of Life, Theatre of Resilience** 1. Act out the story as if they have the power of the Monkey King	1. Color pencils 2. Papers 3. Fabrics 4. Musical Instruments 5. Mahjung papers

(Continued)

Table 10.1 (Continued)

Session	Objective	Activities	Materials to prepare
11		**Story Telling: Journey to the West (Monkey King) Part 3** **Role – Theatre of Resilience** 1. Act out the story as if they have the power of the Monkey King	1. Color pencils 2. Papers 3. Fabrics 4. Musical Instruments 5. Mahjung papers
12	Reclaiming Future + Termination	**Story Telling: Hero Journey** **Projection** 1. Draw the map for hero journey 2. Call for the journey of change 3. Create the ending of the story **Role – Theatre of Resilience** 1. Act out the story	1. Color pencils 2. Papers 3. Fabrics 4. Musical Instruments 5. Mahjung papers
13	Termination	**Story Telling: Hero Journey (Part 2)** **Projection** 1. Draw the map for hero journey 2. Call for the journey of change 3. Create the ending of the story **Role – Theatre of Resilience** 1. Act out the story	1. Color pencils 2. Papers 3. Fabrics 4. Musical Instruments 5. Mahjung papers
14		**Embodiment – finger paint** Finger paint and create empowerment story from the finger paint **Bedtime story**	1. Mahjung papers 2. Finger paint
15		**Projection** 1. I am the Star! **EPR – Rhythmic Play** Create the farewell rhythmic and song, dance, movement, and song **Bedtime story**	1. Apples 2. Knife 3. Papers 4. Color pencils 5. Fabrics 6. Musical Instruments

Following termination, it is imperative to provide ongoing support to both the children and the staff in the orphanages. While the children transition to independent living, they may encounter challenges that require additional guidance and assistance. By offering follow-up sessions and continued support, we ensure that the children have the resources they need to navigate the complexities of life beyond therapy. Also, the orphanage staff's support is necessary to maintain a caring environment that fosters the children's ongoing development and wellness. By providing training and resources, we empower staff members to continue supporting the emotional and psychological needs of the children long after therapy has ended.

The transformative power of NDP

Witnessing the transformative power of NDP sessions has been a profoundly moving experience, illuminating the resilience and growth of children in orphanages. Throughout my journey as a practitioner, I have observed the profound changes that unfold within children at various stages of the NDP process. Each session is a testament to the capacity for healing and self-discovery that lies within each child. One poignant memory that remains etched in my mind is from my time at Rembau Vivakananda Home, where a boy's expression of emotion during messy play left an indelible mark. As he joyfully colored his hand red and pressed it against the temple wall adjacent to the home, his smile radiated warmth and sincerity. Despite the need to repaint the wall afterward, witnessing his uninhibited expression of emotion was a poignant reminder of the therapeutic power of NDP.

Similarly, at PJ Chempaka Welfare Center, I was deeply moved by the bond between siblings during a projection activity. As they collaboratively drew a rainbow, the sister reassured her brother with words of unwavering support, affirming, "Don't worry, I will always be with you." This simple yet profound declaration encapsulated the strength of familial love and solidarity, offering a beacon of hope amidst adversity. Additionally, at KL Tiratana Welfare Society, a young boy's identification with the character of Sun Wukong transcended the boundaries of the literature. Embracing the role with fervor, he drew parallels between his own journey and that of the legendary Monkey King. Reflecting on his support network within the home, he expressed gratitude for the guidance and love he received from the chief (founder of the home), the monks, the caregivers, the volunteers, the teachers, and the peers alike.

These experiences serve as poignant reminders of the transformative impact of NDP on the lives of children in orphanages. From the embodiment of emotions to the projection of inner thoughts and the enactment of roles, NDP provides a multifaceted platform for self-expression and exploration. Through creative activities and symbolic play, children find a voice to articulate their emotions, forge meaningful connections, and discover newfound resilience. As a witness to their journeys, I am continually inspired by their courage, resilience, and capacity for growth. The changes I have witnessed are a testament to the profound impact of NDP in fostering healing, empowerment, and hope within the hearts of children.

Here are some examples of children's artwork that they have developed:

Practical considerations and ethics

Owning and alienation

In the intricate dance of child psychotherapy, the concepts of owning and alienation serve as crucial waypoints, guiding children through the delicate process of self-discovery and expression (Zheng et al., 2015). Within the therapeutic realm, owning allows children to fully immerse themselves in the play, delving deeper into their inner selves with a sense of ownership and agency. Children get insight into their needs and desires and become closer to their genuine selves via this process. Moreover, owning fosters a nurturing relationship between therapist and child, laying the foundation for trust and mutual understanding. As children navigate the terrain of ownership, they

Figure 10.1 The Tree of Life: Piṭṭam (Buttock) Tree

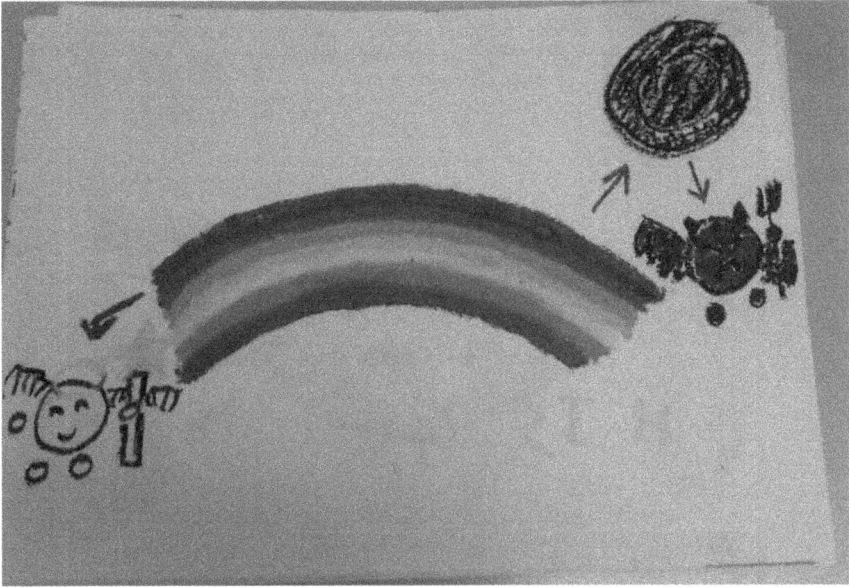

Figure 10.2 The Rainbow: 天使和恶魔的诞生 (The Birth of Angel and Devil)

Figure 10.3 Spectrogram: GTA Animal 5P VS GTA Animal King

Figure 10.4 Mask Making: Journey to the West

find solace and healing in the positive nurturing of play, gradually overcoming the scars of trauma that once haunted them.

Conversely, alienation offers children a pathway to externalize their emotions, enabling them to express themselves to the outside world (Zheng et al., 2015). This process cultivates independence and resilience, empowering children to navigate life's challenges with newfound confidence. Children use play to communicate their deepest emotions and ideas via the use of characters and mediums; the act of expressing oneself releases them. However, it is imperative for practitioners to maintain healthy and therapeutic boundaries in both owning and alienation, particularly for children residing in orphanages. By fostering a safe and supportive environment, practitioners can facilitate the exploration of self and the expression of emotions, guiding children on a transformative journey toward healing and growth.

The greatest companionship

Wholehearted Companionship – As well as active listening forms the bedrock of effective child psychotherapy, embodying a deeply rooted attitude and belief in the value of authentic connection with the child (Zheng et al., 2015). It is essential to set aside distractions such as mobile phones and immerse oneself fully in the child's world, offering undivided attention and empathy. Personally, I find resonance in the traditional Chinese character for "listen," "聽," which intricately combines symbols representing the ears, eyes, and heart. This character underscores the importance of using our senses to observe and understand the child's emotions, thoughts, and behaviors with unwavering focus and compassion. As child psychotherapists, we may encounter challenges that cannot be fully resolved, but our steadfast presence and support can offer solace and reassurance to the child. Simple companionship, devoid of elaborate techniques or criticisms, can provide a comforting anchor for the child, reminding them that they are not alone in their struggles.

Building empathy and understanding with children requires us to engage in basic talks about their thoughts, feelings, and behaviors. These reflections serve as gentle affirmations of our presence and support, allowing the child to feel heard and valued. Sometimes, the most profound form of support lies in simple companionship devoid of elaborate techniques or solutions. A nonjudgmental presence can provide children with comfort and assurance by serving as a reminder that they are not alone in their struggles.

By engaging in reflective dialogue, we demonstrate our willingness to accompany them on their emotional journey, fostering a sense of connection and trust. However, it is essential to ensure that our reflections are subtle and non-intrusive, seamlessly integrated into the flow of play. This delicate balance allows children to feel heard and understood without disrupting the natural rhythm of their exploration and expression (Zheng et al., 2015). Ultimately, we establish a caring environment where children feel respected, encouraged, and equipped to face life's problems with resilience and confidence by placing a high importance on wholehearted friendship and attentive listening. A suitable reflection should complement the child's exploration and expression, enhancing their sense of agency and empowerment. This method builds a strong connection and sense of trust between the children and the therapist, which paves the way for fruitful therapeutic work.

TWO (2) Do not and THREE (3) Must – Child psychotherapy sessions are profound moments of transformation, transcending mere education or task completion. It is a journey of emotional and cognitive evolution, where resilience is cultivated and nurtured. Unlike traditional assessments, there are no grades or right or wrong answers; instead, the focus is on the process of growth and self-discovery. The value lies in the journey itself, where each step taken towards healing and empowerment is celebrated. In these sessions, children find the space to express themselves authentically and find strength in their vulnerabilities. Two crucial "Don'ts" and three essential "Musts" are paramount:

1. Do not ask "why."
2. Do not lead the play.
3. Be interested in the children's performance or play.
4. Be able to accept the ambiguity and silence.
5. Focus on the children as a person, not the pains nor the problems.

Empower freedom to make choices and respect the children

Giving children a sense of agency and autonomy in their lives is an essential component of the therapeutic process, as was discussed in previous sections. Even with the youngest students, empowering them to make their own decisions is a terrific method to support self-determination and empowerment. Therapists should present a variety of options so that children can take charge of their own experiences rather than flatly rejecting their decisions. Whether it is in the context of play or everyday decision-making, honoring the child's choices without interference is a form of profound respect.

In my previous writing, "Using Play as a Counselling Tool in Multicultural Society," I emphasized the importance of respecting children's narratives, even when they involve sensitive topics such as sexuality. By providing unconditional positive regard and genuine acceptance, therapists create an environment where children feel safe to express themselves authentically. This unconditional acceptance lays the foundation for meaningful change to occur organically, as children feel valued and respected for who they are.

Children in orphanages often possess a heightened sensitivity and maturity shaped by their unique life experiences. Therapists have a duty to treat these children with much more consideration and understanding because they are important to their healing process. The way therapists convey care and concern directly impacts how children perceive and internalize these feelings. Even at an early age, children possess an innate ability to discern genuine love and empathy from superficial gestures. By offering unconditional positive regard and authentic empathy, therapists create a nurturing environment where children feel truly seen and valued.

Building a strong therapeutic relationship based on unconditional positive regard and genuine empathy is essential for children to progress toward congruence, as described by Carl Rogers. When children feel that they and their therapist truly connect and that their feelings will be acknowledged without condemnation, they are more likely to be open and fully engaged in treatment. Congruence, or the alignment of their inner experiences with their external expression, is a crucial sign of emotional development and therapeutic advancement.

Empowering children with autonomy and respect is paramount in the therapeutic journey, particularly for children in orphanages who may have experienced significant adversity. By honoring their choices, providing unconditional positive regard, and building genuine connections, therapists create an environment where children feel safe to explore and express themselves authentically. This nurturing relationship fosters emotional healing and growth, paving the way for children to achieve congruence and a deeper sense of self-awareness. In the end, therapists can only genuinely impact the lives of the children they work with by exercising the virtues of respect and empathy.

Future direction and conclusion

In a time when technology is developing at a breakneck pace, children's conventional play activities are changing significantly (Wang et al., 2022; Kim and Kim, 2023). I see a decline in the art of imaginative play with real toys as Artificial Intelligence becomes more commonplace. However, amidst this digital revolution there emerges a promising avenue for therapeutic intervention: the Therapeutic Metaverse. As I delve into the realm of research surrounding this innovative approach, I am shocked by its potential to provide profound benefits akin to those found in traditional therapeutic settings. Using Virtual Reality (VR) technology, the Therapeutic Metaverse has demonstrated extraordinary efficacy in treating a range of mental disorders that children encounter, including trauma, anxiety, and phobias. Furthermore, it minimizes geographical obstacles by making therapy accessible to everyone, no matter where they are.

The utilization of virtual reality (VR) technology and the creation of serious games within the Therapeutic Metaverse have benefited children's psychological well-being (Oberdorfer et al., 2023; Li Pira et al., 2023). Through immersive experiences and interactive gameplay, children can engage with therapeutic interventions in a novel and engaging manner. The potential for integration between Neuro-Dramatic-Play (NDP) and the Therapeutic Metaverse is particularly intriguing. By combining the principles of NDP with the immersive capabilities of VR, we can unlock new possibilities for therapeutic intervention.

In aligning with the first paradigm of NDP, the creation of a SafePlace within the virtual environment becomes a tangible prospect. Within this virtual sanctuary, children can find solace and security, laying the foundation for subsequent therapeutic exploration. Moreover, the second paradigm of NDP, focusing on Embodiment, Projection, and Role (EPR), lends itself seamlessly to the creation of serious games within the Therapeutic Metaverse. By copying practices like messy play in the virtual world, children can explore and express themselves in ways that are not feasible in the real world.

Furthermore, the third paradigm of NDP, Theatre of Resilience (ToR), can find expression in the form of virtual theatres within the Therapeutic Metaverse. Here, children can immerse themselves in theatrical performances, assuming various roles and engaging in creative expression. Through these virtual theatres, children can cultivate resilience and confidence, harnessing the power of storytelling and performance to navigate their inner worlds.

In conclusion, the integration of NDP principles with the Therapeutic Metaverse represents a groundbreaking approach to child therapy. We can develop creative and captivating therapies that address the individual requirements of every child by utilizing the immersive powers of virtual reality technology. We are getting closer to a time when children's lives will be transformed and healed by technology as we investigate the possibilities of this mutually beneficial relationship.

Let's consider this as the future path for both NDP and Therapeutic Play!

References

Achmad, F., Putri, M., Rini, A. P. Nury, D. F. and Suhartono, S. (2022) Trauma Healing Bagi Anak-Anak SDN 4 Sipa Rayo Jorong Bunga Tanjuang Terdampak Korban Gempa Pasaman. *Jurnal Abdi Masyarakat*, 8(1), 7–16. https://doi.org/10.22441/jam.v8i1.15949/

Jennings, S. (2011) *Healthy Attachments and Neuro-Dramatic-Play*. Jessica Kingsley Publishers.

Kim, E. J. and Kim, Y. J. (2023) The metaverse for healthcare: Trends, applications, and future directions of digital therapeutics for urology. *International Neurourology Journal*, 27(1), 3–12. https://doi.org/10.5213/inj.2346108.054

Li Pira, G., Aquilini, B., Davoli, A., Grandi, S. and Ruini, C. (2023) The use of virtual reality interventions to promote positive mental health: Systematic literature review. *JMIR Mental Health*, 10, e44998. https://doi.org/10.2196/44998

Ndlovu, B., Okeke, C., Nhase, Z., Ugwuanyi, C., Okeke, C. and Ede, M. (2023) Impact of play-based learning on the development of children in mobile early childhood care and education centers: Practitioners' perspectives. *International Journal of Research in Business and Social Science*, 12(3), 432–440. https://www.ssbfnet.com/ojs/index.php/ijrbs

Oberdorfer, S., Banakou, D. and Bhargava, A. (2023) Editorial: The light and dark sides of virtual reality. *Frontiers in Virtual Reality*, 4, 1200156. https://doi.org/10.3389/frvir.2023.1200156

Wang, G., Badal, A., Jia, X., Maltz, J. S., Mueller, K., Myers, K. J., Niu, C., Vannier, M., Yan, P., Yu, Z. and Zeng, R. P. (2022) Development of metaverse for intelligent health. *Nature Machine Intelligence*, 4, 922–929. https://doi.org/10.1038/s42256-022-00549-6

Wu, S. (2023) Critically discuss the importance of play for young children's learning and development. *International Journal of New Developments in Education*, 5(2), 27–34. https://doi.org/10.25236/IJNDE.2023.050205j

Yong, J. C. G. (2021) Using play as a counselling tool in multicultural society. In *Routledge International Handbook of Play, Therapeutic Play and Play Therapy*, eds. Jennings, S. and Holmwood, C. Routledge, 181–192.

Zheng, R. A., Zhang, Y. D., Chen, W. R., Wang, Y. R. and Liu, X. J. (2015) *Liao Jie Qin Ting Pei Ban*. Persatuan Lifeline Malaysia.

Chapter 11

NDP in the jungle

Play, enjoy and get stronger

Andy Hickson and Ming Yang

Introduction

We, Andy and Ming, husband and wife, have a long history with the Malaysian jungle and the Temiar people who live there. I (Andy) travelled originally with my siblings and Mum (Sue Jennings) when she studied them as part of her PhD (Jennings, 2018). The Temiars are the major influence on developing Mum's (Sue Jennings) original ideas around NDP (Neuro Dramatic Play).

In the 1970s, the Malaysian jungle (in Kelantan) was abundant, prolific and bountiful. By 2024, an estimated 90% of the jungle has been cleared, 80% of it in the last 40 years. This has impacted negatively on the Temiar and other indigenous Orang Asli people in Malaysia, losing their ancestral homelands, food supply and particularly polluting the rivers. Logging and huge mono-crop plantation corporations have little care for the indigenous people, especially as huge profits are to be made. Despite the huge shift in the Temiar's now not being able to live self-sufficiently due to rainforest destruction, the Temiar's remain a peaceful and powerful people challenging for their rights and living in harmony with what jungle remains. Sharing and a child-friendly model of society are central to the Temiar belief system. This is what helps them survive.

In April of this year, the four of us, Andy, Ming and our young son and daughter, went back to the jungle to learn more about Neuro-Dramatic-Play. We took a group of international adult students with us in addition to Sue Jennings (Andy's mother). We also took our daughter, who is now 6 years old.

The Temiar jungle

Each time we have the privilege of visiting our Temiar friends, it is a magical trip to a faraway land away from our regular life cycles. Each visit gives us precious memories. Our son's first trip to the jungle is where he learned how to walk. He was intrigued by a strange environment: kids running around in groups, chickens wandering everywhere with several chicks behind them, and the tall palm trees and bamboo house. All of these make a strange world

DOI: 10.4324/9781003498209-15

that is not like home. Home in the UK is a typical nuclear family, with Dad, Mum and himself, and later, his younger sister (not born yet). In the jungle, we spent many hours in a big communal house (aka a long house) that everybody in the community had access to, especially kids of his age or slightly older than him. He got interested in them and what they were talking about, what they were eating or drinking and what they were playing. It all looked so fresh and interesting.

As well as the long house, the river soon became their favourite playground. There are several small routes to the river from each house. So, they have access to the river almost everywhere. They soon learned from the local kids where and how to play in the river. They even invented their own games in the river, too. Our daughter saw a piece of bamboo floating down the river. She asked Mum to catch it for her, then she used a little stick as her striker to hit various parts of the bamboo to make music. She called it "soothing music" to "relax me when I lie down in the river". On that afternoon, the breeze blew and took away the heat and fatigue while our little girl made that bamboo music to entertain us. It kept us really close to nature. What an amazing afternoon!

Every afternoon, the river is the perfect place to wash off the heat of the day and have fun. Our son looked forward to going to the river every day. He also learned a new game with other kids in the village: there is a tree hanging over the river from the bank, so the children will swim to the middle of the river, climb on the tree branches and jump into the river. The boys see it as a chance to show their swimming skills and courage, so they keep doing it repeatedly. At first, our son found it interesting and fun, so he wanted to try it, but he soon gave up as he got into the river and realised how fast the current was. Furthermore, he had not learned fully how to swim, so he did not have much confidence in the water. So, he started from the shallow bit of the river and tested the depth and the current to the deeper area of the river slowly. He did this for a few days; once he got more confident, he would do a bit more to be able to catch the tree. Finally, one day, he walked to the upper end of the river, swam to the middle of the river and flowed with the current. He managed to catch the tree branch like the other children. He was so excited and proud of himself that he waved at us, shouting, "Look at me!" Then he let go and flowed down until he got to the bank. Since he managed to do this, he started to love the game and he kept doing it every time he was in the river. After two weeks in the jungle, he became more and more confident with the water, much more than he was in the beginning.

It is almost like the river found a way to regulate their little bodies. They found comfort, fun and power from the river. It also became part of them when they were in the river. They found a way to deal with it, they found a way to tame it and, most importantly, a way to have fun in it and enjoy it.

Besides the river, the children found another thing that was forbidden and fun – fire. At home, both of them are strictly forbidden to play with fire, including lighters and fireplaces. But in the jungle, fire is everywhere – every evening, adults made fire in the village to get rid of mosquitoes and flies. When we went on the jungle trek, our guide would make a bonfire during break for the same reason. At this point, it became perfect timing for our children to play with fire. They would get a stick of a nice length to poke the fire and collect small twigs and leaves to add to the fire. By feeling the heat of the fire, they slowly learned to respect the fire.

Water and fire, as part of nature, have a natural attraction for children. In the jungle, Temiar adults do not forbid children to play with them, but give them the freedom to explore safely. When the little kids are getting too close to the fire or displaying any dangerous behaviours, older kids will naturally remind them to stay safe by stopping them. For us, it just proved the old saying that "it takes a whole village to raise a child".

Bamboo raft making in the jungle

One activity we planned to do in the jungle village was to make bamboo rafts and drift down the river on them. On the day of the raft-making, we trekked a long way deep into the jungle to find suitable bamboo to build rafts. That day was particularly hot. We were surprised to see our children keeping up with the adults and able to have fun during the journey. They found sticks on the way, used them as their walking sticks and pushed away any plants and foliage in their way.

The Temiars used motorbikes to give us a lift for a short distance to make the journey easier. When the children had their motorbike journey, they could not stop talking about it! Their first motorbike ride on a bumpy jungle path!

When we finally arrived at this riverbank with a great deal of massive bamboo, we knew this was the destination. The Temiars started to chop bamboo while we rested and helped. We found a small flat area to sit down in and our guide Jonny brought us food! It was plain rice and some cooked papaya and he magically brought one long bamboo and used his bush knife to cut it in half lengthways and trimmed spoons from the leftover bamboo.

So, each of us had a bamboo bowl and spoon set ready for the picnic. Our children were mesmerised by this wonderful craftsmanship; they stared when Jonny was doing the cutting and trimming and when they received their bowl and spoon, they could not wait to eat with them. The plain food tasted so much better! Even when they finished, they rinsed the bowl in the river to use as toys.

While we were eating, the Temiar villagers did not stop at all. They worked hard at making the bamboo rafts. So, our son was eager to see how they did it. The bamboo forest was across from the other side of the river, so if we wanted to observe and help, we needed to swim across the river and climb the rock for about 20 meters. This would be the easiest way to get to the "bamboo raft workshop". At first, our son watched a few older boys

(12–14 years old) swim across the river and climb the moss-covered rock to reach the bamboo forest. He was eager to try as well, but once he stepped his foot into the fast-flowing river, he backed out and hesitated. Dad decided to go with him to help him conquer his fear. So, they went in together and successfully swam across to the other bank. On the mossy, slippery riverbank, our son got a few cuts from the rock, but overall, he reached the "bamboo raft workshop" in the end. When he came back to the other side of the river, he was so excited to tell us how they made the rafts.

He was so proud of himself! So were we!

Storytelling and games in the jungle

Every day in the jungle, before and after supper time might be the most relaxing time of the day. All the day's work was finished, women were preparing supper in the communal house for the guests while chatting with each other and kids were playing their games, waiting for supper to be served. It did not take long for some of the girls (aged between 10–13) to start a variety of clapping games in a circle. It involved simple words in Temiar and several clapping gestures. The rhythm and the laughter soon attracted more kids to join in and, of course, our two little ones. They had not played such a group game before, not in school or in the family, so they were immediately intrigued. They managed to keep up with the rhythm and occasionally made mistakes, but that made them laugh. This clapping game soon became the routine before supper time every day. Everyone enjoyed it, even the adults.

One night, we decided to do storytelling. It was a bold idea as the Temiar children do not speak English and most of us do not speak Malaysian or the Temiar language, except Dad (Andy). So, Dad started the storytelling session by telling an old Temiar story of a snake called Tagou Relai that he had learned when he was living in the jungle as a teenager. This got the group storytelling session going. It also got everyone in the communal house sitting in a circle and listening. Then it was Mum's turn (Sue Jennings). Those days, Mum was telling the story of "Monkey King" every night to our children as their bedtime story. They both loved this mischievous and clever hero in the Chinese culture. Monkey King followed his master to the West to get the Buddhist Bible and experienced 81 challenges to complete their pilgrim journey. So, it is a bit like "One Thousand and One Nights". Mum decided that since our children both loved this story, she would choose one chapter to tell that night to the Temiar children. The good thing about the "Monkey King" story is that it is like a Hollywood action film, which has heroes and villains fighting each other with a happy ending and lots of funny moments. Mum managed to use simple language and a lot of mimicry, body language and silly moves to finish telling the chapter of "Monkey King against the golden and silver horn monster" and made the children laugh several times.

Mum's attempt at storytelling obviously encouraged our children to be more interested in the Chinese classical story-Monkey King. As a mischievous and powerful monkey, the Monkey King's character can relate to many children who want to be naughty and be able to do things. So, when she said, "Tonight we have a Monkey King story as our bedtime story", our two little ones would be so excited to witness Monkey King's adventure.

Not long before, the two little "Monkey King" fans wanted to do dramatic play and take on roles to play and recreate the Monkey King story. We did not use any puppets; we did not have any props; we just lay on the bamboo floor and used our imagination to recreate the "fire mountain" chapter of The Monkey King story. Our daughter used her squeaky monkey voice to mimic Monkey King's naughty tricks when he transformed into a fly. Our son pretended he was the Iron Fan Lady who swallowed the fly and had a big stomachache. Mum was the narrator of the story to smooth things. We worked together so well that we giggled and laughed, as did all the other Temiar children and adults present.

This game continued when we had another favourite chapter of the long story. This storytelling was highlighted when we left the jungle after two weeks and saw a Chinese temple in another city in Malaysia. There was a statue of the Monkey King in the temple! Our two children immediately recognised him from his signature weapon – the Golden Stick. They were so excited to see him in reality, not in a story.

When we introduced a successful version of the TV series Monkey King to them, they looked disappointed in the characters. They told us that in the story, the Pig sounded funnier and the Monkey felt so much cleverer. We understand the feeling when your favourite book is adapted into a TV series or a film; it never feels as good as the book itself. The imagination you have from the book will always be better.

Building relationships and playing in the jungle's cultural differences

Towards the end of our stay in the Temiar village, our son made a friend with another Temiar boy similar to his age. They soon became quite close, always together at playtime. They chased each other, provoked each other and did some pretend fights. But soon, they made up again. Our son normally has trouble sharing, but this time, with his Temiar friend, he was happy to share his toys and snacks. They did not speak each other's language and did not know each other's history. We were surprised to see how they made friends in such a short time. Just before we left, our son asked us to take a photo with his friend. He even drew a picture of them playing together to give his friend as a goodbye gift. After we left the village, he still talked about his friend for a while. But when we asked him, "What's your friend's name?" he said, "I don't know. It doesn't matter; he is my friend". I am sure he can recognise his friend next time we go to the village again. For our son, the name is not the most important; the memories they share are. At home, he can be very competitive with his little sister, sometimes he almost pays all his attention to her, but here in the village, our son had so much more to explore: the village, the river, the house and other children's games. He did not focus on competing with his little sister any more; he became less aggressive and calmer. When he was bored in one place, he just went to the communal house to see other children or went to the next house to see what was there. So, he never complained, "I am bored", while we were in the jungle like he often did when at home in the UK.

It reminds Mum (Ming) of her childhood, living in a lovely neighbourhood in China. Her parents both worked at that time, so after school, she would finish homework first and go to the yard to play with her friends until her parents finished work. She did not have any digital gadgets or fancy toys at that time. They played games: dodgeball, jumping rope, kick the feather and shuttlecock; they did not have formal play dates and they did not need to worry about going to other people's houses without making an appointment. All the adults in the neighbourhood were so kind to all the children. They helped look after each other's children when they needed to work and they fed other people's children when it was mealtime. Seeing our children live in the village like Mum when she was a little child in her old neighbourhood, she felt a long-lost warmth from the bottom of her heart. This child-oriented community creates a safe, sound place to raise children.

The child's role-play and NDP's inspiration

We have always believed the job of children is to play, which is central to NDP. The Temiar people, their society and the jungle were Mum's (Sue Jennings') major inspiration in developing NDP. It is fitting that our children could learn to play here in a different way than in the UK. Mom noticed how the Temiar children played in her many visits. Here, children learn about themselves, life skills, empathy and more through playing; they learn about the world through playing. Play is their nature. In our big, modern concrete jungle cities, children have limited nature and they are kept at home. Here in the real jungle, they finally have access to unlimited nature; they have full play license to get close to rivers, fire, mud and bugs. They do not have distractions from digital gadgets and are free from "sit-still" classrooms. They are free to play in nature with each other. They play chasing with butterflies, they play hide-and-seek with all the other children in the village and they play all the games they know. The adults here provide the playground for them: their home, the village road and in the jungle. They protect children when they play; sometimes they join them too.

We had so much fun in this whole "back to nature" and "back to the community" play session in the jungle. As adults, we too were able to play in the river and play with children without the need to worry, "Where are our children?" as we knew they were looked after and we knew they were safe.

Neuro Dramatic Play is a child-oriented philosophy, very similar to how the Temiar raise and bring up their children: playful in nature, non-judgmental and skill-producing. The highlight of our year is when we are able to take the time to go back to the jungle and learn more from our Temiar friends.

Final thoughts

The thing that concerns us the most is how long the Temiar culture will survive the ravages of logging, the loss of their ancestral lands and the diminishing jungle. The peaceful protests continue. Temiar lawan.

Reference

Jennings, S. (2018) *Theatre, Ritual and Transformation: The Senoi Temiars*. London: Routledge.

Chapter 12

NDP and performance training in Greece

Rediscovering childhood: Learning to play again

Ros Johnson and Neil Johnson

Introduction

Neuro-Dramatic-Play is described by Dr Sue Jennings as an attachment-based intervention that focuses on the early playful relationship between "mother-unborn-baby and mother – newborn – baby interaction" (p. 31). Through play and drama, it emphasises a combination of basic trust, security and ritual, with stimulation, exploration and risk. Ritual and risk form the basis of children feeling safe in the world, as well as feeling safe to explore it. Neuro-Dramatic-Play enables and encourages one to become more playful and to think creatively. It also tries to encourage independence and self-reliance. It affirms identity and self-esteem and the building of social relationships.

Neuro-Dramatic-Play and Performance (NDPP) is a natural progression from NDP as an innovative and therapeutic approach that intertwines neuroscience, drama and play that fosters emotional and psychological healing. Grounded in the understanding that the brain is highly responsive to creative and sensory experiences. Neuro Dramatic Play and Performance leverage these elements to facilitate developmental growth and emotional expression.

At its core, it is based on the principles that play and drama are not only natural modes of learning and self-expression but are also deeply embedded in our neural pathways. The transition to the performance approach harnesses the power of the imagination, movement and storytelling to engage individuals in a holistic process that supports and promotes mental health and well-being. Learning to play and then to perform as an adult opens up the options for the practitioner to experience the child's journey and help them understand their place in the world.

Core concepts of NDP and performance

1. Neuroscience Foundations: NDPP integrates knowledge from neuroscience to understand how play and drama can stimulate brain function and

DOI: 10.4324/9781003498209-16

emotional regulation. It recognises the brain's plasticity and its capacity to form new connections through creative activities.

2. Dramatic Expression: Drama serves as a medium for participants to explore and express their emotions, thoughts and experiences. Through role-play, storytelling and performance, individuals can externalise internal conflicts and gain new perspectives.
3. Play is a fundamental aspect of NDPP, offering a safe and natural context for exploration and expression. Play therapy techniques are employed to help individuals, especially children, process emotions and experiences in a non-threatening way.
4. Sensory Integration: NDPP emphasises the importance of sensory experiences in emotional and cognitive development. Activities often include elements that engage the senses, such as music, movement and tactile interactions, to enhance the therapeutic impact.

NDP and Performance is versatile and can be applied across various settings, including clinical therapy, educational environments and community programmes. It is particularly effective with children, but its principles can be adapted to benefit individuals of all ages. The approach has been shown to:

• Enhance emotional resilience and self-regulation.
• Improve social skills and empathy through collaborative play and performance.
• Foster creativity and imaginative thinking.
• Provide a safe space for processing trauma and difficult emotions.

Neuro-Dramatic-Play and Performance is a dynamic and integrative therapeutic approach that leverages the power of play and drama to support emotional and psychological growth. By engaging the brain through creative and sensory-rich activities, NDPP offers a profound way to heal, learn and connect with oneself and others. This innovative method opens new pathways for therapeutic intervention and personal development, making it very valuable in the fields of mental health and education.

NDP and performance in Greece

When we think of Greece, we might immediately conjure up ideas about stunning beaches, ancient culture, myths, wonderful food and amazing hospitality (or filoxenia). Or perhaps island hopping as a student or the controversy over the 'Elgin' Marbles, still noticeably missing from the glorious Parthenon on top of the Acropolis in Athens. Greece is also known as the birthplace of democracy, medicine, philosophy and, of course, theatre.

As well as the mainland of Greece, there are approximately 6,000 islands in total that make up the country. Not all of the islands are accessible or inhabited, but one particular island stands out as a jewel in the middle of the group of islands known as the Cyclades (pronounced with a hard C), in the heart of the Aegean Sea and that is the beautiful island of Naxos.

The enchanting Island of Naxos – A playground for Neuro Dramatic Play

Naxos is the biggest and the greenest island of the Cyclades, boasting a magnificent natural landscape. The island's rich history is reflected in the many archaeological sites that embellish it. The most iconic of them – and THE iconic symbol of Naxos – is the Portara, the remaining gate of an ancient temple dedicated to the Greek God Apollo.

Naxos features in the myth of Theseus and Ariadne. Although Theseus is credited as having killed the Minotaur, it was Ariadne who gave him the idea of using a roll of string to help him find his way out. She was indeed clever and sharp and not the pathetic princess of many stories. In one version of the story, on his way back to Athens after defeating the Minotaur in the labyrinth of Crete, having tired of her, Theseus supposedly abandons Ariadne on the island when they stop off for supplies. Another version has Ariadne being abducted by Dionysus, who spots her on the beach, is entranced by her beauty and wants her for himself. Either way, she was not in control of her destiny and in the confusion after departing Naxos, Theseus, either glad to have got rid of Ariadne or distraught about her being kidnapped, forgets to change the sails on his ship from black to white, which was the sign to let his father know that he is still alive. This oversight causes Theseus' father, Aegean, to throw himself into the sea and the mercy of Poseidon as he believes his son to be dead. Thus, the name of the Aegean Sea is born.

So, Naxos, this serene island bathed in sun and surrounded by the calming embrace of the beach, becomes the idyllic backdrop for NDP and Performance. The inviting atmosphere and opportunities for relaxation contribute to the overall experience, creating an environment conducive to shedding inhibitions and embracing the spontaneity of play. We will examine why Naxos is the perfect stage for the exploration of NDP, highlighting the role of sun, beach and good food in enhancing the transformative journey.

The beach plays an important role in the NDP process. Firstly, it is a blank canvas for creating shapes and pictures. A good example of this is creating a sand labyrinth enhanced with beach debris as part of the inspiration when looking at the Theseus/Minotaur story. The beach is a rich source of objects, including driftwood, shells and pebbles of all shapes, sizes and colours and many other items of flotsam and jetsam. Foraging and collecting objects for both storytelling and to create pictures, sand sculptures and other artwork is an important part of the NDP process and allows creativity to begin and the imagination to flourish.

The proximity to the sea provides another source of play material – water, as well as an opportunity to walk barefoot and feel the sand between our toes or run it through our fingers and splash about in the sea. All of which can invoke memories of childhood and holidays.

Finally, at the end of the day, simply lying on the sand, hearing the gentle waves washing onto the beach and watching the sun go down provides a wonderful opportunity for relaxation and reflection.

How does this relate to performance? To become creative, we need to find peace and leave distractions behind. We try to tap into the uninhibited creativity and imagination that often fades with age and remember the freedom we had to play, which encourages our brain to focus and our creativity to begin to germinate.

So, as adults in the world of Neuro Dramatic Play (NDP), our participants in Naxos are taken on a journey to rekindle this essence of childhood. We have already mentioned the evocation of memories of building sandcastles or splashing about in the sea, but one of the core principles of engaging with NDP involves learning to play like a child again. We examine the transformative power of embracing childlike playfulness, exploring how it intertwines with the broader NDP framework. The sea and the beach are the perfect playground for this process to start.

Rediscovering childhood – learning to play again

So, what drives participants, teachers, therapists, counsellors or indeed any parents to engage in Neuro Dramatic Play and what unfolds during these immersive experiences? Firstly, participants have the opportunity to explore the intricacies of NDP, dissecting the elements that make it a unique fusion of play and performance. From the messy and artistic aspects to the utilisation of puppets and masks, participants dive into a world where the boundaries between reality and imagination blur. Then, there is the exploration of the possibilities that performance can give them using the newly found resources and learning. Body language and physical expression is integrated into the next stage of the process and the use of the voice.

Embracing childlike wonder – role play and attachment

The early years form the foundation of attachment, and NDP supports this concept by allowing participants to experience role play as if they were children. We look into the psychological aspects of attachment, exploring how NDP serves as a medium for revisiting and understanding the formative years. Themes and stories, range from Shakespearean dramas to Greek myths and they will serve as the canvas upon which participants paint their narratives.

Building confidence and fostering teamwork

Neuro-Dramatic-Play becomes a crucible for building confidence and fostering teamwork. Through the exploration of characters, participants step out of their comfort zones and embrace vulnerability as a catalyst for personal growth. NDP serves as a dynamic platform for individuals to develop a robust sense of self-assurance and enables them to collaborate seamlessly within a team setting.

Theatre of Resilience (TOR): the synergy with NDP elements

Theatre of Resilience and performance is quite unique in both teacher and therapeutic and parental training. It is very important that we don't just stop at dramatic play, we take it further into drama, theatre and performance. The Theatre of Resilience (TOR) concept takes centre stage, examining how the performance elements in NDP resonate with resilience. As children transition from dramatic play to 'drama for real,' there is a heightened awareness of what feels right and an exploration of characters that can induce inner changes. NDPP explores the intersection between performance, expression, and resilience, unravelling the transformative journey that NDP offers.

Performance, expression and change

The developmental shift from inner to outer expression is a pivotal aspect of NDP in the early years of child development. Theatre of Resilience (TOR) looks at later stages of development from six years of age. As we delve into the psychological nuances, we can showcase how engaging in performance opportunities facilitates the transition from internal exploration to external manifestation. Participants discover the power of performance as a tool for personal transformation, laying the groundwork for a deeper understanding of self-expression and inner change. ToR is also unique, as it works from the outside in; an individual will explore a character from a play and will perform that character in that play they're doing safely because their inner vulnerable self is kept protected and looked after; they'll find that there's some inner change and start to develop new strengths, new skills, new insights.

Aesthetic awakening: text, story and beyond

As participants evolve through NDP, an aesthetic sense begins to blossom. Exploring the intricacies of text and story work, delving into how the exploration of characters and narratives contributes to an aesthetic awakening. From the raw, messy aspects of play to the refined beauty of storytelling, NDP becomes a vehicle for cultivating a profound appreciation for the arts.

Performance is extremely important, and there's something quite interesting about doing this course on Naxos because, after all, Greece is seen as the origin of participating in theatre as we know it today; theatre performances used to be carried out at the order of the state to try and keep a stable society. So, somehow, it's all linked up.

If you engage children in role play in the form of pretend play at an early age, it helps them to express feelings in diverse ways. Piaget expresses this as follows:

1. Simplifying events by creating an imaginary character, plot or setting to match their emotional state. A child who is afraid of the dark, for example, might eliminate darkness or night from the play episode.
2. Compensating for situations by adding forbidden acts to pretend play. A child may, for example, eat cookies and ice cream for breakfast in play, whereas in reality, this would not be permitted.
3. Controlling emotional expression by repeatedly re-enacting unpleasant or frightening experiences. For example, a child might pretend to have an accident after seeing a real traffic accident on the highway.
4. Avoiding adverse consequences by pretending that another character, real or imaginary, commits inappropriate acts and suffers the consequences. Children whose television viewing is monitored at home, for instance, can pretend to allow the doll to watch indiscriminately and then reprimand the "bad child" for unacceptable TV viewing habits.

Children usually have to be a little bit older to be able to take on-board role play in performance. So, we don't really introduce performance elements until the age of six. Before that, it's been very much dramatic play or, as Piaget says, 're-enacting troubling experiences' (Piaget, 1962, p. 171). Children will differentiate between different characters, imitating siblings, imitating something from television, playing a superhero, having a Batman costume, all of these things. Younger children might use puppets, dolls, toys or figures in the sandpit to start telling little stories or enacting scenes, even if it's just a brief scene that they create. They impose a role onto those objects in a similar way, which is much more of an internal process rather than an external one. This is where one sees the movement towards theatre of resilience (ToR) and performance.

However, when they get to six or seven years old, they start to become aware of the sensibilities around a performance. For example, "Grandmas or old people walk like that," "Teacher speaks like this," they can stand outside what they're doing and look in and reflect on it. That's a very big step for children, to be able to reflect on something that they and their friends are doing. It's a big step in maturity that they're not just being fed performances from screens; they are participating in and/or directing a performance and have an opinion about what the outcome might be.

As a practitioner, when we're using this performance work in therapy, it's very useful that we can get insights into the life of the child by the way they will project their personal stories into role-play.

So, what we are exploring is: How relevant is the performance element to the NDP training? The answer is: It is crucial. It's absolutely essential because it is a culmination of all the processes that have happened before. So, all the creativity, the messy play, the rhythmic play, the interactive play, the imitation, all these things that have been going on from birth to six or seven years now come together and are integrated into performance. It is part of their own internal and external growth and development and it's how their social and emotional intelligence will grow.

Claudia Vlaicu says.

It is a well-known fact that school success largely depends on children's ability to interact positively with their peers and adults. In this type of interaction, play in general and role-play in particular are vital both for children's social development and for maintaining the emotional basis for learning.

(2014, p. 158)

So, the performance is the climax of the dramatic process. And we can presume that this helps build confidence for adults who are learning to play again. It allows them to get a better understanding of what it is they're asking the children to do.

Even for children, the whole NDP, EPR and the Theatre of Resilience approach can be applied right through the whole of the life cycle. Particularly post-trauma, post-difficult times in people's lives and times when people are facing an unexpected change, all these times, one can integrate this approach and do something about it in a safe and creative environment.

Training the adult to support the child using NDP and performance

NDP in Naxos is a very practical course. We call it NDP and performance because we encourage participants to explore the very nature of what performance is and how it affects us. This process can be daunting to many who do not use performance in their lives. However, what we want to achieve is an understanding of the child and their experience of their dramatic play. The adult working with the child can use dramatic play to question the child about the experiences they are re-enacting but from the point of view of another character rather than directly to the child. For example: "How did the grandfather feel when . . .?" or "What did it feel like when . . . said (or did) . . .?"

We approach the performance element with participants in a very gentle way, encouraging group work and physicalisation. At the beginning of the process, we invite participants to find a space to relax. This work is all done outside in a sheltered area with a view of the sea or mountains. Participants can lie down or remain seated, and we give them the space to breathe, deepen their breathing, and slowly feel the tension flowing away from their bodies. At this point, we encourage participants to join us on a visualisation story where they can find a safe space to relax and explore. The aim of this is to encourage partcipants to find themselves present and ready to delve into their creative selves.

We will then invite participants to play games. These games can be silly and physical and a way of reminding them about the games they might have played in childhood or would have found useful in their childhood. Examples of these games are:

- Tag
- Splat
- Freeze (in a group)
- Grandmother's footsteps

At this point, the participants are bonding as a group and beginning to trust each other, so we might encourage some more risky trust exercises. Walking around in pairs with one person blindfolded and one person acting as a guide. A very different experience in Naxos than in a drama studio, as the terrain is uneven and ever-changing. You can walk on sand, broken paving, through fauna, up steps and in the sea (if you are brave enough)

By now, we are ready to begin more formal performance skills, and we might start by retelling the stories we have chosen to explore (latterly, this has been one of the Greek myths). We might create five freeze-frames of the story, adding a spoken line per freeze-frame to further illustrate the important moment in the story. This helps participants gain a sense of ownership of the story and encourages them to delve deeper into its important themes.

Our first course in Naxos was based around Shakespeare and we did some work on the Iambic Pentameter with participants creating their own pieces of verse. This gave them a wonderful sense of achievement, as many only had bad memories of being taught Shakespeare at school. However, on the next courses, the Greek Myths beckoned and being on the island where Ariadne's statue welcomes you as you arrive by boat, we felt it was only right that we explore her story, reimagine her reality and those of other strong but abandoned women. There are many of them in the Greek Myths!

The next phase is to treat the participants as actors and teach a few of the techniques actors may use. We look at breath not only as a tool for speech but also as a tool for relaxation and focus. Breathing and breath control are taught in all drama school training and learning the power of controlling your breath can enhance performance skills. Cicely Berry, in her book *Voice and the Actor*, says that breath work helps actors feel "comfortable" (pg. 28) with their own voice, and that learning to breathe from the stomach rather than the upper thorax is all part of this.

So, we encourage participants to lie on the floor or sit on a firm chair, breathing in and feeling their stomach inflate, gently encouraging the breath down to the stomach and then using the stomach muscles and diaphragm to control the breath coming out – in a sort of pop. We might get them to breathe in and count to 10 while allowing the air to come out in time with the counting. We can start with a lower count and build up to 10/20. (I precis the work here. There are many books which will give you rigorous voice workouts.) This is not something that happens overnight. Actors will have a voice warm-up most days at Drama School and, in turn, will build up the muscles required. When we breathe in and out, there should be as much air at the beginning as at the end of the counting so the breath does not tail off and the words feel strained and forced out. We are not forcing the breath out and our bodies are relaxed. We can then add speech from text. This is where Shakespeare is so useful – having the ability to speak a line in one breath, giving as much power to the beginning of the sentence as the end of the sentence, is a wonderful skill. We will massage faces, work on diction and use the piece of text to explore different ways of speaking it. An interesting exercise is to try saying a line stressing a different word each time you say it and see how the sense changes.

Here is an example:

"To be, or not to be: that is the question." (Emphasising "to be," focusing on existence and the struggle of life)

"To be, or not to be: that is the question." (Emphasising "not," contemplating the alternative of non-existence)

There is a famous sketch (that can be found on YouTube: 'Shakespeare live from the RSC') where many well-known actors and King Charles argue for different stresses on this line.

Once we have looked at the voice, it is time to look at characterisation and we do this through physicalisation – there are many ways to explore character, but for this journey, we feel working from the outside in is the best way. We have already looked at freeze – frames and the next part of the journey is developing the characters. We ask participants to create a labyrinth or minotaur as a group with their bodies. We may suggest creating a journey with their bodies, asking each person to create a barrier or a bridge while the other actors find ways of travelling through this obstacle. The process is not only an acting technique but offers group work, collaboration, and mutual respect because of the work. We first discovered this technique when working with the inspirational Antigone Gyra in Athens. Antigone studied at Laban Dance Theatre in London. She is now a well-renowned and celebrated physical theatre practitioner who founded the Kinitras Studio and Performing Arts Network in Greece.

Participants often find the journey to Naxos an adventure in itself and this can inform the performance process. It can be a technique for further development of trust, but often recreating the journey becomes the basis for a final showing at the end of the course.

Another element of the process might be looking at choral work both vocally and physically. Participants start by walking round the room together, 'balancing the space' while they have to react to instructions thrown at them – clap, jump, sleep, etc. They are beginning to work as an ensemble. We might ask one of them to sit while the others remain standing without discussion and the opposite. By now, participants are feeling more comfortable with each other and with the practical work. We will then take a piece of the story and re-write it from a minor character's perspective. We began by looking at the character of Penelope, Odysseus' wife in the Odyssey. We explored what her thoughts and feelings might have been abandoned by her husband for 20 long years, leaving her to bring up her son alone and fight off the many suitors. This then formed the basis for a script and was adapted for part of the group to discover how the whole group can tell Penelope's story. What techniques can we use? We experimented with a section of the script which suited each performer, saying one word each and another section where the performers speak in canon. We might ask one person to say the line echoed as a whisper by the other members of the group. There can be repetition of lines to create a more dramatic effect or playing with volume and the often under-used technique of silence. Alongside this might be synchronised movement – e.g., everyone moving and then stopping together as one body.

In the second NDPP course, we introduced the idea of puppets. The National Theatre (UK) has a video of how to make a puppet out of brown paper and also gives brief instructions as to how to bring the puppet to life. The participants made their puppets and embellished them to personalise their creations. Puppets are well-known for their use in therapy work with children, and they can be the vehicle in which the child talks about trauma. The use of them in performance gives us the option of bringing an alternative voice into a world that has been created by the students. The group has to work together as a team; the puppet is operated by two or three people. It can also be an alternative way of creating a monster or child.

After all these techniques, it is then up to the participants to use them and create their own performance. The performance is a retelling of the story we have chosen using all the elements we have introduced and how they fit into the NDP/ToR story.

Finally, we reflect on the holistic journey of Neuro Dramatic Play and Performance, weaving together the threads of learning to play like a child again, the enchanting Island of Naxos, the transformative elements of NDP and the profound impact on confidence, teamwork, and resilience. As the curtain falls on this exploration, participants emerge not only as more confident performers but as individuals who have rediscovered the essence of play and harnessed its power for personal growth and transformation.

References

Berry, C. (1973) *Voice and the Actor*. London: Harrap.
How to Make a Puppet | How You Can Make It | National Theatre. https://www.youtube.com/playlist?list=PLJgBmjHpqgs41un5eRyQFIYrL42qWjE5U
Jennings, S. (2011) *Healthy Attachments and Neuro Dramatic Play*. London: Jessical Kingsley Publishers.
Piaget, J. (1962) *Play, Dreams, and Imitation in Childhood*. New York: Norton.
Vlaicu, C. (2014) The importance of role play for children's development of socio-emotional competencies. In *Logos Universality Mentality Education Novelty, Section: Social Sciences, Year III, Issue 1*. Lumen Publishing House, 157–167.

Chapter 13

The journey of learning with NDP within a collective

Pre-pandemic, during and after the pandemic

Akansha Rastogi, Lavina Nanda, Ashima Kandwal, Sukarma Dawar, and Kavita Arora

Authors

This authors' collective is part of the Developmental Services team at Children First, India. The team has developed an Early Intervention Model which attempts to combine the neurobiological understanding of childhood and developmental needs with therapeutic approaches rooted in playfulness, respect and wonder for neurodiversity. They constantly strive to create approaches rooted in local knowledge and culture but informed by global perspectives.

Setting the context

The Developmental Services at Children First have a dedicated team of psychologists, occupational therapists and arts and movement-based therapists that work with toddlers, children and early teens presenting with neurodevelopmental differences. A large section of the families and children who come have diagnoses like ASD, ADHD, Dyspraxia, Learning Disorders or have had adverse experiences in early years resulting in differences in development. While many of the principles of the prevalent behavioural intervention models were learnt and tried over time, we had not found enough resonance with existing behavioural models for intervention.

Over the years, what has emerged is an Indigenous intervention model built on establishing positive and meaningful connections through play while retaining the dignity of the child and the essence of their emerging profile and childhood. This is the Children First SMART-Connect Model. In parallel, the aim is to enable the family to have this expertise reside equally in the parents and caregivers over time. Most behavioural models do not address this directly, as they are targeted at predominantly developing the child's skills and reducing symptoms. However, we experienced that most parents felt deeply and grieved about the absence of a reciprocal connection that was expressed and overt. The team also experienced repeatedly the effortfulness of eliciting reciprocity despite the efforts of the family as well as the therapists in many of these children. At the same time, eliciting and developing

DOI: 10.4324/9781003498209-17

spontaneous connections with other children of the same age group but different profiles led to a significantly different quality and pace of skill-based intervention; therefore, this ingredient of "Connect "started emerging as a foundational effort of the intervention with neurodivergence.

A deeper dive into the possibilities of what constitutes human connection in the early years and how to foster it when it was not effortless or naturally being created and nurtured has been an ongoing journey. This has meant a constant search for developing an understanding of attachment models and how they fit into what was traditionally seen as developmental milestones. A more defined curiosity also emerged about the attachment model within children developing or emerging with the profile of Autism Spectrum Conditions. This was the set of families where the children did not seem to attempt to connect in conventional ways. Parents were left confused about how to intentionally form connections that elicited consistent reciprocal responses from their children. The intention to connect with each other often appeared skewed, with parents going to extreme lengths to get the attention of the child. The child, on the other hand, seemed to find their own ways to play and seemed to prefer or get attracted to aspects other than the usual primary need to connect socially to their caregiver.

The intrinsic preference to connect was seen by us (The Children First Connect model) as a precursor to building the intention and desire to communicate. The aim was for the child to "want to connect," and we hoped this would mean an increase in self-initiated attempts to connect by children in their own ways. We hoped that this would increasingly bring more awareness of their social world, which could then help them explore it and make choices in their interactions. In parallel, therapists and parents could understand the unspoken language that their child was communicating in an attempt to understand and foster the "connect" through non-spoken ways that seemed to have a higher likelihood of being received by this subset of children. The medium we found most relevant in this continued to be play. Play provided a wider canvas and did not heavily rely on spoken language, which has emerged as a predominant tool in the early years of our civilised world.

We also saw that play was present in various forms in all children. There was a clear preference in many children for a certain kind of play which was rhythmic, often repeated and often precise. We had started getting trained in and applying sensory Integration therapy (Jean Ayres) and sensory play was emerging as a medium to intervene with that framework. At this time, we came across Dr Sue Jennings and the NDP paradigm (Jennings, 2011) based on attachment (Bowlby, 1988).

Pre-Covid journey of "why we started, how we started and what we were hoping to find

Initially, it was a tentative discovery and examination of the framework because we felt drawn towards the drama and resonated with the sensory play (finally, someone understood the value of child-led sensory play!) (Kilroy et al., 2019). Though we were intrigued that the lens was different from Sensory Processing Framework, it felt that we were arriving at the same conclusion through different approaches.

Some of the team attended NDP workshops by Dr Sue Jennings between 2016 and 2019, which were mostly an exploration of the NDP paradigm (Jennings, 2011), with no idea about whether it could be applied in any shape or form to the ongoing work of our developmental services. We found increasing resonance as we explored it deeper. The use of rhythm and rituals, especially in group work, was already an established part of the intervention in the service; however, we began to understand its significance from a different lens via NDP. At the two sites of our Developmental Services, there was a parallel journey of an increasing number of families seeking intervention at CF for the changing age group of 5–14 years.

Many of these children and families brought in a different need, with manifests of anxiety, loss of trust in the world around them, and the avoidance of structures that demanded skills without providing emotional safety. The team started applying some of the NDP principles with some of these children and called it "socio-emotional-play-based work." It was difficult to find vocabulary except for the all-encompassing "play-based work" for this effort. But within the team, some of us were becoming fairly convinced of its value despite questions and confusion about its form and structure. Within this space of confusion and "chaos," some of the team decided to formulate and approached Dr Jennings for developing a tailor-made NDP course for us. The course started with 11 people, with some time spent in person with Dr Jennings, a peer group tutorial and supervision model and a full group collective learning model as well. The intention was to explore the NDP principles and then see whether applying them could serve and converge with our ongoing intervention models.

One such initiative was applying NDP principles in intervention at an ongoing feeding clinic that we had started in 2018 at CF. This started as a unique service with a team of paediatric gastroenterologists, developmental psychologists and occupational therapists for children under 10 years of age. Children who were neurodivergent and had feeding difficulties resulting in nutritional as well as emotional difficulties would attend this clinic. The team developed a model of intervention based on neurodiversity-affirming principles. Two of the team members at the feeding clinic had joined the NDP course. They initiated applying some principles using the rationale of the child's "relationship with food" and how families carried the relationship with mess and food.

The use of sensory and messy play and EPR as a paradigm emerged as helpful in this project. Conviction started, developing a series of intervention outcomes through experience. In parallel, in a different subset of under-12 age group, the journey of "Mess to form," or form to mess and then to form, emerged as a highlight. Our understanding of it changed from applying it not just for rapport building and to "Connect" with another over an activity to the emergence of a lens that looked at this journey as connecting to the aspect of the "dramatic self" that the NDP paradigm proposed. Increasingly, the language of messy play and sensory play became part of the team's vocabulary and many of the developmental psychologists started using sensory, messy and rhythmic play not just from the point of view of sensory processing and integration but also from the NDP lens of exploration of attachment, as well as to the concept of healing and the socio-emotional lens. The translation of this knowledge into practice and relaying it to the families and parents had started becoming resonant and meaningful.

NDP during the COVID era

And then came the lockdown: March 2020, the time that changed everything

In 2020, as COVID hit, we were in a world that was suddenly surrounded by uncertainty, loss, disconnect and confusion (Singh et al., 2020; Berard et al., 2022). There was fear where once there had been comfort in a gentle, reassuring touch, a hug, an intimate conversation. There was a sense of loss of community and belongingness, and an impact on physical health (Teich et al., 2023). The routine and the rituals that were sustaining us were proving to be unsafe. Each of us reacted differently, but we all relied on our connections and connectedness, as well as our language and ability to comprehend the information around us in a big way. In parallel, the Developmental Services had created and graduated to an online intervention model for the first time, delivered via video, relying heavily on parent-facilitated playful interventions. We faced numerous apprehensions, given our previous reliance on hands-on experience and in-person interactions with children. This shift presented unique challenges as we adapted our methodologies to maintain the quality and effectiveness of our interventions in a virtual environment. We also lost touch with many of the families that we used to meet regularly. While we were all coping with this shift in our lives, we would often ask each other with urgency, *"How are the children we haven't reached coping with this?" "What do they understand about this world?" "What is the looming fear and disconnect doing to them?"*

At this time, an online seminar with Dr Jennings offered a space to reflect on how we felt being part of the child and family's inner circle in the current times. To learn from her and get reminded of the possibilities that existed within this framework made us all think about "creating safe spaces" and its implications for us, the children and families that we work with.

We often revisit some themes and collective thoughts shared in the online seminar. Some shared narratives from the session are shared below:

> Creating a safe space activity' was personally a comforting experience to remember that there is always an agency in me to be able to create or find shelter in and how in these times that is such a privilege and a gift.

It also got me thinking of the little children who may not be able to express what safety means to them. Tents, scarves, little hideouts, etc. are all so important.

The stories that we remember and tell our children were another theme that was spoken about. "Goldilocks and three bears" was one story often used with kids; however, discussing the "unsafe" component when she left the home was something we never addressed earlier. *"Connecting to the joys of rhythms and repetition"* – be it allowing space to go from form to mess or mess to form or attuning to what our children find comforting. As a team, we met online regularly and we decided to reclaim the journey of learning and applying NDP with Sue that we were on just prior to the pandemic. As the online medium persisted with the second and third waves of the pandemic, what started as a tentative foray into the online world – was proving to be a set of learnings.

Even as we each sat in our own bubbles, continuing to explore the sense of "connect and community," we now understand how intangible yet powerful this experience was. We increasingly witnessed and realised how much could be felt and shared even through the sparse "connect" that the small screen window provides, play is such a powerful medium. One of the main themes that emerged was the one of loss and grief. It came in different forms and ways. Adults may see "loss" as the absence of a loved one by death, loss of income and loss of the freedom of the outdoors, but loss as an experience may look very different in children. It is reassuring for children to know that their profound sadness and/or loss is allowed rather than resisted. Hence, we felt an urgent need to create a space to express/playout/share/experience their grief in their own way and own time. With this intent, a set of seven stories was written with the lens of development, neurodiversity and curiosity in order to witness the child's loss and grief and to facilitate healing.

A culmination of these written documents is to be turned into a workbook that could eventually aid the therapists in their intervention. In this workbook, each story is written in three sections. This sectioning is done to facilitate thinking and reflection as one reads it.

Section 1 – is aimed at identifying a child's responses to loss/grief. The question we stayed with was: What does loss manifest as in children?

Section 2 – of each story attempted to understand what the therapist did to encourage the expression yet maintain safety. The brief descriptions of what happened in therapy are illustrated with examples of an activity/art/ritual/narration/and how sessions progressed.

Section 3 – is to understand what healing looks like.

The question we often ask ourselves is, "Beyond just the expression of grief, what changes occur to indicate healing?" Is it more a journey rather than an endpoint and, if so – what clues help us understand that this journey is proceeding towards a desirable outcome? At the end of each story is a reflection by the therapist (section 4).

One such story is of K.

Section 1: How does loss manifest in children?

This story is about a 7-year-old girl called K who lived with her mother and father. In the middle of the pandemic, her family was displaced from their home overnight due to a financial dispute. K lost her home, her toys, her belongings, her safe place; in her words, "her everything." Her parents quickly moved to a hotel so that it was comfortable for her until they solved matters. In her father's words, "K has all the comfort of the hotel staff, big lawns and swimming pool, but she truly misses home."

Despite all their attempts, parents observed a significant increase in K's meltdowns and separation anxiety. During the first intake, when the therapist asked her age, K insisted she was 6 years old, even when her father said she was 7. Her parents later shared how she does not want to remember the past year and wants to believe that her last birthday did not happen. Hence, for her – she is still 6 years old.

While managing their financial stress, the family also got COVID in April 2021. K and her mother recovered fast; however, her father got seriously unwell due to the virus. During that unprecedented time, K would witness her mother crying and being worried about her father's health. K and her parents have managed to cross the turbulent times and her family is now doing better financially; however, K is left with a lot of anticipatory anxiety, as shared by her parents.

Section 2: What did the therapist do to encourage the expression yet maintain safety?

Therapy sessions for K began online. After the first few sessions, her mother shared, "It felt like she wanted to attach to anything comforting." K would insist on sitting at a spot where it did not feel or look like a hotel. She would share make-believe stories about an imaginary pet and an imaginary sister sleeping in the room upstairs to give the impression that she lives in a house.

During her sessions, it was observed that K wanted to talk about everything beautiful, grand and fantastical, like unicorns, rainbows and shiny toys and she felt extremely unsettled and unsafe to talk about anything which does not fit her story of "happiness." The therapist helped to create a "happy jar," which she filled with all the things she owned that made her happy. We hoped for her to see, visualise and create a jar full of happy resources that go beyond her "things."

K loved her session time, so much so that she would eagerly wait for it and had very big emotional responses if she was unable to attend or if the session started a few minutes late. She also had meltdowns at the end of the sessions as she did not want this time with the therapist to end. We used a starting and an ending ritual to help with transitions. The weather map embodiment exercise was repeated every session, with the aim of feeling safe after it closed. The idea of creating another unique rainbow in the next session became a symbol of continuity and safety. It felt that the rhythmic and ritualistic quality of the weather map allowed some sense of grounding and a check-in by the weather map before we left about "her heart."

We used art and drawing regularly in our sessions and once played a game where we took turns creating an image by adding our own elements to it. K struggled with each picture being left on how she made it and wanted to improve it or change it again and again. Providing that space for change yet giving her a count to be able to move onto the next one helped us move towards creating a story about her "home."

Section 3: What does healing look like?

K had created an attachment to the therapy space and found it comforting and joyful. After around five sessions, it was observed that K was not bringing up her imaginary stairs or imaginary dog or sister anymore during the session. K initially found it extremely hard to talk about anything stressful; however, as she felt anchored in the therapist, she felt safe to talk about difficult things for, e.g., online classes, wish to leave the hotel room and her broken unicorn toy.

In her mother's words, K's "perfectionism" used to show the depth of her fears. With the help of eight "perfectly imperfect" picture series, K created a story about her home. The story was filled with themes of sunlight, flowers blooming, a heart full of love and comfort and lots of kindness. During the course of therapeutic play sessions, her mother shared that K felt more comfortable with her parents' movement. The big news around the ninth session was that she was moving to her new house, but she did not want to speak about it as she felt she might jinx it. Instead, we created a story that allowed the experience of the resolution of the story. The process of healing for K is rooted in her experience of her home and her relationship with her loved ones.

Process notes: Reflections from the therapist

When I first met K, her exaggerated happiness and intense need to communicate felt like a loud cry, even if she was smiling ear to ear. Even though it made me very happy to interact and play with K each week, her sadness was palpable. What started as a happy session would often turn into a crying event for some reason. She was aching to grieve (Helbert, 2013). Sad tears, angry tears, happy tears, tears of victory. I think I felt a deep sense of resonation with K in more ways than one. In the middle of the pandemic, I became a mother; I have a baby who is healthy; I am healthy. We have all the things in the world and, hence, there is an unsaid pressure on me, from my social context and sometimes myself, to be grateful for all the things I have. And here I am in the first year of my motherhood, finding every opportunity to break down. I felt what K was feeling, every day. That made me think about how there was an expectation for her to be "grateful" for what she has versus grieving for what she had lost.

K's heart was hurting and I think we are often conditioned to think that once the child stops crying, the child stops hurting. But I feel during the experience of loss, when I was stopped from crying, I was being stopped to heal. And that is what I felt I needed to share from the collective wisdom of the children and families I have worked with. I felt that K needed that space to cry on little things to start the healing process. Working with K reminded me of what I read once:

> I am homesick for a place I am not sure really exists one where my heart is full, my body is loved and my soul understood.
>
> *– Mellisa Cox*

K needed to retreat, cuddle up and find the circle of containment to feel safe and she was better once she found predictability and grounding. It also made me reflect on her clinginess to the therapeutic space. She wanted that safety feeling to extend and expand and the ending of the session felt like an end to the safety for her. But knowing that she feels so safe in the therapeutic space gave me the courage to help her hold it in our hearts with the metaphor of the rainbow. I realise that I needed that ritual as much as she did. How my rainbow looked each day helped me map my feelings as well and I also managed to authentically share that with K.

Meanwhile, as our online programs of intervention were developing and evolving with the experience of therapists and feedback from the community, we were able to be dynamic in approaching the community's needs using the NDP framework. We conducted "Enrichment sessions" online with a group of children based on the principles of Messy Play, creating rituals and using stories. This was a module-based program for young children to find their communities and play spaces again with the tools and experience-based learnings from NDP. We also used sensory play with conviction with families to understand and work on feeding differences and concerns. This also helped us build a structure and framework around rhythmic play and dramatic play to work in groups with children in different capacities. The children had started looking forward to that time of the day when they would meet the therapists online and be ready to engage in their co-created space, their little corner in the house that had become a consistent space of connecting, sharing and exploration.

NDP at CF was where the world opened as we converged the work with a training course

As COVID receded and the world reopened, developmental services resumed in-person sessions. Although we had newfound conviction in our work, over the next two years, we realised that we were continuing to see the impact of the lockdown. This included the absence of a multisensory environment, the unexplained anxiety created by the practices we had to follow during COVID and the prolonged close proximity of parents and children. We realised that while grief and loss were one aspect, there seemed to be several other dimensions of development that were affected.

Children were presenting with a sense of mistrust in unfamiliar spaces, people and experiences, thus having a heightened sense of anxiety or avoidance. We also observed a subset of children with increased separation anxiety and others who seemed easily overwhelmed by the sudden influx of sensory stimuli. Additionally, due to the lack of opportunities for physical activity, motor skill development was adversely affected and we observed an increase in cases of dyspraxia and coordination disorders as well.

The team felt the need to skill up and build capacity outside of therapeutic spaces to address these emerging community needs. In 2023, after substantial planning, a reviewed curriculum was offered for an Advanced Diploma in Neuro Dramatic Play. The course was then slightly modified, with initial modules being more about theoretical aspects of understanding NDP and attachment, moving towards EPR and theatre of resilience. As part of our understanding and working towards the TOR paradigm, we delved into "A Midsummer Night's Dream," creating puppets, building character, taking on different roles and understanding the depth of drama work. This journey took the shape of a theatre box for the group; it was an enriching ensemble of our inner selves poured into each character we created.

As a group of facilitators as well as supervisors, and sometimes participants, it was enriching to witness the shifts in both the cohorts-participants and us. As trainers, we had understood that we had a paradigm to work with and we had developed a framework to work in sessions, groups and coursework. The group comprised a unique mix of 5 NDP trainers, who had gone through the collective journey of being long-term participants and, thereafter, practitioners of the NDP approach. Meeting with Dr Jennings periodically, to hone their own skills of both NDP application as well as training and supervising 11 students who were approaching NDP for the first time.

The students travelled on a journey from "Chaos to form" while holding the concept of Nurture and Nesting, Rhythms and Rituals, EPR and Theatre of Resilience. Participants were from different spheres – pre-school teachers, therapists and parents and they all were attempting to understand NDP and the neuroscience of Early development to work collaboratively with children. The course consisted of eight modules which were delivered in a mix of online and face-to-face sessions. Each module came with specific assignments and a supervision space was created to work on the groups' engagement with the course.

Employing NDP principles within the pedagogy

While delivering the NDP theory as trainers, we were quite aware that the modality of NDP is not didactic but is process-oriented. Therefore, all the modules were delivered with thought provided to the actual process of learning and experiencing through the following structure.

1. **Warm-up activities:** These were an essential part of the course structure and served as the first activity to lead into the day's content. This coming-together ritual allowed participants and trainers to be playful and co-create intentions for learning together. Trainers were seen as play partners and facilitators of shared meaning. Starting from where the participants were, these activities helped tune into the group's energy, set the tone for the day and build complexity from simple to advanced. The warm-ups usually ended by bringing everyone into a circle so that everyone could see each other. The warm-ups on a particular module held the central principle for the module as the anchor.
2. To share an anecdote, during day one, a warm-up activity was facilitated by two trainers, involving an imaginary ball to engage all the participants. The trainers led the group through various visualised games with the ball, culminating in everyone collectively holding and carrying it forward.

Figure 13.1 Imaginary ball warm-up activity

This activity transitioned from individual participation and effort, then in pairs to eventually centre a collective experience holding the biggest ball together with collective effort. Participants reported that, though initially cautious and anxious about being in a new space, they eventually felt able to let go of these feelings and come together. The activity fostered a sense of safety and connection among the participants.

3. **Sharing the theoretical content of each module:** Involved presentations and discussions through which we understood the key concepts of NDP, EPR and TOR. Dr. Jennings would often connect the concepts to her lived experiences, which helped to enhance our understanding.

4. **Experiential activity:** Theoretical understanding was deepened through experiential activities that allowed participants to engage with the material in a hands-on manner, either in groups or individually. Thereafter, they would share collectively and discuss what they experienced. We realised that these insights were invaluable for them to open up the possibilities of how others may respond when they facilitated and to understand the possible impact of these activities on a group.

For example, on Day 1, we spoke about the principles of NDP and immersed ourselves in messy play – our first experiential activity with the group. Participants were asked to go through the stages of mess to form and end by creating a childhood toy and a story in their sub-groups. In the end, when reflections were shared, some participants found that the

Figure 13.2 Group Collective Experience

Figure 13.3 Messy Play

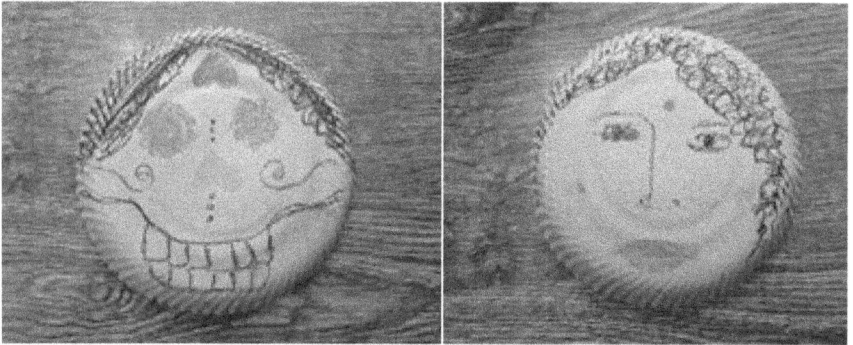

Figure 13.4 Mask Work

experiences evoked childhood memories, leading to feelings of nostalgia. For others, it triggered deeper emotions, while some found it a moment of reflection, allowing them to connect with their past in a meaningful way. This also led to questions about how to handle such evocations when working with children. We held these as a group and discussed the application of messy play, underlining the process and experiences during the activity.

5. **Application of the principles of NDP:** This was fostered through giving participants assignments. Some were to create therapeutic tools, others for self-reflection and yet others about applying learnt knowledge to explore with a group. These encouraged participants to internalise the concepts

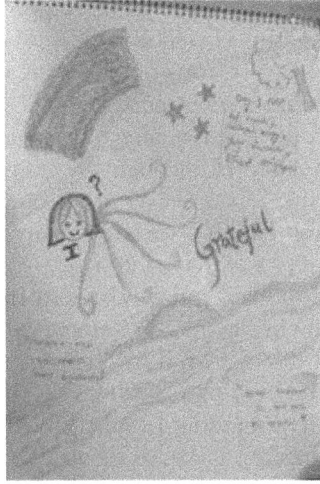

Figure 13.5 Reflections

through real-life application. This hands-on approach helped bridge the theory, self-reflection and applied practice.

In one of the assignment, participants had to draw their inner and outer self through masks

6. **Inviting participants' reflections through journaling:** Lastly, we would close the session by inviting participants' reflections through their chosen mediums. They were asked to draw, write, create poetry or use craft as a medium to share their experiences. We would then end with a story either from Sue or creating a story with each other.

Supervision sessions

For the supervision sessions, the participants were further subdivided into two groups and each group was led by two trainers. The supervision sessions were thoughtfully set for 90 minutes, usually placed two weeks after the direct teaching module, to encourage participants to bring in their dilemmas and hold a space for discussions. Our supervision sessions became the ground for people from various walks of life to come together and share their experiences of taking the concepts into their work. The supervision structure included:

1. *Starting ritual:* where we intended to bring the participants' reflections and intuitive knowledge to the group before their queries were voiced. We would ask each member to share one thing that stayed with them from the teaching module.

2. *Invite experiential knowledge:* During reflections, we would pick certain themes arising for the group as well as collectively try to resolve each other's challenges. As supervisors, we would use this space to share theoretical knowledge about childhood or principles of NDP to bridge the intuitive awareness that the group was reaching. We would also share and invite Experiential knowledge gained through the assignments. As supervisors, we would share our lived experiences from our group through sharing PPTs/Stories. We attempted not to use too many words to let the essence of NDP stay and for others to delve into it.

3. A *storytelling* session followed and we chose stories per the themes emerging in the group. In one of the initial sessions, we narrated a story of Jennings' "Moose and Mouse get Muddy" addressing themes of trusting the process, uncertainty and inviting playfulness in the setting.

4. At the end, we made a grounding ritual that would *close the session* by sharing one word/feeling about where we were.

While the webinars became playgrounds for inner work and supervisions became spaces to build safety reflections and take the work to our actual setups. As supervisors, we were constantly tasked with providing safety to participants, bringing provocative memories from their childhood while attempting to help the group look beyond their evoked experience. The group constantly struggled to shift to a group-based learning process. We had to iterate the sense that the group had the expertise to solve their challenges and dilemmas. What also helped us were the debriefing spaces with Dr SJ and Dr K, along with peer-supervisions, to share felt knowledge as well as revisit the theory time and again.

This process evolved as a unique group experience for everyone. By the end, each participant shared noticeable shifts within them. Moreover, the group became one entity and we worked towards consolidating the collective. Many of us reached the awareness that learning is Circular and not linear, i.e., we will revisit each stage of NDP at different points in our life/work but derive meaning from the repetition of the principles. We started to look at ruptures within sessions as opportunities to repair, leading the participants as co-creators of learning experiences honing their ability to stay with the process. We observed the progression of attachment (Sensory-messy play) within the group, which led the space for emotional sharing and growing empathy (EPR) to work towards the group's ability to work from the outside to within and develop resilience.

The essence of the participants' journey could be captured through these anecdotes.

• "It started with chaos, but as the course ends, I experience an internal shift within myself . . ."

- "I really enjoyed sharing my experiences with my small group, as well as listening to them. It was such a rush of diversity – and it was so powerful to feel connected in these differences . . ."
- "I was amazed to see how our childhood experiences shape our actions and behaviour. When we did the activity of choosing an object from the environment and creating a safe space for it, I chose to do exactly what I missed in my childhood."
- "As I sit here, reflecting on the process of creating masks, I find myself drawn into a profound exploration of the human experience. Each mask I made is not merely a piece of art. It is a manifestation of the intricate dance between the roles we play and the personas we project onto the world. In this enthralling journey, I am reminded of how individuals seamlessly transition between various roles in different settings."
- "I got intrigued by how we can use our folk Indian stories in the contemporary context and make out the meaning of them."
- "I was always scared to use a loud voice, but playing out embodying and enacting different characters seemed to shift something within."

The participants' journey began with feelings of anxiety, uncertainty and curiosity about NDP as a modality for intervention. "What will we get out of it?" was a central theme, with an initial focus on seeking answers to the "how" and "why" of everything. This primary concern gradually shifted to a greater emphasis on viewing the "process" as more important than the "outcome." Hands-on learning and a non-judgmental environment created a sense of safety, aiding participants' exploration. Engaging in activities such as making different kinds of puppets, enacting characters and creating life-size puppets brought about a significant shift. As participants immersed themselves in these activities, they reflected on how the process of making puppets involved a part of themselves and was therapeutic. These experiences encouraged them to be present in the moment rather than focusing solely on the final product.

Taking NDP forward

Continuing our journey of NDP in intervention as well as some new projects. We continue to evolve as a group and how to refine the course for the next batch in 2024–2025. We continue to apply principles in our daily intervention practices and we hope to bring new projects like the Nesting circle.

Nesting circle is rooted in the NDP paradigm. It is an endeavour to offer a nurturing space to parents and their babies that contains them and brings insights into a child's healthy development that aims at building a strong foundation of attachment and connection. It is for infants and early movers (5 months to 18 months) accompanied by one caregiver, coming together in a facilitated small group.

Even as we write this, our first attempt at the Nesting Circle is starting. We intend to invite new parents into our Nesting circle, circle of Containment and build a Circle of trust.

- Understanding the Significance of play from the beginning of life.
- Connecting to their "inner child" as a playful parent.
- A step towards postpartum recovery – self-care to caregiving.
- Opportunity to engage in playful partnership in their parenting journey.
- To offer insights into their attachment and bonding with their baby through the approaches of the research-based paradigm of Neuro-Dramatic-Play.

At the very end, we often have a story to close the chapter

Once upon a time, there was a handful of people who happened to come together because they were fascinated by childhood. They went by the name "Children First." They wanted to find out more about the inner worlds of children, especially when babies could not yet speak. They wondered how to find out more from the little ones themselves as the children did not seem to have words like adults do. So, they started spending dedicated time in the children's world to find out more. They realised with time that they often felt a tug somewhere inside whenever they met these babies and the "tug" would make them do certain things intuitively, like create sounds, smile, laugh and play. What was wonderful was that the babies' eyes seemed to sparkle and they would often join in, so the Children First team called it "*Connect*." As the team at Children First went about trying to find the language of Connect in more and more children and even adults – they realised it gave them meaning and joy, too, and families started bringing their children to explore this language of "Connect."

There were some children the team felt especially drawn to – these were the little ones who were not actively searching for their *Connect* and *did not feel compelled yet to tell their own stories*. It seemed they had not yet felt the tug or their way of "Connect" was different and unique, which CF had not yet discovered. Their parents seemed worried and baffled in equal measure.

The Children First team devised a small set of discoverers who called themselves the *Developmental Services team* and they set about finding how they would find the Connect or any other way to explore the "tug." They met many parents who brought to them their children who had languages other than the spoken word; some immediately responded to the language of "Connect" and others did not seem to know it at all.

They met many children, from little babies to teens, whose inner stories were not understood because their language was different. Some spoke through their bodies, some relayed messages through their play and others made rhythms that seemed like invitations. They tried to observe these children and explore other ways to play and communicate. It was also a journey of curiosity about how other human babies found Connect, discovered words and language and made stories of and for themselves.

On this journey, they explored many different vistas. They tried to understand how all the senses came together for a baby human, how their bodies instinctively seemed to know how to crawl and walk.

The story will continue . . . .

References

Berard, M., Peries, M., Loubersac, J., Picot, M. C., Bernard, J. Y., Munir, K. and Baghdadli, A. (2022) Screen time and associated risks in children and adolescents with autism spectrum disorders during a discrete COVID-19 lockdown period. *Front Psychiatry*, 13, 1026191, December. https://doi.org/10.3389/fpsyt.2022.1026191. PMID: 36532191; PMCID: PMC9751585.

Bowlby, J. (1988) *A Secure Base: Parent-Child Attachment and Healthy Human Development*. Basic Books.

Helbert, K. (2013) *Finding Your Own Way to Grieve: A Creative Activity Workbook for Kids and Teens on the Autism Spectrum*. London: Jessica Kingsley Publishers.

Jennings, S. (2011) *Healthy Attachments and Neuro-Dramatic-Play*. Jessica Kingsley Publishers.

Kilroy, E., Aziz-Zadeh, L. and Cermak, S. (2019) Ayres theories of autism and sensory integration revisited: What contemporary neuroscience has to say. *Brain Science*, 9(3), 68, March 21. https://doi.org/10.3390/brainsci9030068. PMID: 30901886; PMCID: PMC6468444.

Singh, S., Roy, D., Sinha, K., Parveen, S., Sharma, G. and Joshi, G. (2020) Impact of COVID-19 and lockdown on mental health of children and adolescents: A narrative review with recommendations. *Psychiatry Research*, 293, 113429. ISSN 0165-1781. https://doi.org/10.1016/j.psychres.2020.113429; https://www.sciencedirect.com/science/article/pii/S016517812031725X

Teich, P., Fühner, T., Bähr, F., Puta, C., Granacher, U. and Kliegl, R. (2023) Covid Pandemic effects on the physical fitness of primary school children: Results of the German EMOTIKON project. *Sports Medicine Open*, 9(1), 77, August 14. https://doi.org/10.1186/s40798-023-00624-1. PMID: 37578660; PMCID: PMC10425322.

Chapter 14

Neuro-dramatic-play and postcolonial African theatre – performing resilience

David Evans

Introduction

Conceived in the street theatre style of *Agbo Play* from Freetown, Sierra Leone, **Native Wit** stages memories from the West African childhoods of two actors, Ayodele Scott and myself. In my work with children, I have explicitly embraced Sue Jennings' developmental theory of Embodiment-Projection–Role (EPR) (Evans et al., 2009; Evans, 2022). What, up until now, has been less clear is the salience of the whole Neuro-Dramatic-Play (NDP) paradigm in my personal theatre-making practice. This chapter questions if, and how, NDP processes are reactivated in the creative discoveries of two established and award-winning artists.

Does the NDP paradigm have a transcultural relevance? I have chosen the descriptive methods of an autoethnographic account as the lens through which to examine the creative dynamics of two artists from contrasting cultures. On undertaking this journey, both Ayodele and I tacitly acknowledged it might be a therapeutic pathway. This chapter examines if the aesthetics of *Agbo Play* intersect with NDP/EPR and if the processes confer a novel 'Theatre of Resilience' (ToR) (Jennings, 2023, p. 2).

On friendship, kinship and creative allegiance

The words, "He's absolutely wired!" fizzed into my mind as he stepped into the dance studio. His presence created in me a dramatic immediacy, an existential urgency that I have always found irresistible on recognising the potential of a new playmate. Resting his hands on the congas, he introduced himself as Ayo, a Freetonian. Then his fingers began to dance, caressing the skins, coaxing sounds of startling lyricism from the resonating belly of the drums. This was around November 1993. He'd travelled down from Birmingham and announced his intention to work in Imùlè,[1] a cross-cultural theatre company I'd founded four years earlier.

Ayo spoke a form of English which had familiar West African rhythmic and melodic qualities but was peppered with words I recognised from

DOI: 10.4324/9781003498209-18

Yoruba,[2] French and Nigerian Pidgin. This was Ayo's English, but it was far from his native Krio, the language learned in his mother's lap in Freetown.

Born in Ibadan in 1957, two years before Ayo, Nigeria was my home until the age of 16. Despite my childhood in which I had communicated using limited forms of Pidgin and Yoruba, once Ayo was in story mode, I could only decipher around 30 percent of his Krio. My linguistic deficit was of little consequence since his accounts were vividly embodied with gesture, dance, mime and physical characterisations.

I have rarely been perturbed by my failure to understand everything being verbally articulated, particularly during cross-cultural interactions. There have always been other clues, and the semiotics of tonal variations, non-verbal utterances, facial and gestural signals are sources of delight and meaning.

Imùlè Theatre and the *Agbo Play* style

Imùlè is a form of company-devised theatre performances and workshops drawing on West African myths and histories. Ayo was a seminal influence in the canon of Imùlè productions. He instituted theatre-in-the-round and 'Agbo Play' from Freetown, which became our house style and aesthetic touchstone.

Typically, Imùlè Theatre worked in primary schools. Our company varied in size and make-up from two to six players of African, Caribbean, British, European and Middle Eastern origin. We would start the day in a school hall. The children would file in excitedly as the company drummed, each class arranged around the four sides of the *Agbo* – "Our African playing space." The children were never quite orderly but would skip, rock, clap and bounce to the rhythm and the cast reciprocated, indulging them with smiles, claps and verbal greetings.

We would quickly introduce ourselves, explain that all of us here were going to make a story and teach them a Yoruba song of welcome – *"Káàbọ̀."* This was achieved in the traditional West African style of call and response and the lyrics, accompanied by drumming and harmonies, unified us as "Children of the Earth."

The theatre works were always energetic and playful, with the climactic moments taking the form of dance and physical motifs, underscored with vibrant drumming, songs and chants. The multi-cultural cast often spoke and sang in their mother tongues mixed with English, so it was accepted that no one could understand all the words.

The 30-minute performance over, excited children would restlessly antici-pate the ensuing workshops. Disassembling the story into the most dramatic episodes, four workshops introduced rigorous performance techniques, ensuring participants experienced maximal visceral engagement.

The expanded cast could run to 100 plus. As each workshop group presented their episode, the narrative, drum and song linked it to the next, creating a coherent story.

Imùlè never performed biographies of the cast. We judged that situating the stories of individual company members in wider historical narratives of slavery, colonialism and environmental exploitation detracted from the mythopoeic and play aesthetic of Imùlè. Moreover, whenever we inadvertently touched on such sensitivities, the experience was debilitatingly awkward and painful.

After ten years, our paths separated in confusion and disharmony, with a saddening erosion of trust. Ayo focused more on his music and dance while I redeployed my theatre and science education practice in Apause, a relationships and sex education programme at the University of Exeter (Evans, 2022). Predating this rupture, we had made a pact to set aside some future time for a personal project, an Imùlè piece about our childhoods in West Africa. We already knew the title – **Native Wit**.

Reunion

Despite notable successes in our respective fields, the ensuing 15 years also brought us domestic upheavals with mental and physical health challenges.

My Apause retirement party was the auspicious occasion of our reunion. We undertook the devising of an Imùlè event with me reciting a history of the Apause achievements at home and abroad. An adapted form of Yoruba oratory meant Ayo could drum while I enunciated in a heightened form of rhythmic prose. By joining the call and response of the West African song, the gathered party punctuated the Apause milestones with a traditional Yoruba chorus of praise. The celebration ended with drumming and dancing.

We knew we were ready to create **Native Wit**.

New beginnings and messy play

Our first **Native Wit** session was riven with mutual trepidation. How does one prioritise memories from a kaleidoscopic array of impressions? Was there a meaningful relationship between our disparate recollections? Could we heal our disharmony? We cooked Krio food together. Washing, chopping, frying, spicing, stirring, sampling and washing up constituted our messy and sensory play. Moving around each other, kitchen rhythms were a comfort, the matrix into which we stitched the patchwork of our dialogue.

Ayo challenged me.

"Dis your PhD, what will it bring?"
"Play," I reposted.
"I've been writing academically about play for six years."

"That's all I'm interested in. If we can't play together in **Native Wit**, then the work has nothing to offer me. Nothing to offer the world."
"David. Put it there, Bra."

With loosely folded fingers, Ayo offered the knuckles of his left hand. I met him with my own left-handed fist punch, confirming this was what Imùlè theatre has always done for us: found a way of playing.

Childhood, taboos and hidden transcripts

I posited that the most formative moments in my childhood had often arisen in secret and from the breaking of taboos. These included: comparing my 'uncut' penis with my friends' circumcised counterparts; using a powerful catapult to fire stones at my Yoruba friend; and speaking in Pidgin. I explained these were the hidden, subversive and fertile transcripts of my childhood. (Sutton-Smith, 1997, p. 116) Furthermore, I had been aware that many of my interactions with my Yoruba childhood playmates, the charismatic market women and inquisitive manual workers, were manifest in the same terms of secret transcripts of complicity shared among the subjugated. My whiteness, conspicuous privilege and childhood naiveté were all sources of humour and played into a parodic game in which my apparent social advantage was merely an ephemeral contrivance, lasting just as long as the others agreed to indulge me.[3] But with a trick of language, a sneaky bargain or pointed observation, I could be gently reminded of my subordinate status and cultural ineptitude. Notwithstanding the shapeshifting and paradoxical nature of these playful encounters, I always felt safe and some tenets of the Yoruba culture became normalised into my sense of personhood. Comforted by our kitchen rituals and recognition that we were in a complicit space, the stories began to flow. Ayo was galvanised by the proposition that my breaking of taboos was formative. He launched into his highly embodied storytelling manner, rich in ethnographic detail and domestic drama.

Taking his mother's cups and saucers down from an out-of-reach shelf, he'd tested them with teaspoons. Tapping her chinaware, the classy tones had thrilled him and, tinkling with delight, he had drummed them into pieces. In another story, he had knowingly addressed one of his mother's friends by his secret title of "Cowfoot," a name to be used exclusively by members of her 'social club' the "Kalelu Squad." Breaking this taboo was a grave affront to Cowfoot and despite his crippled left foot, he had chased Ayo home through the shanty alleyways of Freetown. Ayo's mother (who herself had to be born three times before agreeing to remain in this world and, hence, been named Akpara Moleh, 'the snake that sheds its skin') had to beg Cowfoot's forgiveness. She explained that the young Ayo, "aka Headache," had an affliction. His incapacity to be still and yield to social constraints was akin to her own restlessness, inherited. Deformed since birth, Cowfoot offered to pay for Ayo's treatment. There was a kind of complicit acceptance that Ayo, his mother and Cowfoot were all born with afflictions – but in the world of Krio, they were a source of solidarity and resilience.

We soon recognised in each other iconoclastic tendencies. The adult social worlds of our childhoods – the strictures, the sense that authority, formalities and binary distinctions – were merely constructs. We surmised these contrivances were founded on false certitudes. We trusted the truth of our senses, we trusted our imperative to play and its heuristic mechanisms and we trusted the intimacy of family and friends, but so much outside those immediate realms presumed too much credulity.

We confessed that we had often proceeded into situations of social jeopardy with open eyes. Our play did not always protect us from its consequences rather, its conventions created a permissive framework in which we were emboldened. Despite an awareness that our actions were usually socially situated and might impinge on the general order of things, paradoxically, the sheer intensity of the game or performative (Austin, 1962) generated its own intrinsic motives and rewards. Our childhood play was autopoietic (Fischer-Lichte, 2008) and as adult performing artists, we resolved that **Native Wit** would restore that aesthetic for ourselves and our audiences.

As we deepened our creative processes, the experience took on an oscillatory quality. Hence, whilst the autopoiesis of our play generated its own benefit and intrinsic pleasure, it simultaneously described wider personal and cultural points of reference (Lyotard, 1988). This is all about power. The church, circumcision, adult power over children, white over black and colonials. We experienced both a childlike absorption and strange omniscience. The unresolved tensions which precipitated our going separate ways began to dissolve. The emotional content of certain disclosures inevitably prompted awkwardness, but the intransigence of one language form could be playfully transmuted into another and we were rejuvenated.

Agbo Play and NDP

Originating from the Yoruba, the word *agbo*, typical of Krio, is polysemic, indicating the multifunctionality of a communal space. As a domestic compound or yard enclosed by houses, it is sanctioned as a playing space for children. It is a venue for family storytelling, theatre, rituals and celebrations. A seamless interplay of the domestic, children's play and performative functions is commonplace in the *agbo*.

Having designated *agbo* as our term for a rehearsal space, NDP/EPR seemed an intriguingly appropriate and subtly powerful paradigm. We felt 'natural', frequently inhabiting a state of 'flow' (Csikszentmihalyi, 2002) and on entering that state, there was little cognition of the regulative frameworks or set rules which held us. Only on reaching some kind of emotional or creative impasse did we consciously shift between the conventions of embodied play to say, role-play and projective play. Oscillating between role-playing, scripting and back again, even these processes seldom felt discrete.

Cooking together also felt natural, but instead of impatiently treating it as a domestic chore, I was content to reframe it both as a form of messy play and ritual in the 'ritual-risk' cycle (Jennings, 1999).

We often started with drumming. The challenge for me was to stop 'forcing' the rhythm. Ayo coached me to just listen and be absorbed by his playing. It was like waiting to laugh; I felt a tingling and widening space in my chest. This rhythmic play was not a lesson in drumming but in empathy (Jennings, 2011, pp. 124–125).

Out of the habit of repeatedly misplacing my glasses came a game, exploring the interplay of oral rhythms, chants and dance steps.

"I lost my glasses."
"When?"
"Just now."
"When do you need it?"
"Now, now!"

These utterances could be translated into a pleasing drumming phrase which, as an isolated rhythm, was indecipherable but nevertheless quite coherent as a percussive accompaniment to a chant and dance. In performance, the audience quickly recognised the time-honoured predicament and were empathetic, joining the geriatric actors in their chorus of exasperation at having once misplaced their glasses, realising they were too visually impaired to find them again.

Having been released through rhythm, our bodies were ready for stories. But, in the tradition of *Agbo Play* and the storytelling of Ayo's mother and grandmother, Ayo insisted we 'inhabit' the stories rather than 'tell' them, conjoining the audience through play.

Characterisations were instantaneous creations. What emerged were those distinguishing qualities, speech patterns, physical shapes and gestures, anything that would invoke and manifest the 'spirit' of the being and 'flavour' of the event into our bodies and the *agbo*. Hence, in one scene, I played variously myself as an enquiring ethnographer, Ayo's childhood friend, Ayo himself, a mating frog, members of the Kalelu Squad and Cowfoot Cole. This freewheeling flow and lack of concern for explanatory detail, instead privileging the sensual and affective essence of the story, was entirely commensurate with the dramatic games and stories I had been playing for months with my partner's granddaughter, aged 3.

By the time I took on the role of scribe, we had already encountered the story as a physical and embodied phenomenon. This collaborative 'scripting' process was our default mode of Projective Play. Documenting formal dialogue was very important. It authenticated our rhythms, patterns and repetitions. I could codify Krio and Yoruba phrases by forming verbal fixed points or scaffolding around which languages of movement and gesture could be articulated. The script was artefactual, emergent from and a servant to our performative explorations. Phrases carefully crafted to invoke a symphony of childhood impressions became instated as a part of our 'regulative framework' (see later on), further emancipating our creative impulses and challenging us to achieve choreographic complexity and precision.

Kriolisation and the aesthetics of *Agbo Play*

As we explored our understanding of childhood languages, Ayo began to articulate his thesis of 'Kriolisation'. A 'patchwork' was a recurrent metaphor. It was emblematic of his knowledge that Krio was a language born out of multiple colonial influences with a syntax integrating elements of Yoruba, Temne, Mende, French, Portuguese and English. His slave forebears had long since been severed from their West African mother tongues. Having fought with the British in the American War of Independence, their reward was to be returned to the African colonies. Patchworking family histories, then, was also a survival response to the multiple displacements and 'repatriation' of his ancestors.

His grandmother had carefully stitched together the salvaged fragments of worn-out garments to create his sleeping quilt – a light cotton bedding nightly rolled out onto the floor. Each fragment bore its own family or Krio story. More recent pieces were vivid cotton cloths based on Indonesian batik, while more ancient fragments were of a deep indigo ádìrẹ, a starch resist technique commemorating events such as a coronation and national Independence Day. Role-playing his granny, Ayo invoked her into our *agbo*. He mimed her random pulling of rags from the sack to trim and smooth them, performing their individual stories as she juxtaposed them on the ground. As each fragment joined its companion, songs and family histories were conjured, stitching their provenance into the present.

Ayo told me of his 'meltdown' some ten years ago and how he'd voluntarily sectioned himself, how he'd worked with an art therapist to create a montage of coloured paper. There were no pictures or explanatory stories for the therapist, just hours of carefully cutting, arranging and sticking down the fragments. The final composition was not figurative; nevertheless, the abstract patching had restored his functionality.

We concluded that our understanding of 'Kriolisation' is synonymous with the restorative processes of patchworking. **Native Wit,** our *Agbo Play,* would be the theatrical manifestation of patchworking. Our performance of patchworking did not arise by conforming to the familiar narrative arc of Western dramaturgies. Ours was a more heteroglossic and messy sensibility. We created our play in multiple and simultaneous languages with memories experienced not as coherent stories but as vivid, episodic, iconic and random fragments. Accordingly, in performance, each memory was given a cryptic title and used to label a piece of card which was placed in a market trader's basket. Audience members were agentic in forming the narrative by drawing each card or fragment 'blindly' from a market woman's basket. The surprise revelation of our next memory would prompt us into playful banter with the audience as we reconfigured props, costumes and drums in preparation for the shared discovery of the ensuing scene. We performed ourselves into a present being out of the remnants of broken histories and audiences became complicit participants in the *Agbo Play*.

Our manifesto was not an uttered declaration but a performed commitment to an ethos of resilience, our 'Theatre of Resilience'. The play theoretician Thomas S. Henricks encapsulates this understanding.

> Play, I – like some others – argue, is a fundamental way creatures make coherent their possibilities for acting in the world.
>
> (Henricks, 2014)

Transitions

From this account, a reader familiar with the NDP paradigm and its constituents of messy play, rhythmic play, embodied play, projective play and role-play can discern how, at any point, the subjects are engaged in one or more elements. Also, there is something of a sequence in so far as the whole process begins with sensory, rhythmic and embodied play, passes through the reflective deliberations of projective play, before role-play culminates in the public performances and a manifesto of resilience – 'Theatre of Resilience'. Each scene was an affirmation that our stories will not easily be broken and when they are, we can restore them through our patchwork of play and the heteroglossia of performance.

Nonetheless, no two stories emerged according to a common prescriptive framework and choosing how and when to move from one set of creative conventions to the next required great sensitivity, demanding an aesthetic judgement in its own right.

Our *agbos*, or play spaces, occurred variously in the kitchen, the patio, the conservatory, the sitting room and the sunlounge, with the latter being most formally arranged as an 8' x 11' performance area. In the kitchen, we would listen to music which was personally moving or created the necessary affective disturbance (Williams, 2005, p. 79). Viewing YouTube revealed the astonishing physicality and metaplay of Max Wall and Charlie Chaplin (Sutton-Smith, 2009). Occasionally, I would read excerpts from my PhD thesis. They all created certain permissions, challenging us to disrupt our existing understandings. This was messy work, an ordeal with long periods of uncertainty, requiring trust in each other's creative capacities. Despite apparently destabilising the 'safety' of our established Imùlè theatre-making conventions, the jeopardy only served to draw us more deeply into a childlike present – a more visceral acknowledgement of our connectedness, interdependence and vulnerability. We were inventing a new childhood friendship, needing to take risks and trusting each other's survival skills.

We verbalised painful, sometimes buried memories of hurt, abandonment and feelings of being the imposter. Formulating such disclosures as mundane utterances in a quotidian context risked us feeling personally exposed, awkward and too cerebral to play creatively. We had no adequate language forms with which to articulate these affective states, far less interpret them meaningfully. As with my work with adolescents, the art of transitioning was crucial and I have dubbed the process 'the creative transmutation of awkwardness' (Evans, 2022, p. 230). We trusted each other to introduce or develop the activity that corresponded to our immediate affective and aesthetic needs.

After one breakfast, we went to the living room and drummed a particularly taxing rhythm to accompany the *Iko, Iko* song, then, for relief, started talking about catapults – in Krio, *Robba thack*. Using my hands and toes, I mimed in detail how I was taught to fashion one from a forked stick, tough catapult rubber and a bicycle innertube. I conveyed my pride in mastering the craft. Wearing it around my neck, it emblemised my belonging to my Nigerian peer group and our 'hunting parties'. Finally, I confessed the shameful story of using the weapon on my friend. But we could go no further with the story; we were immobilised with awkwardness and, in the absence of mitigating socio-cultural norms, it remained as an unresolved disturbance (Kotsko, 2010).

Some weeks later, in the sunlounge, we suddenly knew how to begin to stage it. It started as a pair of friends sculpted into a composite motif of hunting with catapults; this moved into a precise, mirroring and slow motion, rhythmic dance sequence. I asked in Pidgin whether he'd watched through my window the home film show projected onto the wall. Instantly Ayo was Charlie Chaplin, the champion of the poor, the marginalised underdog surviving on his wits alone – his indomitable capacity to play and make a satirical game of hegemonic posturing. Suddenly, I transitioned to another kind of movie – cowboys – playing John Wayne, with my father's English private school accent, no trace of Pidgin. I shot him with my catapult.

Cowboys and Nigerians *(Transcript from the scene in* **Native Wit***)*

(Opens with the slow motion, mirror 'Rubber Thack' motif – boys are hunting a squirrel)
D: *(In Pidgin)* I see you watch dat film last night?
A: Eh?
D: Tru my window.
A: Tru de wire na de window. Because we are not allowed inside your house.
D: Dat wire is to stop de tief.
A: Well, tru dat wire we are watching – we are not stealing.

D: You like dis film?

A: The man wid de stick. *(Chaplin business with cane)* Dat man he makes me laugh. Oh . . . Nah me Nigerian brodda.

D: Why is he your brodda?

A: He never have much money! And he is very witty!

D: Witty? Charlie Chaplin Witty?

A: Because dey can nevva beat him.

D: But he nevva win.

A: But he's always playing wid dem. Dey are VEX . . . de more dey vex, de more he PLAY.

(Ayo points Dave in direction of a squirrel; he creeps towards it preparing to shoot. Ayo taps him on the shoulder; Dave spins round; Ayo has slipped behind him and surprises him with a Chaplinesque kick up the arse. Angrily, Dave shoots Ayo in the foot. Ayo feigns pain. Dave leans in out of concern; Ayo tweaks his nose)

D: *(Indignant – In received pronunciation)* What about the other film?

A: Which one?

D: *(Angrily)* Cowboys!
(Mimes shooting Ayo with a rifle)
(Twisting, dropping slowly to the ground and letting out a choked howl of pain, Ayo dies)

A: You kill your brodda? Oh ho . . . Cowboys and Nigerians. Why dey don't fight man man? Hand to hand?

There was no resolution to the global narrative of colonialism. I was a white boy born into colonial privilege, the beneficiary of this historic shame. Did this make Ayo a victim? Would it help if I said sorry?

(Horrified at the enormity of his own actions, Dave takes Ayo's hand and assists him from ground – a slow lifting and balance motion arriving at a motif of the fingers of both left hands clenched, forming an arch framing our heads)

A: No guns!
(Ayo leads Dave in a drum sequence, rising in intensity)

A: NO GUNS!

In the sunlounge, he drummed. A slow, doleful thud of execution. Then came the signal. Was it a call to accompany him? Tentatively, I joined in with a simple repeating phrase. Ayo drummed with a surging complexity and ferocity. This was not lyrical; it was a call to arms, a pulsating throb echoing across the generations of hurt, frenetic patterns of rim and slap rose from his djembe. In the ludic spirit of *agon* (Huizinga, 1949), Ayo challenged me to stay with him. Without elaboration, I tried to keep my rhythm honest. Out of the frenzy came the drum call to end. We closed in unison and it was out. We had played it, shouldering the burden and sharing our tears.

Discussion

Alongside the priceless healing of our personal friendship, in what other sense could the making and performing of our *Agbo Play* be adjudged to have engaged the restorative processes of NDP?

We believe we performed our own version of an Imùlè ritual or pact. Our enterprise was to enjoin, through performance, our public in the childhood experiences of two boys occupying opposite poles of multiple binaries, including: white versus black, coloniser versus colonised, rich versus poor, hegemonic versus subjugated, English versus Krio and formal versus informal education. Through play, we endeavoured to expose and destabilise the assumptions and norms that maintain those binaries.

My interpretation of NDP has engendered in me a gentler, more empathetic way of being present. Accordingly, we aspired to demonstrate that there are simple, creative ways of being together, even as adults, which can be deeply fulfilling. Ways which make modest demands on resources without implicating us all in conspicuous shows of consumerism and inhuman acts of cultural and environmental destruction. The *agbo* invites all to share in the sensibility of Kriolisation, salvaging and patching the fragments of our pasts. We performed our manifesto and it is our Theatre of Resilience.

In experiencing the intersectionality of NDP with our ritual of *Agbo Play*, I was guided by Jennings' notion of the interplay between regulative and constitutive frameworks.

> all rituals are performative and as such are subject to two different sorts of rules: regulative and constitutive, the former orienting a pre-existing activity and the latter created and understood within the activity itself.
>
> (Jennings, 1995, p. 16)

Within our creative partnership, I was the only one with prior academic involvement with NDP. Hence, to avoid replicating existing imbalances of power and privilege, during our devising phases, there were few explicit references to the paradigm. Nonetheless, as a way of being with each other during the processing of highly personal material, we shared tacit sensibilities, many of which, for me, could be ascribed to NDP as a regulative framework.

As with NDP, prioritising safety, trust and only moving forward on the basis of consensus was axiomatic. Not every day of rehearsal was equally exposing, but we always started and finished each day in the kitchen preparing and eating food. The processes of dramatic exploration and manifestation, corresponding to our constitutive framework, were often messy and inchoate and always had the potential to provoke anxiety and stifle play. We flowed in and out of all the phases of NDP, not always chronologically, but secure in the knowledge each one would reveal its own developmental function and place. Enabling us to sustain the liminality of our *agbo*, prior knowledge of NDP helped us avoid prematurely imposing a sense of order or closure extrinsic to the play imperative.

Historically, evidencing unequivocally the processes of personal development through play has proved elusive (Burghardt, 2014, p. 94; Sutton-Smith, 1997). It can take place in the individual on an intrapersonal and neurological basis, but neuroscience has demonstrated that plasticity within the brain is not a process which occurs in isolation from somatic stimuli or social contexts (Blakemore, 2018; Burnett, 2023). Changes are affected on interpersonal bases between two people, with respect to individuals' status within a peer group and the wider community (Yeager et al., 2018). Like others, I am arguing that consistent with the social function of *Agbo Play* within the Krio community, the heteroglossia of NDP and theatre can be the nexus for change in multiple interactional contexts and dynamics (Sutton-Smith, 1997, p. 222; Thompson, 2003, 2009; Okagbue, 2007; Evans, 2022).

Conclusion

As our manifesto of ToR (Theatre of Resilience) (Jennings, 2011) emerged, so, too, did our personal bond of trust deepen and our status amongst friends and communities consolidate. We enjoyed an invigourated sense of our own virtuosic qualities as artists but, more importantly, a sense of purpose. We learned that despite neither of us feeling 'native' to England, our divergent personal and cultural perspectives shared critical commonalities with our audiences and we had something important to share. Perhaps, above all else, it confirmed that play and its capacity to embrace paradox has a universal appeal in its performance, engendering amongst participants feelings of empathy, unity, hope and human potential.

Notes

1 "Imùlè" is the Yoruba name given to a covenant or pact. It literally translates as "Drinking together from the earth" and describes a ritual act performed before an earth divinity. The covenant commits its performers to reciprocal obligations, typically extending to the carrying out of a collective enterprise with the utmost integrity. Critically, the Imùlè ritual must be performed and honoured by all the participants if they are to benefit from the binding force of the covenant. Whilst the enterprise is sanctioned by the divinity, failure to execute it with integrity places the wellbeing of the transgressor in serious jeopardy (Evans, 2022).
2 Yoruba is a language spoken in West Africa, mainly in Nigeria. The number of speakers of Yoruba in Nigeria alone is estimated at 45 million, excluding non-Yorubas who speak the language (Evans, 2022).
3 Play in my childhood was predicated on my childhood apprehension of power structures. As Sutton-Smith argues, we recognise and operate within hierarchies in order to ensure the play takes place. Play and power dynamics are acknowledged, if not explicit.

References

Austin, J. L. (1962) *How to Do Things with Words: The William James lectures Delivered at Harvard University in 1955*. Oxford: Clarendon Press.

Blakemore, S.-J. A. (2018) *Inventing Ourselves: The Secret Life of the Teenage Brain*. Random House, Penguin.

Burghardt, G. (2014) A brief glimpse at the long evolutionary history of play. In *Animal Behaviour and Cognition* (vol. 2). Sciknow Publications Limited, 90–98.

Burnett, D. (2023) *Emotional Ignorance – Lost and Found in the Science of Emotion*. Bloomsbury House, Faber and Faber Ltd.

Csikszentmihalyi, M. (2002) *Flow: The Classic Work on How to Achieve Happiness* (Rev. ed.). London: Rider.

Evans, D. (2022) *A Theatre of Applied Performativity: Play and the Aesthetics of the Scripted Performance Workshop in Peer-Facilitated Relationships and Sex Education*. PhD, Goldsmiths, University of London.

Evans, D., Akerman, S. and Tripp, J. (2009) Where professional actors are too "good". In *Dramatherapy and Social Theatre: Necessary Dialogues*, ed. Jennings, S. London: Routledge, 220.

Fischer-Lichte, E. (2008) *The Transformative Power of Performance: A New Aesthetics*. London: Routledge.

Henricks, S. T. (2014) Play as self-realization – towards a general theory of play. *The American Journal of Play*, 6, 190–213.

Huizinga, J. (1949) *Homo Ludens: A Study of the Play-Element in Culture* (Angelico Press, Copyright 2016 ed.). Kettering: Routledge & Kegan Paul.

Jennings, S. (1995) *Theatre, Ritual, and Transformation: The Senoi Temiars*. London: Routledge.

Jennings, S. (1999) *Introduction to Developmental Playtherapy*. London: Jessica Kingsley Publishers.

Jennings, S. (2011) *Healthy Attachments and Neuro-Dramatic-Play*. London: Jessica Kingsley Publishers.

Jennings, S. (2023) *Managing Social Anxiety in Children and Young People*. Abingdon, Oxon: Routledge.

Kotsko, A. (2010) *Awkwardness: An Essay*. Ropley: O Books.

Lyotard, J.-F. O. (1988) *The Differend: Phrases in Dispute*. Manchester: Manchester University Press.

Okagbue, O. (2007) *African Theatres and Performances. Theatres of the World*. Oxon: Routledge.

Sutton-Smith, B. (1997) *The Ambiguity of Play* (2nd ed., 2001 ed.). Harvard University Press.

Sutton-Smith, B. (2009) *The Ambiguity of Play*. Harvard University Press.

Thompson, J. (2003) *Applied Theatre – Bewilderment and Beyond* (2nd ed., 2012 ed.). Oxford: Peter Lang Ltd.

Thompson, J. (2009) *Performance Affects Applied Theatre and the End of Effect* (Paperback edition published in 2011 ed.). Palgrave Macmillan.

Williams, J. (2005) *Understanding Poststructuralism*. Chesham: Acumen.

Yeager, D. S., Dahl, R. E. and Dweck, C. S. (2018) Why interventions to influence adolescent behavior often fail but could succeed. *Perspectives on Psychological Science*, 13(1), 101–122.

NDP and diverse populations

Chapter 15

Taking care of pregnant womens' mental health through NDP, a model

Ulises Moreno-Serena

Pregnancy, as important as it is for the continuing of the human race, has been overlooked and left solely to the responsibility of those bodies who carry the life-giving process. Modern societies have moved far from those traditions in which pregnant women were to be holistically sheltered, privileging physiological care (Jennings, 2011).

Taking care of the biological dimension has given positive results. However, the need to attend to psychological well-being during and after pregnancy has surfaced. Globally, the estimated burden of disease of perinatal depression ranges from 10–20% (Van Niel and Payne, 2020), constituting a public health concern. Through the following chapter, the reader will find the practice-based evidence from which this NDP intervention outline emerges.

It is possible to argue that, drawn from the natural origin of conception, individuals and society have overlooked the necessity of taking care of the mental health of bodies in gravidness. Even though pregnancy carries positive reactions among the diverse cultures, their efforts are focused on taking care of the future newborn and the wellness of the bearing body to fulfill this task (Maldonado-Durán, 2011).

A pregnant woman's mental health

Bodies in pregnancy go through several biological changes that impact on a psychosocial level. As the pregnant woman deals with the changing of their body, identity and society's treatment, they would also have to answer and negotiate those concepts of what motherhood must be. An idealized role that has been rehearsed from early childhood informs us of what pregnancy and motherhood is all about or is supposed to be (Maldonado-Durán, 2011).

Gestation entails changes in body rhythms and patterns of movement, habits and conduct, which will continue to develop in a new lifestyle as the dyad evolves from the birthing stage and into the primary caregiver for the newborn (Nillni et al., 2018). Elaborating from Low (2020), it can be sustained that changes in rhythm are a challenge for the individual as in the

DOI: 10.4324/9781003498209-20

adapting process, arrhythmia might be faced. They will need some time to cope and for a new rhythm to emerge and establish.

Images of the expecting womans' body are often related to a moment of pure joy, relaxation, filled with love, a blessing; they relate little, if none, to mood swings, sleep pattern changes, lower-back pain or the uncertainty of being capable of enduring the whole of the giving birth process. Pregnancy, from a biological and physical perspective, entails more stressors than what collective images tell us about (Jennings, 2011).

Pregnant women are crossed with impressive challenges, frequently not considered from the perspective of the bearing subject. From those that have to do with deciding how to accommodate nurturing alongside professional life, economic situations, personal and the baby's health, stressors related to the partner and those derived from familial and societal relations (Nillni et al., 2018).

Adding up to the previously mentioned stressors, that might be considered normal, there are well-identified risk factors which augment the possibility of compromising a pregnant womans' mental health, which might lead to perinatal depression. Drawing from Lara et al. (2017), Van Niel and Payne (2020) and Maldonado-Durán (2011), Table 15.1: "Experienced Stressors by pregnant women," of the authors' own elaboration, displays the mentioned experienced stressors:

Table 15.1 Experienced stressors by pregnant women (own elaboration)

Individual psychological sphere	Societal sphere
High risk pregnancy	Facing barriers to obtaining medical care
Personal or baby's health issues	Lack of support during pregnancy and after birth
Difficulties in coping with body changes and discomfort	Facing economic distress
Previous mental health conditions (personal or from family of origin)	Facing trouble within the couple or with the partner
Substance abuse	Suffering violence in any of its forms
Unwanted pregnancy	Rape victim
Fears (irrational or real)	Pressure to adopt a preestablished motherhood role
Uncertainty	Having to make sacrifices for the welfare of the baby
Difficulties in coping with changes in lifestyle resulting from changes in rhythm	Having to conciliate between motherhood and professional life
Overattachment or under-attachment	Teenage pregnancy
Difficulties in allowing the motherhood role to emerge	

DSM-5 (Asociación Americana de Psiquiatría, 2013) criteria for diagnosing peripartum depression advises to observe the depressive symptoms' appearance within pregnancy and not over four weeks after delivery to be considered as such. Pregnancy can be read as a special moment of vulnerability for a pregnant womans' mental health, which impacts far beyond the scope of time suggested by diagnosing criteria, as Dagher et al. (2021) affirms, experienced stressors during the first year after giving birth are related to the appearance or recurrent manifestation of depressive episodes.

Perinatal depression consists of depressive symptoms related to pregnancy, motherhood and the challenges of coping with changes in lifestyle resulting from the novel experience. Its symptoms include those at present in depression and feelings and behaviors related to the baby, its needs and its existence expressed as an over-attachment (an excessive preoccupation about its wellbeing) or a total lack of interest (the desire for its death or them both dying), resentment or anger acted out towards the baby or constant irritability sustained over a 14-day period (Van Niel and Payne, 2020).

Described symptoms are worrying as they not only jeopardize the birth giver's mental health but also put at risk the development of a healthy and sound relationship with the baby to the extent of risking the life of them both. A depressed caregiver cannot give proper attention to the newborn's emotional needs, compromising early childhood development and thus affecting newborns' mental health (Van Niel and Payne, 2020).

Evidence-based practice has shown that the most effective treatments for perinatal depression are Cognitive Behavioral Therapy (CBT) and Interpersonal Psychotherapy (IPT) as shown by the systematic review conducted by Nillni et al. (2018). Their effectiveness can be attributed to behavioral activation and cognitive restructuring (CBT), interpersonal relationships and social support (IPT).

While A CBT approach deals with perinatal depression by not allowing the client to withdraw into the avoidance behavior and rumination that strengthens depressive maladaptive behavior and works with those beliefs and automatic thoughts that support the depressive state (Diego et al., 2020), IPT centers its actions into aiding the client to attain a support network taking into consideration the relationship style of the client, changes in role and societal interaction and the developing of assertiveness (Maldonado-Durán, 2011).

Why NDP?

The Neuro-Dramatic-Play paradigm centers its attention and benefits on the mother–child dyad, as it considers it to be the foundational milestone for the healthy development of the newborn. NDP has been demonstrated to be effective in building positive and nurturing relationships where security and confidence can thrive and aiding persons in repairing and expanding their welfare (Jennings, 2011).

Aimed first for pregnant womens' and children, its applicability has come to expand to address a wide range of ages as it can aid those populations in restoring basic experiences needed for positive mental health. As her creator, Sue Jennings posits, "it is 'value free': it does not rely on a particular school of psychological theory; indeed, it can be integrated into any psychological model or therapeutic or educational practice" (Jennings, 2011, p. 17), as her latest work, "Managing Social Anxiety in Children and Young People" (Jennings, 2022), shows.

Pairing the NDP paradigm with the CBT approach to dealing with social anxiety has many positive aspects both for the therapeutical process and for the client. First, the creative and playful approach entailed in NDP makes therapy enjoyable and less stigmatizing, which leads to therapeutic adherence. Second, involving creativity helps clients find new and unexpected answers, aiding them in the process of developing and incorporating new behaviors.

Jennings (2011) stresses the need for the pregnant woman to keep in a relaxed and stress-free environment as their main objective is that of building an emotional relationship with the unborn; in other words, she advises pregnant women to enjoy pregnancy. This proposal takes a step further in affirming that more attention needs to be paid to the person and that the emergence of motherhood needs to be placed to protect their mental health and the NDP paradigm can aid in doing so.

The proposed intervention aims to support the client in using their inner resources, develop and channel them to feel secure, have the capability to adapt to changes and the capacity to give an appropriate response to present challenges. This is proposed as, for example, sensory play promotes relaxation, a quality needed to differentiate oneself from the context, which allows one to establish and distinguish boundaries between what one can control and what not. Messy play promotes tolerance towards uncertainty. Rhythmic play is an important tool in understanding the inner body rhythm and external rhythm and how they affect us. Dramatic play is useful in aiding the client in allowing the emergence of new roles.

The approach promoted by NDP constitutes a behavioral activation as it offers the client pleasurable activities with the possibility of rediscovering play and playfulness. Cognitive restructuring will be addressed through exploration within the proposed dynamics as well as with stories, another important resource to the NDP paradigm. IPT therapeutical objectives (conforming a support network, client's relationship style, changes in role, assertiveness and societal interaction) will be incorporated within the specially designed activities of EPR (Embodiment Projection Role) and ToR (Theatre of Resilience).

Expected outcomes

Through this proposal, pregnant women will:

- Find a secure space where they can reflect upon their identity and the changes that they are experiencing, reconcile with their body and relate in a respectful way with the unborn child while deciding how to approach motherhood.
- Develop tolerance towards uncertainty while fostering a perspective of positive outcomes, learning to rely on their own resources and finding support either with institutions or with their support network.
- Learn to listen to their inner rhythms while having the opportunity to adjust to the emerging rhythm demanded by a new lifestyle.
- Reflect towards their introjections of motherhood, setting functional boundaries according to their reality and life goals having in mind the concept of "good enough attachments" (Jennings, 2011, p. 35), allowing the role of motherhood to emerge.

The intervention proposal

The intervention outlined consists of a 10-session plan; however, this is not to be taken rigidly as it is more important that the client achieves the therapeutical objective rather than advancing through each step. Some clients might need to spend more than one session on some of the proposed steps.

Sessions can be grouped within each of the frameworks pertaining to the NDP paradigm:

1. Neuro-Dramatic-Play: Sensory and Messy Play in sessions 1 and 2.
2. Embodiment-Projection-Role: Involving the work with Rhythmic play, working with embodiment and projection and then into role in sessions 3 through 6.
3. Theatre of Resilience: The main tool in sessions 7 through 9.
4. Finally, in the tenth session, a ritual-like experience is developed as a closure of the experience, traveling through what has been achieved and synthesizing it into an artwork form.

It is advisable not to skip any of the steps, as they can help the client work on their own attachment issues, which are core to establishing a secure relationship with the unborn. In this sense, it is preferable that the client engages in the proposed step in a light manner or to review more than one step in the session.

First session: "Oasis."

Assess whether the following is suitable for your client. If there seems to be acceptance towards pregnancy and the unborn, it would be advisable to proceed with the activity of applying cream onto the belly; if not, it would be preferable to distance further and employ water and jelly in a separate container.

Materials: Have water, vegetal coloring, jelly with different consistencies, some scents and different bowls or have body cream, vegetal coloring, several cups, toothpicks and scents. Always have enough moist tissue at hand!

If the activity is led towards applying colored body cream in the body make sure you have prepared a private place for your client and have proper consent, as the activity must not, in any way, result in stress or discomfort; it should promote the experience of a secure, safe and intimate moment for the client with themselves.

Present materials to your clients, allow them to examine them through their senses, have them try to mix them as they prefer and reserve those that are more pleasurable in separate bowls. During the activity, you can prompt your client to share feelings, thoughts or memories that come to mind. Facilitate the emergence of play and playfulness through exploration.

Alternative 1. Working with water and diluted jelly

Once the warm-up activity has evolved into a natural ending, proceed to the following: prompt your client to pick a desired bowl of water and to think of it as an oasis, a place for setting oneself apart from all and everything and where to feel secure and in no need to answer to demands of others. Invite them to submerge their hands and delve into the sensation of peace and relaxation until they can feel as if they are the oasis themselves. Invite your client to change the bowl to one of very light or diluted jelly (unadvised if a phobic trigger), ask them to feel the consistency and the feelings that might arise and prompt them to imagine how it must feel to be floating in this light jelly. How much support must one feel being covered and at rest? Let your client enjoy this for a moment, prompting them to channel this sensation to the whole of their body. Reaffirm to your client any emotion that might need to surface or be expressed. After the moment has passed, invite your client to recognize themselves; begin with thoughts and memories, then skin, breathing, sensations, feelings and emotions and ask them to feel the difference between them and the light jelly.

Alternative 2. Working with body cream

Let your client explore the material, little by little, applying small amounts in hands and forearms. Prompt them to feel the difference in temperature and the silky-like feeling. By expanding it and caressing themselves, their sensations are awakened; ask them to define them and, if comfortable and pleasurable, invite them to carry them all throughout their body. Ask them, once they have distributed the whole cream through their hands and forearms, how does the sensation of being covered feel? Once again, invite them to channel that sensation through the whole of their body, invite them to imagine how it would feel if they were covered in this silky sensation and invite them to imagine being carried away into an oasis where they could indulge and delve into this feeling of relaxation, calm and carefreeness. Invite them to allow themselves to imagine as if they were an oasis. Advise your clients to allow themselves to express any emotion that might need to surface. Then, invite your client to go to a private space and prepare and negotiate in advance, carrying the prepared mixes of colored body cream. Invite them to gently body paint on their belly the image of that oasis, narrating to the unborn what they are painting and how it looks and invite them to imagine how the unborn might experience this listening from the oasis. As the activity resumes, invite your client to recognize themselves; begin with thoughts and memories, then skin, breathing, sensations, feelings, emotions, the womb and the baby and ask them to feel the difference between being the oasis, the baby and themselves.

As your client cleans themselves, offer the following story:

> Once, there was a drop of water, so afraid of falling to the ground. "I will not be the same," she thought, "I will be lost, perhaps for good, and never to be back again." When the moment of rain came, she struggled hard not to be one of the drops falling from the cloud, yet the moment arrived. She fought and tried to grab herself onto anything that might prevent her from falling into the soil. Irremediably, the moment arrived and as she touched the ground and felt how she integrated with the earth, she discovered a moment of peace and relaxation and as she expanded, she could feel others than herself. A new sensation of, while knowing who she was, being something more and new.

Reflect with your client

How was the experience?

- How was allowing yourself to be the oasis? (if an emotion was allowed to surface) How was it for you to allow the emotions to flow while having this containment?
- Did you manage to stop thinking, even for a moment, how was that for you? How would this be of help during this stage of your life? Do you imagine how you can expand this ability throughout your life?
- For the body paint activity, how was it for you to establish contact from the oasis with your baby?

Regarding the story, do you find it useful for your actual stage?

The facilitator must pay attention to the client's verbalizations, addressing appropriately any automatic or intrusive thought as well as any opportunity to assess the improvement of intra and interpersonal functioning by bettering the relationship of the client with themselves or others, be cautious about it, at this point, referring to the relationship with the baby.

Second session: "Colors of life."

Materials: Be aware in advance of the preferred coloring materials for your client and have them prepared; they can be finger paints, crayons, chalk or whichever coloring materials your client is comfortable with and a large piece of paper. Have the coloring materials at hand, but scattered.

Invite your client to take a comfortable position with the paper and coloring material in front of them. Invite them to take a few deep breaths while noticing the materials, then instruct them to draw in whichever way is meaningful to them; emotions may be present in their life, whether they are pleasant or disturbing. When you have finished, ask them to circle with a specific and different color those related to people, changes, challenges, pregnancy or the baby.

Invite your client to explain it. This is an opportunity to apply cognitive restructuring, address interpersonal problem areas and improve communication skills. When finished, ask your client to observe the painting again and ask if something needs to be changed in any way; if so, ask your client to make those changes. Ask your client to think about whether those feelings expressing discomfort can be improved. This is an opportunity to work on exploring options and decision analyzing and making.

For the closing of the session, tell the following story:

The King who hated green

It was spring and while for many people it was a time of enjoyment, the people of Warasu were faced with an enormous task. No one knew why, but the King hated green. He couldn't stand seeing it and, because of that, he had ordered that all the green of the kingdom must be eliminated. And, because of that, the subjects of Warasu had to color or paint everything that was green. It was funny to see blue, white, yellow or red grass; despite making their kingdom a very colorful place, one couldn't avoid missing the green hills or eating a green salad that had not been modified. The situation was coming to a breaking point when one of the chancellors had an idea. He told the King he was at imminent risk since green was more present than what he was led to believe; as it is considered a primary color, it was present in many other colors. The only way to protect the King was by using a pair of lenses which would show everything in gray. In panic, the King agreed to wear the protective glasses. At first, he felt alleviated as his life would not be jeopardized, but soon, he found himself trying to watch over the lenses to see some of the colors surrounding him. Gray was not enough! The King called the chancellor and asked for the lenses to be removed. "But, your majesty, if the lenses are removed, you are at risk of having to tolerate some or all of the green present in other colors," said the chancellor. The King said, "I know; however, I have discovered that I value being able to see those other colors more. If having to learn how to tolerate green is the price I have to pay for not having to see life in gray color, so be it; I will learn to tolerate it."

Third session: "Living as a symphony."

Materials: Prepare in advance music with several rhythms; it must fluctuate from adagio type of rhythms to a chaotic rhythm. You can ask your client for help with making the playlist. You will also need A1, A2 or A4 size white paper, markers and a drum or percussion instrument.

Invite your client to listen carefully to the music while drawing lines with the markers to represent the rhythm of the music played. Have them change colors for each piece listened to; they can even number or name them for clear identification. After all songs have been heard, ask your client to choose, from the represented rhythms in the sheet, those present in their lifestyle before getting pregnant and play them with a drum. Suggest they play the drum having in mind different moments of their lifestyle, exploring several contexts in which their rhythm might change. What was it like before pregnancy? Now, invite your client to play what their natural rhythm might be while not being pregnant and draw the rhythmic line into the chart. Repeat this exploration now whilst pregnant and draw the rhythmic line of the natural rhythm while in pregnancy.

Reflect with your client on the differences – how are they coping with these changes? Are there things they are longing for? Rhythms they are having trouble adapting to? Can they identify rhythms that might be too demanding or that they are pushing too hard to apply? Perhaps there are other things that might be stressful? This is the right time to elaborate strategies for coping, identify people to bring into the support network and challenge preconceived ideas of what a person ought to do.

For the last part, invite your client to elaborate on what their personal rhythm *might* be once they give birth and on into early motherhood. Support them in considering several contexts that might make the rhythm change, for example, the baby crying all night, sickness or returning to work.

Next, invite your client to choose a rhythmical pattern that might be soothing and relaxing for them and assist them in recognizing that a self-care practice would acknowledge when some changes might be needed in the rhythm; this can be achieved through the body by breathing, dancing, drawing or some creative approach of their choosing.

Finally, have your client reflect on their transition from their natural rhythm before pregnancy, the emerging rhythm now and what their future changes may entail. What are they missing? What is new and pleasant?

Are there any expectations to return to their personal rhythm before pregnancy? To what extent would that be possible? Would they resent if old rhythms cannot be reestablished? Elaborate with your client with negotiating role transition.

Fourth session: "Nesting."

Materials: According to your training and your client's preferences, you can have props, art materials, sand tray or some other way to make a visual representation.

Have your client select a space in the room where they feel most comfortable and secure. Invite them to relax and close their eyes; you can aid them by employing some progressive relaxation, mindfulness or WOSI (Weight, Outline, Skin, Inside) techniques. Once finished, invite your client to visualize themselves walking calmly on a path. Their steps guide them to a place that feels secure and calm. Invite them to enter and take in the sensations as they allow themselves to put everything in the space they might need to make it secure, a nest-like space. Have your client acknowledge their feelings and thoughts while being in this special space. Allow the fantasy to last for a few minutes, when it is time to move on, prompt your client that it is time to leave, bearing in mind they can always return to it. Perhaps your client would like to thank the space. Guide your client to exit the space, back through the path and, while walking, notice the temperature of the room, the sounds of the room, feeling their feet, the floor and opening their eyes when ready.

Elaborate with your client about the experience and benefits of it, how being in a safe place, a nest-like space, changes our feelings and thoughts and our general attitude and disposition and, from that, the way we perceive things. Invite your client to discuss their preferred expression of their nest and have them replicate it with as much detail as possible. Have them acknowledge how having a tangible representation of it calls upon the experienced state.

Next, ask your client how it would be to have their maternity process in a nest for a while. What would it look like? Would it take some things from the previous one? What would be needed for it to be purposeful for the maternity process and the pregnant woman? Have them discuss it in detail. When finished, reflect with your client on the things present in the nest. What are those things that promote their wellbeing? Do those things find correspondence with people, places or organizations in real life? Write those identified resources on a card, as they could be integrated into the support network.

Repeat the process, now elaborating a nest for the future baby. Beware of impulses of self-demanding, self-criticism, perfectionism or any form of over-demanding behavior which would result in a stressful relationship with the baby and feelings of failure in the motherhood role.

Reflect with your client: What does this activity let them know about their approach to the baby? How do they perceive the baby, the baby's needs, their relationship with it and their role as primary caregivers? How do they evaluate being a successful or inefficient caregiver and how does this affect them? Ask if there is some other part of themselves or role that might benefit from this exercise; if so, invite them to repeat the steps whether during the session, if time allows or in their own time.

Fifth session: "Motherhood, a landscape."

Materials: Prepare in advance an A3 or A4 white sheet of paper placed horizontally for a layout of a drawing shown in Figure 15.1.

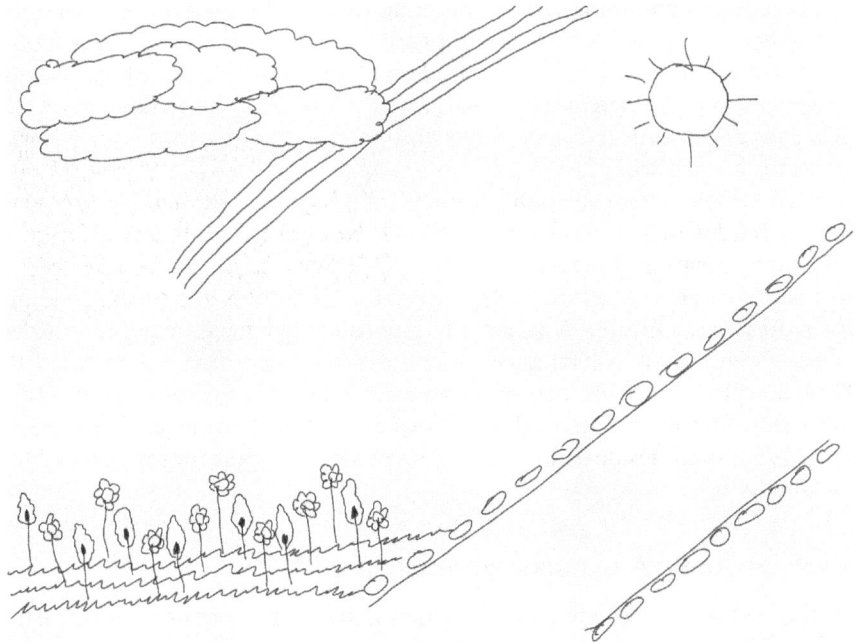

Figure 15.1 Landscape map of the author's own elaboration for you to get inspired!

Invite your client to put on the image with a marker or pen or, for better visibility, place a post-it over the clouds with those things or situations that during the pregnancy process are or have been stormy clouds. Allow your client to elaborate on them and intervene through cognitive restructuring when appropriate.

Have your client think about which of those challenges have resulted in new discoveries, the emergence of new qualities, relying on new talents or new alliances. Have them place them as rain falls from the clouds.

Direct your client's attention to the garden and the flowers. What of their lived experience during pregnancy could be represented as such and how have they nurtured from the rain and the challenges still present in their lives? How does this make them feel?

Not everything is gloomy, as even when we can't see it, brightness is always present. What are those things present or things to come that could be represented as the sun? Have your client elaborate on this aspect and reflect upon them.

Rainbows can represent many things; for us, now, it will be a way to acknowledge the many emotions experienced and to come during this process. Which have been new or experienced in a different way? What meaning did we give them then and what meaning can we give them now? How does this ability to reflect and transform the meaning we give to emotions make us feel?

Have your client see the whole picture and the things that have been expressed and placed into the layout. How have they been transformed and how might they be potentially transformed? How does this make them feel? What thoughts come to mind? What meaning do they give to this and themselves in this process?

Expectations, dreams, confidence and hopes give us strength to follow a path, a road. Considering the previous elaboration, has your client reflected on their motivations to travel the road? What does the actual road represent for them? What are the things they expect for themselves and the baby along the road and the future? What are the tools do they have to travel this road?

Close the session by having your client express what their general mood is. How do they feel about themselves and the pregnancy process? How is this exercise useful for them? And how does this translate to a real-life dimension? What qualities does this exercise show us are important for our wellbeing and living?

Sixth session: "A mandala of motherhood."

Materials: Have an A4 white sheet of paper, markers, crayons or coloring materials preferred by your client. Lay out four concentric circles on the paper; the space between them is divided by lines, first section 4, next 8 and last 16. Have the following Figure 15.2: Mandala layout of own elaboration as reference:

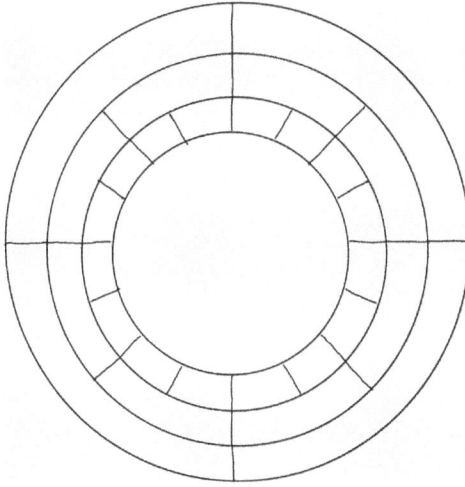

Figure 15.2 Mandala layout (own elaboration)

Invite your client to think about the closest references of motherhood they might have, if appropriate, their mother, their mother's mother, the mothers of their cousins or close relatives, friends or even from fictional sources. Have them notice the difference between their role as a mother to their child and other roles as aunt or grandmother. If needed, have another sheet of paper where they can list the different qualities that can be noticed between them. Have them appreciate how there are several ways of exercising motherhood.

Place the mandala layout in front of your client and invite them to represent the several qualities discovered through coloring, beginning from the outside part to the inside. The outer part would be used to represent big categories of motherhood, such as bad mother, caring mother, discipline mother and so on. As we advance to the inner circle, we would be representing the qualities we would like to exercise during motherhood, those needed and those I haven't experienced personally but want to incorporate. Place any other you or your client might think useful. At the center of the mandala, draw color spots of each quality selected as desirable and some of those that are disliked or considered useless.

Once finished, reflect with your client. Why was it important to place some representation of the disliked qualities at the center? How was it for you to think about the several models of motherhood you have had during your life? Tell me about your dislikes – what have you discovered? Some qualities of motherhood are, at essence, good but sometimes expressed in a bad manner. Can you tell me if you discovered some under that assumption? What do you think, and what does it feel like having the possibility to reflect upon these models of motherhood and selecting those you want to portray in your own motherhood style? How would this be achieved?

Have your client take the mandala or a digitalized image of it with them.

Seventh session: "Playing the baby."

Materials: Have several stuffed toys or puppets which will stand in as babies. A white sheet of paper and pen or pencil.

Invite your client to identify and list how a newborn (0–180 days) can communicate; aid them in the process. Once finished, have your client empathize with the situation of the newborn – what would it be like to be inhabiting the child's body? Not understanding what you hear and not being able to say what you need? Is there a feeling of discomfort? Have your client imagine that and discuss their findings.

Invite your client to choose as many stuffed toys or puppets to represent several states of the baby: aching, hungry, playful, joyful, in discomfort, soiled, sleepy, not sleepy, angry or as many others that your client can identify. Having the previously made list as a guide, invite your client to consider how the baby might express each state.

Once each baby has been labeled with a state and their expressive means defined, you can play them or invite your client to play them first and exchange roles, whichever is more appropriate. Reflect with your client on the experience and the feelings they might have. Does the exercise aid them in feeling more capable of understanding the baby's communication?

For the last part of the session, you and your client will play the caregiver-baby dyad. Invite your client to play the caregiver role while you take on the baby role. Whenever your client states that they do not know how to respond or you observe they are having difficulties responding efficiently, invite your client to reverse roles and model the appropriate behavior; once modeled, have your client play it back. When all or most important states have been played (depending on time available), have your client reflect on their displayed behavior when they were responding to the baby's demands effectively and missed when they were ineffective. Does their performance improve when they observe the modeled behavior? Can they identify states that are easier to handle or more difficult for them? Would there be a key behavior to tackle communication with the baby to provide care better? Celebrate findings with your client.

Eighth session: "Rehearsing the good enough attachments."

Materials: Have several props and art materials (paints and sheets of paper). They will be used to symbolize qualities. In advance, find a deck of cards that might prompt baby demands or reactions and situations.

Have your client remember the sixth session, "A mandala of motherhood," where they reflected upon desirable motherhood traits they would like to exercise and guide their behavior. Ask them to share their feelings and thoughts about that today. Introduce them to the concept of the good enough attachment figure as an affection that is warmth, has a regular, almost predictable manner, which one can depend upon, someone who is emotionally available and tunes in finely to the needs of the baby. Who offers a bond of mutual awareness, emotional resonance, playfulness and turn-taking. Providing nurture and has a primary maternal preoccupation that promotes trust and is predictable (Jennings, 2011, p. 35).

Discuss with your client what they think of these qualities and why they are qualities of a good enough attachment. Ask them to appreciate the difference between their desirable motherhood traits and the basic good enough attachments. Invite your client to represent through the available props or with painting good enough attachment qualities; go further and ask your client to name some behaviors which are congruent with each quality.

Once the good enough attachment has been mapped out, invite your client to play the role of the good enough attachment figure while they react to the stimuli prompted by the cards. At the same time the game is developed, aid your client in recalling the good enough attachment qualities. When they have finished exploring the cards, reflect with your client about the implications of the good enough attachment. How is the good enough attachment concept useful for them and when are the desirable traits of motherhood applicable? Do they conflict with each other? How important was it for them to notice when they were giving more than what was a good enough attachment? Think about motherhood as a long run rather than as a short race. Desirable traits of motherhood are an aspirational guide rather than a recipe.

The importance of this session is to model the concept of the good enough attachment through the body and the deployment of behaviors. This allows the client to experience what they should give, not more nor less, and sets them apart from the idealization of motherhood and feelings of guilt from trying to be perfect. It makes motherhood achievable and bearable rather than something that feels like it requires a great extent of sacrifice and effort.

Ninth session: "Rehearsing reality."

Materials: Prepare a deck of situation cards considering personal expectations, needs, baby's needs, returning to school or work and professional or personal goals. Leave some cards blank for your client to fill them out. Have some props at hand or fabric from different colors to aid your client in enacting different roles.

Invite your client to recall their work on rhythm, desirable traits of motherhood and the good enough attachment. How do they feel about this work? What is their current sensation towards their motherhood role? What is their current sensation towards the baby? How are they feeling about their future incorporating this role and relationship in their lives? Are they confident about their future and the challenges they might face?

Frame the session as a rehearsal. Explain to your client there are several kinds of rehearsals for discoveries, to learn new ways to act and react, to affirm those ways of acting and reacting, to deepen their performance and incorporating missing details. As such, there is no failure in rehearsals but learning.

Share with your client that the objective of the session is to rehearse how to use the rhythm to preserve a good enough attachment and decide whether it is pertinent to keep on pursuing the desirable traits of motherhood while also responding to reality. If appropriate, negotiate with your client some visual or verbal cues to support them and agree with them on the blank cards.

Instruct your client to choose props that can enact their diversity of roles that might coincide with that of motherhood and all the other roles that go with being a parent. The game consists of your client choosing and taking on a role while they are enacting and reporting what they would be doing, having to respond and switch or take on diverse roles to answer to the demands of real life, which stem from the situation cards. For example, if your client is playing the partnering role, describe an afternoon meal, being joyful and relaxed. Then, the card of having to bathe the baby pops up. They can remain in the partner role and negotiate with their partner to take on that task. Think with them about their process, reminding them to pay attention to the rhythm, their preservation of the good enough attachment and choosing their desirable mother traits.

After several scenarios have been rehearsed, reflect with your client. How does this exercise aid in weaving the work they have been doing up to now? What are their discoveries? It is helpful for decision-making to have the objective of exercising a good enough attachment in mind and assess that through acknowledging the rhythms they are in. What is the toll of assuming several roles? When is it helpful or necessary, and when is it not? Invite your client to congratulate themselves for those things they achieved and identify those things that need to be developed. Agree on a way to practice them in their everyday life.

Tenth session: "Motherhood, a journey."

Materials: A variety of art materials.

The purpose of this session is to reflect on the whole process. If your client is more comfortable with symbolic communication, they might prefer to begin working with art materials or through talking if they prefer.

1. You can employ an Embodiment–Projection–Role (EPR) approach by inviting them to represent with paintings the situations, emotions and discoveries they've experienced in the discovering of their motherhood style, things they must remember and keep on developing.

2. Employing the six-part story-making method (Lahad in Jennings, 1992). Invite your client to storyboard first the character they were and their context at the beginning of the process; second, what was their objective; third, the obstacles they were facing; fourth, discoveries and helpful factors; fifth, what changed, the impact in their lives and the discovering of their motherhood style; and sixth, the present situation with themselves, the baby and their expectations for the future.

3. Put a timeline on the floor or on a sheet of paper, marked by evolutions or significant milestones. First, invite your client to reflect upon the process and indicate through labeling on the floor or chart. Ask if all the important moments are there. If you think there might be some missing, ask your client permission to add them. After this has been completed, invite your client to point out things in the chart or position themselves on the line, stepping onto each milestone. Allow them to express in a sculpture or movement the feelings, thoughts or context they experienced at that point, then verbalise how they feel now about it; repeat this for each milestone marked.

4. Another useful way is the Narradrama practices of remembering and active role interviewing (Dunne et al., 2021). Invite your client to represent, through fabric or paper in the play space, those figures of motherhood (living or not) who would recognize and appreciate their discovered motherhood style and place them in a circle; then invite your client to consider placing their motherhood style at its center.

Next, have your client enact how their motherhood style would present to the circle of wise mothers by telling them what has been overcome or discovered. How might the motherhood role emerge and what are their aspirations and compromises they make towards themselves and their baby?

After your client has finished affirming the motherhood role, invite them to take on any of the wise mother roles and allow each one to tell what they appreciate from their journey of the motherhood role at the center. What traits or qualities do they admire or welcome, words of love and hope or best wishes? Finalize with a guided fantasy of the wise motherhood welcoming and incorporating the motherhood role into the circle.

Whichever way you have worked with your client, close the session with an art and craft, dreamcatcher, rock painting, painting or collage. Invite them to reflect upon the exercise and find a way to resume it and capture its best. I wish them a merry journey!

Closing comments

The intervention model you have read interweaves CBT and IPT work and delivers them through the NDP paradigm, which, in doing so, opens space to creativity, imagination and play. Incorporating these qualities into the process is helpful as it makes it less threatening to approach the motherhood role and negotiate its emergence. At the same time, it allows the client to establish contact with those basic qualities needed to promote a good enough attachment.

Although CBT and IPT maneuvers are emphasized during the first sessions, it doesn't mean they shouldn't be used later during the process if needed. It is recommended that the mental health specialist pay close attention, especially during those first sessions, as the rest of the sessions build and practice the motherhood role.

Therapists do not push the client into assuming or accepting motherhood. This is a work of discovery and through it, we allow the emergence of the motherhood role while negotiating with the other aspects and roles present in the client's life. As such, this model is not advised for pregnant woman who are unwilling to exercise motherhood or are looking to terminate their pregnancy. In such cases, several adjustments must be made to be beneficial. Nonetheless, it is worth embarking on such a task as it would allow the baby to have a good enough beginning and for the pregnant woman to have a less traumatizing process.

Although it is advisable to implement this intervention at the early stages of pregnancy (best after the first trimester), as it may aid the client and prevent perinatal depression, a postpartum person can also receive treatment through this model as it would still be addressing the risk factors responsible for depression, aiding them in negotiating role transition and working with beliefs and automatic thoughts.

Finally, sex and gender of the therapist must be considered, as well as the gender identification of the client. Therapists must check with the client if they are feeling comfortable during the process. Sex and gender bias must be observed, noting motherhood or a particular style.

References

Asociación Americana de Psiquiatría. (2013) *Guía de Consulta de los Criterios Diagnósticos del DSM-5*. Arlington, VA: Asociación Americana de Psiquiatría.

Dagher, R. K., Bruckheim, H. E., Colpe, L. J., Edwards, E. and White, D. B. (2021) Perinatal depression: Challenges and opportunities. *Journal of Women's Health*, 30(2), 154–159. https://doi.org/10.1089/jwh.2020.8862

Diego, J. de, Soler, J. and Domínguez-Clavé, E. (2020) Abordaje del paciente con depresión mayor. In *Depresión y Suicidio 2020. Documento estratégico para la promoción de la Salud Mental*, eds. Navío, M. and Pérez, V. Madrid, España: Wecare-u. Healthcare Communication Group.

Dunne, P., Afary, K. and Paulson, P. (2021) Narradrama. In *Current Approaches in Drama Therapy*, eds. Johnson, D. and Emunah, R. (3rd ed.). Springfield, IL: Charles C. Thomas Publisher Ltd.

Jennings, S. (2011) *Healthy Attachments and Neuro-Dramatic-Play*. London: Jessica Kingsley Publishers.

Jennings, S. (2022) *Managing Social Anxiety in Children and Young People*. London: Routledge. https://doi.org/10.4324/9781032256641

Lahad, M. (1992) Story making in assessment methods for coping with stress, six-piece story making and basic Ph. In *Dramatherapy and Theory in Practice 2*, ed. Jennings, S. London: Routledge.

Lara, M. A., Patiño, P., Navarrete, L. and Nieto, L. (2017) Depresión posparto, un problema de salud pública que requiere de mayor atención en México. *Género y Salud en Cifras*, 15(2), 12–25.

Low, K. (2020) *Applied Theatre and Sexual Health Communication. Apertures of Possibility*. Londres: Palgrave Macmillan.

Maldonado-Durán, J. (2011) *Salud Mental Perinatal*. Washington: Organización Panamericana de la Salud.

Nillni, Y. I., Mehralizade, A., Mayer, L. and Milanovic, S. (2018) Treatment of depression, anxiety, and trauma-related disorders during the perinatal period: A systematic review. *Clinical Psychology Review*, 66, 136–148. https://doi.org/10.1016/j.cpr.2018.06.004

Van Niel, M. S. and Payne, J. L. (2020) Perinatal depression: A review. *Cleveland Clinic Journal of Medicine*, 87(5), 273–277. https://doi.org/10.3949/ccjm.87a.19054

Chapter 16

Emotions neuro-dramatic play in forensic settings

Rowan Mackenzie

Prison would not usually be a place associated with playing or with theatre, but Shakespeare UnBard facilitates theatre companies and creative workshops in several English prisons. This chapter explores the ways in which playing and the principles of neuro-dramatic play can be used as a tool for developing 'positive autonomy' (Mackenzie, 2023, p. 7), emotional resilience and self-identity for those in custodial environments. Many adults within the criminal justice system have had childhoods which have been significantly less than ideal and have not had the opportunities to develop positive bonds with their caregivers or others through the modality of play. This, in turn, can impact their development in other areas of life, including their social interaction with others and their decision-making. Whilst society and the media tend to vilify and other those who have committed crimes (Spivak, 1985), the reality is that almost all of the people incarcerated in the United Kingdom will be returned to the community in the future as whole-life sentences are rare. Albeit some hospital orders may continue throughout an individual's life unless it can be demonstrated that their mental health is sufficient that they no longer pose a threat to society. Yet, the amount of rehabilitative work which takes place in forensic settings is limited by resources, funding and staffing levels. Shakespeare UnBard aims to enable participants to develop skills, creativity and self-esteem by using drama and enacting characters.

I began working in prisons in 2017, starting with a one-off two-hour workshop on Othello as part of HMP Leicester's Talent Unlocked Festival (Mackenzie, 2023, pp. 34–39), which showcased a variety of artistic mediums as a way of encouraging new interests. From this, I truly saw the power of theatre within carceral settings and developed relationships with several other prisons to enable me to work with a wider population across the English prison system. Within that initial session, a group of men, many of whom did not know each other well (HMP Leicester is a remand prison with a high turnover of prisoners), coalesced from a collection of disparate individuals into a cohesive group. They discussed the themes of jealousy, betrayal, love and toxic friendships, which are encapsulated in Act 3, Scene 3, where Iago plants the seeds of doubt regarding Desdemona's fidelity. Many of these men

DOI: 10.4324/9781003498209-21

chose to share their own concerns about whether their partners would be faithful to them whilst they were in prison and the potential impact on their relationships should they receive lengthy custodial sentences. In an environment which is often known for its 'hypermasculinity' (Morey and Crewe, 2019, p. 38), such honesty about their fears was unexpected and I genuinely believe it would not have been voiced without the 'dramatic distancing' (Jennings, 1992, p. 17) provided by the text.

Since 2017, I have worked in eight English prisons, facilitating creative workshops and forming collaborative theatre companies and I continue to develop my creative practice within forensic settings. I currently work within the adult male estate as over 90% of those incarcerated in England and Wales are adult males and, therefore, most prisons hold this population (Ministry of Justice, 22 March 2024). Forensic institutions are dehumanising by their very nature and the removal of almost all decisions from those imprisoned erodes their sense of self (Warr, 2016, p. 593). The intention of my work in prisons is to reverse this process to some extent and to give those involved a sense of ownership and 'positive autonomy' (Mackenzie, 2023, p. 7). By enabling those involved to make decisions, suggest their own ideas and work collaboratively to take account of the suggestions of their peers, they are able to develop skills which will enable them to better navigate their time in custody, strengthen familial bonds (where possible) and equip them for their eventual return to the community. My work embodies the concept of theatre of resilience (ToR) (Jennings, 2011, pp. 233–238), with the men experiencing modelling of pro-social behaviours as we move through each of the three stages of ToR. All of my work is underpinned by the principles of trauma-informed pedagogical practices (SAMHSA, 2014), as a large percentage of those in forensic settings have both experienced and inflicted trauma (Bradley, 2022). Therefore, it is imperative to understand the way in which these experiences may influence an individual's behaviour and responses and to develop the work in a way which takes account of the need for safety, trust, collaboration, choice, empowerment and cultural consideration (SAMHSA, 2014).

Some organisations that work within prisons, such as Pimlico Opera who stage a biennial large-scale production where prisoners work alongside a professional cast, have a pre-defined methodology and process to which prisoners must adhere (Pimlico Opera website, n.d.). However, I work differently, encouraging the participants to choose which plays will be used to edit, adapt and develop their own elucidation of Shakespeare's works. I use Shakespeare as the basis for the work I do as the characters, stories and themes of the plays are relevant, multi-dimensional and allow for diverse interpretation. Although I describe my work in detail in Creating Space for Shakespeare (2023), a brief outline is prudent for this chapter as well.

The Creative Workshops are ideally a 12-week programme of a three-hour session each week (this can be adapted to fit with the prison requirements as working in carceral settings requires a great degree of flexibility, especially during this time of severe overcrowding). For the first ten weeks, we look at one play per week, acting out selected scenes and discussing the topics raised by the play and then the final two weeks are for the men to work on their own performative piece, which they share with the group in the final session. They can elect to work alone or in small groups, perform a scene verbatim or create their own version. Pieces have ranged from adaptations of Richard II's prison soliloquy to Shakespearean versions of an *8-Mile* rap battle (Hanson, 2002); from a lyricised version of the Seven Ages of Man speech to an emotional suicide note of a man developing dementia. I selected a play for the first session, but the group then agreed on the other nine plays to be included so that from the outset, they have autonomy in defining their own learning around Shakespeare. Through the course of the programme, we work through the three stages of ToR; interweaving storytelling, roles and communication skills. For each play, there is an activity pack which includes a synopsis of the play, the edited scenes and a number of creative activities for them to complete in a cell. One man, Tony,[1] found such delight in the activities and his newly discovered creative writing skills that he has gone on to write a full-length play combining Shakespeare and the Christmas truce of World War I (which was performed by our theatre company, Emergency Shakespeare, in December 2024).

The theatre companies are formed in prisons where the population is more static and there is the opportunity for the men to engage in at least six months of work with me. Many actors will remain for multiple productions, often only leaving due to transfer or release. Each theatre company has its own unique feel based on the men who are a part of it. Formed of up to 15 men and myself, we work collaboratively to edit, adapt, rehearse and perform productions. Every decision is made democratically, from the choice of play to casting, set design and music. The production cycle usually takes six to eight months (again, this needs to be relatively flexible as prison regimes can affect rehearsals) and culminates in a number of performances for prisoners and one for families/invited guests to attend. These performances for loved ones are particularly poignant (Mackenzie, 2023, pp. 102–107, 116) and can rebuild or strengthen the 'golden thread' of family support, which Lord Farmer (2017) identified as crucial to reform and desistance. It is through the process of creating the theatre company and rehearsing the production that the participants have the opportunity to develop their skills, work together and develop positive relationships, which often permeate far beyond the confines of the rehearsal room. The culmination in performances is also crucial as it gives the men the opportunity to be seen as actors rather than prisoners, a deeply heterotopic experience for both the cast and the audience. Working together to put on a performance also gives a focus to the work we undertake and changes the dynamics from what they would be in the context of simply exploring play texts.

In the context of this chapter, the elements of the process and the inherent playing and playfulness are the focus rather than the final performances. It is the process of exploring their own experiences through theatre and playing roles, which they then perform before others, which is important. Emergency Shakespeare is one of the collaborative theatre companies, founded in 2019 and now entering our sixth year of existence (a hiatus during Covid-19 impacted in-person sessions for circa 18 months). As we chose and then began to rehearse The Tempest in December 2021, a new member, Wyn, joined the group, bringing with him a wealth of musical experience. The choice of play is made through each actor suggesting their preference for a specific play along with a brief plot synopsis and the reasons they think it suitable for the ensemble before being put to a vote. One of the reasons for the selection of The Tempest was the inherent musicality of the play, which would be a new challenge for the company and one to which Wyn would be able to contribute with his prior expertise. We decided to create a soundscape to underpin the production and to emulate the magical sounds and underlying rhythm of the enchanted island.

Whilst rhythmic play is often seen to be predominantly for young children, we used this as the basis for creating the soundscape, encouraging everyone to become a part of our ensemble orchestra. The actors created rudimentary musical instruments using items they could appropriate – coffee tins to become drums, elastic bands of differing thicknesses and tautness stretched across an empty sweet jar and then plucked, a small plastic comb used to be pulled against a piece of wood, a small wooden box made of balsa wood to be used as percussion, a wind-chime effect created by stringing together hollowed out plastic biro casings with the ends removed and which could then be shaken. Within a prison, there are limited resources, but between discussing the idea and running the first soundscape session in early January, they demonstrated great creativity in finding and repurposing objects to create the instruments we were going to use, often asking others on the wings for suitable objects.

To open the session, we sat in a circle and spoke about how rhythm and music can often be a way of regulating emotions, slowing an individual's heartbeat, bringing back positive memories, etc. I briefly explained Kelly Hunter's concept of the Hunter Heartbeat method (2015) and we began by beating out 'hello' on our chests for a few moments as a collective. We spoke about the natural heartbeat of iambic pentameter and some of the actors spoke about how the rhythm of the lines helped them with line learning and in knowing how to speak to them. We then shared the instruments so that each of us had one in front of us and they were encouraged to play for a few moments without worrying about how the cacophony sounded, instead focusing on the feel of the instrument they had chosen, how they could use it to make sound and any sensory impact the object had. Obun spoke of the aroma from the empty coffee tin and how this linked to his love of drinking coffee, while Bert had a larger tin which had held nuts and was decorated with festive images. This made him think of the recent Christmas which had passed and how he had felt very low being separated from his partner for the first time in almost two decades.

After the men had explored their instruments and we had discussed the sensory elements arising, Wyn allocated numbers and actions for each person to create a preliminary soundscape (for example – on the number two, one individual was to do two staccato beats on their 'drum' whilst on three another was to pluck the elastic bands one at a time left to right – dum, dum, dum, dum). We spent some time making this soundscape by using the instruments in the agreed sequence, with Wyn marking out time and calling the numbers so that everyone knew when to make their sounds. We then progressed to 'performing' the piece without anyone marking time. Afterwards, we discussed how everyone felt about the work in the session. The actors commented that it sounded much better than they expected it would do, given the homemade/recycled nature of the instruments. Harry publicly commented that he had been incorrect in his original assessment that this soundscape would make the production appear amateurish and that he now thought there was an additional dimension to be created from using this within the play. Simon, also recently joined, noted that this session had brought people together to feel very much like a community of equals, as each one of us had our part to play in the rhythmic sounds we created.

There was also the opportunity for people to try different instruments and Wyn played a classical guitar accompaniment for some of the soundscape. As a group, we spoke about how rhythms can evoke powerful memories and remind us of previous experiences, good and bad. This widened into a conversation about how rhythms and chanting can be used in ceremonies and religious festivals and the sense of occasion created by seeing marching bands and other rhythmic-based spectacles. By drawing on the men's life experiences and stories in relation to rhythm, we were able to develop their sense of belonging to the community we have created in Emergency Shakespeare, developing their emotional resilience.

We discussed the songs within the play and ways in which to use this rhythmic quality of the group to make these more substantial parts of the performance than perhaps would usually be the case in this company's productions. Taking Caliban's 'Ban, ban, Caliban' song, we worked on making it more rhythmic. The result was Caliban jumping onto a table, which was part of the staging for the production and beating out a rhythm with his bare feet before he began to sing the song. He chanted each line, and this was then echoed back to him by Stephano and Trinculo. Marcus, a long-standing ensemble member who was playing Stephano, also wrote a sea shanty to end with the lines

I shall no more to sea, to sea,
Here shall I die ashore (2.2.41–42).

He performed this acapella piece as he came onstage with the rumbling of thunder echoing around the island, to great acclaim from the audience.

Theo, who played Ariel, made himself a bodhran from cardboard and tightly stretched polythene, playing it throughout the play as an audible marker of his presence when he was invisible to others onstage.

Wyn wrote a song for the Gods' blessing of the young couple, creating a three-part song sung in the round, with harmonisation provided by those cast members off-stage.

JUNO

Honour, riches, marriage-blessing,
Long continuance and increasing,
Hourly joys be still upon you.
Juno sings her blessings on you.

CERES

Earth's increase, foison plenty,
Barns and garners never empty,
Vines with clust'ring bunches growing,
Plants with goodly burden bowing;
Spring come to you at the farthest
In the very end of harvest.
Scarcity and want shall shun you.
Ceres' blessing so is on you.

IRIS

You sunburned sicklemen, of August weary,
Come hither from the furrow and be merry.
Make holiday: your rye-straw hats put on,
And these fresh nymphs encounter every one

Juno's part (spoken by Walter, a young man who felt uncomfortable singing) was spoken as a gentle rap to a beat of de-dum, de-dum, de-dum, de-dum and after he had spoken his lines through once Ceres (Wyn) then sang his lines over the top of the rap which Juno continued. Ceres sang a descant through fully and then repeated it whilst Iris (Bert), then sang his lines over the two existing songs. The result was a harmonious one, rich with rhythm and melody, which perfectly complemented the sound-rich production of *The Tempest*. As one audience member noted:

The Tempest is one of Shakespeare's most musical plays, and it was a delight to hear how you dealt with this aspect of it – I really enjoyed Marcus' songs and the way Wyn layered the sound (Rudd, 2022).

A long time ago on an island far away
the winner of *Which Witch?*
Magazine's annual 'Rich or Itch'
competition Sycorax began a new life
with her son Caliban. They were not,
however, alone.

Figure 16.1 Image from Obun's cartoon book image 1

This production also inspired Obun to create a cartoon version of the play for me to use with a group of young adults with complex special educational and mental health needs whom I was introducing to drama for the first time. The young people had no prior experience of drama or knowledge of Shakespeare so I asked him if he would be willing to create some images which could be shared with them as a way of making the plot and characters more accessible. This project with teenagers was designed to encourage them to engage in the stages of embodiment, projection and role (EPR) (Jennings, 2011) to explore a reality other than their own. Obun developed my request into a cartoon book which included contemporary images and a satirical storyline based on Shakespeare's original play but with modern references to enhance the appeal. (See Figures 16.1 and 16.2).

The young people took delight in reading each new page and we then used these as a way of delving into the characters, acting out each role to feel the physicality of Prospero, Miranda, Caliban and others. Obun's dedication and commitment to the intricate drawings he produced were praiseworthy. This commitment aligned with his assertion that he wants to use the opportunity afforded to him of joining Emergency Shakespeare and the self-development

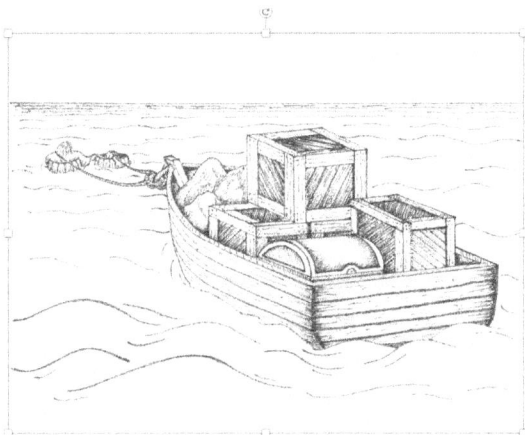

Prospero's best friend, Gonzalo, helps
them by packing all their belongings for
their holiday. So begins the longest
holiday in history, with father and
daughter drifting out to sea and words
of revenge and hating holidays.

Figure 16.2 Image from Obun's cartoon book image 2

this has offered him to build a legacy for the future and to help others (Obun, 2023). He articulated this in a poem entitled 'Unknown entity' in which he describes:

> I have travelled on this adventure
> Following an energy I can't truly explain;
> But as I stand in front of a door, that wasn't there before;
> Leading to unforeseen adventure and achievement;
> Realisation dawns.
> Where once I looked for a saviour;
> Someone to rescue me from the darkest chasm;
> I now look at her and see the truth.
> She isn't there to save us,
> She's there to guide us,
> So we can save ourselves (Obun, 2022).

Obun attributes the work we have done through Shakespeare to much of his personal progression through his sentence and his desire to contribute positively to society upon his release. He has developed talents in visual art, creative writing and acting whilst in prison and he plans to use those skills in the community when his sentence ends in two years' time. He has also co-written, with myself and prison governors, about the theatre company and how this has helped him to develop his own non-offending identity. In *Othello* (Shakespeare, 2001), he played Iago, a role which he found challenging as the worst of Iago's characteristics were reminiscent of the behaviours, Obun himself exhibited when he committed his offences (Mackenzie et al., 2024, pp. 217–220). Through the embodiment of the role of Iago, Obun was able to explore those elements of his own psyche, which he was deeply ashamed of. The feeling of utter revulsion he felt at speaking the misogynistic lines of Iago and then killing Emilia onstage took him back to the time in his life when his behaviours and mental state were at their very worst but confirmed to him that he felt no affinity to that person now. Whilst addressing this in an offending behaviour programme was a formal part of his sentence plan, Obun himself acknowledged that the enactment of the role was a far more visceral exploration. Through becoming Iago, Obun was able to turn his individual 'areas of distress' (Jennings, 2011, p. 238) into both a powerfully performed character and a confirmation of his own development.

In contrast to the deeply personal role of Iago, there are other instances where the actors engaged with much more light-hearted characters but can still take from the experience some fundamental insights into their own life. One such example is that of Riley, who joined Emergency Shakespeare just as rehearsals began for King Lear, chosen as one of Shakespeare's most iconic plays to commemorate the 400th anniversary of the publication of the First Folio in autumn 2023. Riley had undertaken the Creative Workshops programme at the suggestion of someone who had completed a previous cohort, saying at the outset that he had little interest in Shakespeare and didn't expect to stay for the duration of the sessions. He has been diagnosed as having attention deficit hyperactivity disorder (ADHD) and admitted that he rarely completes anything he starts as his interest wanes. However, he began to enjoy acting and explained, 'being on my feet and doing stuff means I don't get bored like I do with formal education classes' (Riley, 2023a, 2023b). He began to help one of the members of the ensemble with some set design for the production we were working on at the time and gradually became more involved with the Shakespeare UnBard work in the prison.

After completing the Creative Workshops, Riley asked to join the theatre company. He was cast as the Fool and developed a great working relationship with Obun, who was playing Lear. His enthusiasm and commitment to rehearsals were exemplary, and he spoke in the group about how much he was taking from this process. He brought energy to the Fool but also worked closely with Obun to develop some moments of real empathy and emotion, crafting a surprisingly quiet and contemplative Fool, using the character to explore alternatives, unlike his natural persona. Around three months before the performance, Riley's Parole Hearing was held and the Parole Board explained the timescales for release should his Parole be granted. This would have meant him leaving a few weeks before the performances were scheduled. He asked the Parole Board that if he was granted Parole, it be delayed until after the performances and explained that he wanted the opportunity to show his commitment to the ensemble. He described that he wanted his family to see him do something they could be proud of him for and he felt this was the perfect way to show them that he had matured and changed. His request was granted and he was released the day after our final performance. When we debriefed the production before he left, he spoke eloquently about how he had taken so much from the group and felt he was 'a better person for all I've learned from you all and from Shakespeare, I'm not so selfish or hard work now' (Riley, 2023b).

For many of the men I work with, their behavioural response to any form of challenge or issue is aggression, whether verbal or physical and it is through role-modelling pro-social responses within the group that this pattern of behaviour can be altered. In another prison where a theatre company was founded in 2023, there were a number of men to whom this applied. One poignant example was during rehearsals for our inaugural production of *Macbeth* where the man playing the lead role (Mahajan) arrived to discover his script was not in his bag. He asked the others if they had seen it, and a thorough search of the rehearsal space was conducted but yielded no results. He began to get agitated and said that someone had obviously taken it to mess with his head; the others laughed at him and said he was being ridiculous and must have forgotten it. His rising stress levels were visible, so I spoke to him separately and we discussed how he was feeling and why he felt that way. He said that in this type of scenario, he would usually lash out physically as this was the way he had learned to deal with issues from a very young age. However, we discussed it and the possibilities as to where his script could be and he managed to retain his temper, borrowing a spare for the remainder of the session. The following week, he apologised to the group and explained that someone had taken it from his bag when he popped into his place of work before joining the rehearsal. This acknowledgement of his behaviour was a real step forward for Mahajan and he said to me that it was the first time he had ever managed to do this (Mahajan, 2023) due to the skills he had developed within the group.

Another actor in this ensemble, Gary, elected to play Lady Macbeth despite having never acted before. He learned his lines quickly and would seek suggestions on how to develop the character, pushing himself well outside of his comfort zone. Initially, he was worried about how others in the prison would react to him playing a female role, but he soon grew in confidence and elected to wear a dress and wig for the production. He began to support some of the newer members of the group and to help with line-learning tips as his confidence in acting grew during the eight-month rehearsal cycle. During a one-to-one conversation with him, he said, 'you're not teaching me acting, you're teaching me human. You make me want to be a better person and you're helping me with the skills to do that' (Gary, 2023). Our theatre of resilience work enabled him to embody different roles and use those experiences to reflect on his own behaviours and beliefs. As someone who had experienced significant substance misuse issues which had blighted his life and led to the actions which he was in custody for, he had never felt that he had alternatives to the life he led, but he began to talk of a future upon release, a future which he hoped would involve him being able to have a positive relationship and a family, a life free from drugs and crime. Whilst acting is unlikely to be a career choice for Gary (or many of the others I work with), the skills and desire for an alternative way of life to their experiences to date cannot be underestimated.

This is also true of Emergency Shakespeare actor Bradley, who was originally talked into attending by his friend on the wing. It was several weeks before he lifted his eyes from the floor and his voice could barely be heard as he was so introverted. He said that there would be no way he could perform in front of others and that his memory was poor, so line learning was not an option. It was evident (he has also since confirmed this to be accurate) that his recent sentencing had shattered his identity and his self-esteem was non-existent. However, Marcus began to mentor Bradley and he slowly integrated into the group. Seeing him laugh for the first time at a joke made during rehearsal was truly special; he began to relax into the work we were doing and to find pleasure in Shakespeare. His memory was far better than he gave himself credit for, and whilst he was very quiet in his first production, he has continued to grow in confidence and gone on to play increasingly large roles. He has, to date, played Ferdinand, Brutus and Edmund and is currently rehearsing Henry IV. His role as Assistant Director in the Creative Workshops gives him the opportunity to pay forward the support he received from Marcus and his confidence has grown exponentially.

In a recent A Midsummer Night's Dream workshop where we were using Quince's prologue (5.1.126–150), Bailey played Bottom and was demonstrating to the others how to inject comedy through over-acting the roles as Quince diligently tells the story in full before its enactment. Playing on Bottom's earlier desire to play all the roles, Bailey then suggested he could be all of the workmen acting out the prologue and proceeded to race around the stage as I read out the lines: rushing from daring lover Pyramus to sweetly innocent Thisbe being frightened by the 'grisly beast' (5.1.138) lion, shedding his mantle, mauling it and then dying onstage, twice. This comedic interlude was reminiscent of the 'fast, funny and physical performance style' (website, n.d.) of the Reduced Shakespeare Company. The group was delighted with his impromptu performance, and it imbued the remainder of the session with playfulness. Reflecting afterwards on just how far Bailey has come during the two years of his involvement with Shakespeare UnBard, his journey epitomises the importance of playing and of projection and how this can be transformative for adults in these austere institutions. Bailey described recently how

> coming to prison has given me a life; through finding Shakespeare and the group I have found something I truly care about, and I never had that before. I'm ashamed of why I am here but for the first time in life I can see a future, I can achieve things.
>
> (2024)

As Jennings writes '"dramatic reality" . . . allows people of all descriptions . . . to challenge their ideas of self and the world' (2023, pp. 14–15). For the incarcerated people I work with, this is particularly true as many of them have lacked stability and positive, nurturing relationships prior to their incarceration. Being labelled as an offender compounds this. Braithwaite's (1989) notion of 'disintegrative shaming' is prevalent in Western culture and prisoners are aware that they will be vilified by the media and society even when their sentence is served. A custodial sentence should be the deprivation of liberty; it should not be the deprivation of humanity, but often, the two become conflated. Shakespeare and drama are not a panacea for all, but in many instances, they have become a way of engaging with the world and finding a place in which someone may feel valued and a sense of belonging. Sadly, for many, this may be the first time they have felt this. Michael articulates the value of this work as:

> For a few short hours each week we are free; although physically we remain within the boundaries of the prison our spirits soar far above the walls and fences. . . . This is a true sense of freedom, one that is rarely found anywhere in life, let alone within the high security estate. It offers each of us a few brief moments of Nirvana.
>
> (Micheal, 2019)

Perhaps in playing and in being someone else, there is a way for people to find themselves; as Shakespeare said, it could be an opportunity to 'turn mine eyes upon myself' (Richard II, 4.1.247) (Shakespeare, 2002) and to develop that self into a person they can be proud of.

Note

1 Pseudonyms are used for all prisoner names to anonymise their identities.

References

Bailey. (2024) *Verbal Comment Made to the Author During Emergency Shakespeare Rehearsals.*
Bradley, A. (2022) *Prison Safety and Security: Exploring the Impact of Trauma-Informed Practice and Trauma-Responsive Interventions.* https://crestresearch.ac.uk/comment/prison-safety-and-security-exploring-the-impact-of-trauma/#:~:text=public%20health%20crises.-,The%20prevalence%20of%20trauma%20within%20prisons%20is%20extensive%20and%20pervasive,minutia%20example%20of%20known%20disclosures
Braithwaite, J. (1989) *Crime, Shame and Reintegration.* Cambridge: Cambridge University Press.
Farmer, M. (2017) *The Importance of Strengthening Prisoners' Family Ties to Prevent Reoffending and Reduce Intergenerational Crime.* Ministry of Justice. https://assets.publishing.service.gov.uk/media/5a81d6b2e5274a2e87dbfc00/farmer-review-report.pdf
Gary. (2023) *Verbal Comment Made to the Author During Macbeth Rehearsals.*
Hanson, C. (Dir.) (2002) *8 Mile.* Universal Pictures.
Hunter, K. (2015) *Shakespeare's Heartbeat: Drama Games for Children with Autism.* Oxon: Routledge.
Jennings, S. (1992) *Dramatherapy: Theory and Practice* (vol. 2). London: Routledge.
Jennings, S. (2011) *Healthy Attachments and Neuro-Dramatic Play.* London: Jessica Kingsley Publishers.
Jennings, S. (2023) Thither and back again: An exploration of a midsummer night's dream. In *Shakespeare and Social Engagement*, eds. Mackenzie, R. and Shaughnessy, R. London: Berghahn.
Mackenzie, R. (2023) *Creating Space for Shakespeare: Working with Marginalized Communities.* London: Bloomsbury Arden.
Mackenzie, R., Lubkowski, R. and Obun, P. (2024) "If to do were as easy as to know what were good to do": The rehabilitative potential of collaborative theatre companies in English prisons. In *International Perspectives on Gender-Based Violence*, ed. Pandey, M. Cham: Springer, 209–226.
Mahajan. (2023) *Verbal Comment Made to the Author During Macbeth Rehearsals.*
Marcus. (2022) *Here Shall I Die Ashore.* Not Published.
Micheal. (2019) Verbal comments made to author.
Ministry of Justice. (2024) *Prison Population Figures: 2024*, March 22. https://www.gov.uk/government/publications/prison-population-figures-2024
Morey, M. and Crewe, B. (2019) Work, intimacy and prisoner masculinities. In *New Perspectives on Prisoner Masculinities*, eds. Maycock, M. and Hunt, K. Cham: Palgrave, 17–42.
Obun, P. (2022) *Unknown Entity.* Unpublished.
Obun, P. (2023) *Verbal Comment Made to the Author During Emergency Shakespeare Rehearsals.*
Pimlico Opera. (n.d.) https://grangeparkopera.co.uk/pimlico-opera/
Reduced Shakespeare Company website. (n.d.) https://www.reducedshakespeare.com/about/complete-timeline/
Riley. (2023a) *Verbal Comment Made to the Author During Creative Workshops.*
Riley. (2023b) *Verbal Comment Made During the Debrief of King Lear.*
Rudd, L. (2022) *Feedback from Emergency Shakespeare's The Tempest.* Unpublished.
Substance Abuse and Mental Health Services Administration. (2014) *SAMHSA's Concept of Trauma and Guidance for a Trauma-Informed Approach.* https://www.cdc.gov/cpr/infographics/6_principles_trauma_info.htm

Shakespeare, W. (2001) *Othello*, ed. Honigmann, E. A. J. London: Bloomsbury Arden.

Spivak, G. C. (1985) The Rani of Sirmur: An essay in reading the archives. *History and Theory*, 24(3), 247–272. https://doi.org/10.2307/2505169

Warr, J. (2016) The prisoner inside and out. In *Handbook on Prisons*, eds. Jewkes, Y., Bennet, J. and Crewe, B. (2nd ed.). Oxon: Routledge, 586–604.

Wyn. (2022) *A Marriage Blessing*. Not Published.

Chapter 17

A research project considering the adaptation and practice of NDP for adults with a diagnosis of young onset dementia

Clive Holmwood, Gemma Collard-Stokes, and Alison Ward

Introduction

Neuro Dramatic Play (NDP) is an overarching approach comprising three distinct phases NDP, EPR (Embodiment Projection Role), and ToR (Theatre of Resilience), developed over several decades by pioneering play and dramatherapist Sue Jennings (1993, 2011). Firstly, NDP is pre-birth from the first trimester to when the child is born. This is when the unborn child begins to have an awareness of the world around them in the warm, dark, safe, wet womb. This is the time when the mother is in a unique position to form a bonding relationship with their unborn child through singing to them, massaging the womb, and feeling the baby when it kicks (Jennings, 2011, p. 81 ff).

The second phase, known as Embodiment, Projection, and Role, is divided into three distinct phases and focuses on the first seven years of life. A time of huge development for newborn babies as they grow into young children and need appropriate stimulation and activities for normal development (Holmwood, 2023). Embodiment, the first phase, is from birth to approximately 13 months; the child is beginning to process the world outside of the womb, what is me, what is not me. The frontal cortex of the brain begins to develop, and the newborn begins to gain control over their limbs and their own body. Then they realise that they are a single-being and not attached to someone else as they were in the womb. Projection, the second phase, occurs from about 13 months to the age of three when, using their newfound skills, the young child begins to reach out to touch and affect things in this new world. Toys are introduced that they can manipulate and move. They can form playful relationships with objects around them. Finally, in the third phase, from about three, sometimes earlier, the child begins to create their own stories with the objects around them. This is the role phase. Through taking on and giving roles and through a story, children begin to make sense of the world around them, as Gersie states:

> [W]hen our life is complex, which it is more often than not, we hope to find within the story images relevant to our own predicament, hoping

DOI: 10.4324/9781003498209-22

maybe against hope, that an answer to our problem might dwell within the story, not yet realising that the solution often merges from our heart-felt response to the tale.

(1992, p. 15)

The world may not be difficult, (hopefully) for the young child, but it is certainly complex. Navigating the world and everyone and everything in it for the brain of a young child is both exhilarating and exciting. The use of character, role, and story allows them to begin to process aspects of the world around them in a more general and embodied way. This is a central tenant to such approaches as dramatherapy (Jones, 1996). He suggests that through 'embodied play,' we can make 'life drama connections' to the world around us. Even at a basic level, young children can do this and process their joys, anxieties, and fears in a playful way.

The final stage is the Theatre of Resilience (ToR), which supports older children from seven upwards, but especially geared towards teenagers. Supporting young people through a second chaotic phase in their young lives as their bodies, attitudes, and minds change. In the same way that coming into the world as a newborn is chaotic, turning into an adolescent is also chaotic. Their bodies and brains go through a whole series of changes as the adult brain begins to form. Their ability to question their identity and relation-ships, both romantic and otherwise, comes to the fore. Through both games and social theatre (Jennings, 2009), young people can again begin to make sense of the world around them. They, too, need to understand their indi-vidual place in the world, and for teenagers, this is more important than ever as they navigate their way towards adulthood.

So, how is any of the previously mentioned information relevant to adults with a diagnosis of Young Onset Dementia? At face value, it might appear that there is no connection at all between the development of a child from prebirth to birth, to childhood to adolescence and young adulthood. We shall come to this shortly. However, it suffices to say there is a developmental pro-cess in both the growth of a child and in the way that all forms of dementia affect the individual, and NDP mirrors this developmental process through these three distinct key phases with children and young people. Firstly, it is important to understand the significance and relevance of dementia and to define it.

Dementia and younger onset dementia

Dementia is a term that encompasses several diseases that affect the brain; the most commonly known is Alzheimer's Disease, which affects between 60–70% of those with a diagnosis. Symptoms may include a loss of mem-ory, changes in behaviour, and in a person's ability to take part in everyday activities. The World Health Organisation (2024) estimates that 55 million people are affected worldwide and that there are nearly 10 million new cases every year. Dementia affects both the individual with the diagnosis and their carers (quite often, these are informal carers such as family or friends). In the UK, there are nearly 1 million people estimated to be living with dementia, a figure that is due to increase to 1.4 million by 2040 (Alzheimer's Research UK, 2024). One explanation for this expected rise is due to a growing ageing population globally, with the majority of people affected by dementia being aged in later life and with age being a key risk factor for developing dementia.

However, younger people may also develop dementia, and this is termed 'young onset dementia', or working age dementia. This is typically defined as those who are under the age of 65 years. Dementia at this age may be due to one of the rarer forms of dementia, such as frontotemporal dementia, a lifestyle-related (alcohol abuse for example), or a genetic condition, although Alzheimer's Disease remains the most prevalent regardless of age. Globally it is estimated that the prevalence of young-onset dementia is 119 for every 100,000 people aged between 30–64 (Hendriks et al., 2021). In the UK, there are over 70,000 people with a diagnosis of young onset dementia (Carter, 2022), a population that Carter (2022) considers to be a 'hidden' group with specific health and social care needs that are often left unmet.

What sets young onset dementia apart from those in later life is the life phase at which it occurs, the range of types of dementia, and the resultant symptoms they experience. Symptoms can be similar to those of dementia in an older population; however, they also include changes in behaviour, personality, and challenges with language and communication, often before memory is affected. Young-onset dementia can be particularly challenging, as it affects people who are of working age, looking after family, and may be caring for elderly relatives. A diagnosis at this age can have an emotional, financial, and social impact. Often, diagnosis is delayed as it can be misdiagnosed for stress, menopause, depression, or other conditions. This is further challenged by a lack of awareness about young onset dementia in health and social care and with members of the public.

Early diagnosis and tailored support are crucial for managing the condition and helping those living with dementia to navigate changes to their sense of self and their personal and work lives. However, the service provision for those living with dementia is not widely available or is offered alongside people who can be 30–40 years older, whose needs, both physically and emotionally, are different from those in a younger age group. This younger age group can experience challenges emotionally, dealing with feelings of loss and grief, but also anxiety and depression. There is stigma around a diagnosis of dementia, which is especially true of young onset dementia, with a lack of understanding and misconceptions. This can result in a loss of social connections with friends and family who can distance themselves or because it becomes difficult to relate to your peers. Isolation can, therefore, result as social circles diminish. This may also affect family relationships, with spouses/partners or children taking on a caring role at a time when they are not expecting to. This can put a strain on relationships and lead to shifts in roles within relationships and an individual's sense of self that can be uncomfortable and difficult to navigate (Greenwood and Smith, 2016; Hayo et al., 2018). Research into the experience of living with young onset dementia has identified that many feel a loss of doing a meaningful activity and that they are no longer able to take part in their community or feel relevant and valued individuals. However, many can find meaning and value by connecting with other people living with dementia and finding support through peers (Greenwood and Smith, 2016). Finding services that can support families and individuals to manage these changes and help them plan for a different future than expected requires a combined holistic approach, one that is tailored to the needs of this age group, supports peer-to-peer engagement, and provides meaning in an important way to support those with a diagnosis of young onset dementia (Greenwood and Smith, 2016; Hayo et al., 2018).

Dementia and creative arts

Creativity can be a valuable way of working with a person living with dementia and it has become increasingly incorporated into services (Camic et al., 2018). Furthermore, creativity does not decline with dementia in the same way that cognition may decline (Ross et al., 2023). There are various ways that the creative arts have been used in this field; some of the most researched approaches are through the use of music, through initiatives such as Singing for the Brain (Alzheimer's Society, 2024), engagement with museums, with the Museum of Modern Art in New York (2024) which has developed a prestigious programme of activities for both family members and the person living with dementia, and many other creative activities that are delivered as one-off sessions or through programmes of work in the community and in care homes. Work by TimeSlips (Basting, 2024) (who offer storytelling), Turtle Key Art's intergenerational creative music programme, Turtle Song, and the Alzheimer's Poetry Project (Glazer, 2024) are just some examples of a variety of good practices in this field. The benefits of engagement in such practices have been shown to improve an individual's self-identity and expression, improve social connections (and thus reducing feelings of isolation), be a way to support emotions and improve quality of life and wellbeing, and sense of accomplishment (Camic et al., 2018; Palmiero et al., 2012; Ross et al., 2023).

Many of the approaches are aimed at those in later life or who are in care homes, as with many dementia services. There are examples of work that are both community-based and aimed at people with young-onset dementia, such as the music and memory project with Manchester Camerata. Or the Together Stronger project brings together children with a parent with young onset dementia to take part in weaving, storytelling, and other creative activities (Moiseyeva et al., 2023). However, these are rare, and the evidence base for such programmes of activity is limited. Creative arts can be a way to meet the needs of those with young-onset dementia by focusing on shared life events and social engagement and doing this in a safe and fun environment. However, there is a gap in our understanding of how to develop and deliver creative activities in a way that can plug the gap in provision for those within this younger age group and their families. A focus on community-based activities is particularly important for this age group, as many will still be living at home and want to engage with others who experience a similar diagnosis. As discussed, those with young onset dementia need tailored services designed to support their needs and the needs of their family. This group requires community-based services, which provide opportunities for engagement in 'normal,' everyday activities that can offer a sense of purpose, time to socialise, and to support them in managing changing roles and relationships (Hayo et al., 2018; Carter et al., 2018; Rodda and Carter, 2023; Mayrhofer et al., 2018).

NDP – adaption for younger onset dementia

As has already been described, the overall purpose of NDP as a framework was to offer an overall philosophical approach to working creatively with babies and children from the first-trimester pre-birth through to adolescence, considering brain development, neuroscience, and attachment. However, when considering the human life span there are other ages/times in life when individuals go through rapid and challenging changes. Old age is a good example of this. Due to the avalanche of modern medicines and their success, humans are living much, much longer. It is not unusual for people to live into their 80's and 90's and even into their early 100's. As we have seen, this adds increasingly to the risk of people developing dementia.

Jaaniste (2016), an Australian Dramatherapist, was the first person to consider adapting aspects of the NDP framework by adapting EPR due to her interest in working with seniors and developing support for adults in later life. One area of consideration was that despite cognitive decline in dementia, 'sufficient account of how latent knowledge remains accessible to people with dementia' (Jaaniste, 2016, p. 264) had not really been considered. Her research, which used mixed methods, including quality of life questionnaires, hypothesised the reversal of EPR (Embodiment Projection Role) to RPE (Role Projection Embodiment), which offered 'a safe structure for clients to validate their inner life when approached phenomenologically' (Jaaniste, 2016, p. 267). In other words, using role-based approaches in the early stages of dementia, projective techniques with people with moderate levels of dementia, and then embodied approaches with adults with late-stage or severe dementia. So, offering an overall philosophical approach for older adults with varying stages of dementia in the same way that NDP had for babies and children. Thus, suggesting that NDP should not necessarily be used with babies and children alone but had the potential to be used across the life span.

The beginnings of a research project

Early in his career, both before and after training as a dramatherapist and NDP practitioner, Dr Clive Holmwood (2021), currently an associate professor at the University of Derby, had developed an interest in working with older people. His colleague at the University of Derby, Dr Gemma Collard-Stokes, who specialised in community-based approaches to dance and movement (Bird et al., 2023; Collard-Stokes and Irons, 2022), invited him to deliver a short open lecture about NDP and its potential for working with older people as part of the Research Arts and Wellbeing (RAW) cluster at the University of Derby. On a separate occasion, she invited Dr Alison Ward from the University of Northampton, who specialises in the use of stories in relation to adults with younger onset dementia (Ward et al., 2018). Gemma noted a synergy between these areas of interest. Especially noting that the area of young onset dementia and connections to creative approaches were under-researched and that NDP as a framework had some limited research in dementia (Jaaniste, 2106) but no research in the field of young onset dementia. The idea of a possible collaborative, creative, attachment-based research project with an overall EPR lens was born.

Creative support: building bonds through play for people with early onset dementia and their caregivers

Recruitment

During the conception of the project, we formed a partnership with Dementia UK to assist in thinking through our recruitment strategy. With collaboration a key facet of the project, our connection with Dementia UK was useful in furthering our understanding of the distinctive needs of people under 65 with a dementia diagnosis, contributing to our focus on family relationships, community, and selfhood. In forming a Patient and Public Involvement (PPI) group to consult from their unique position as experts by experience, named the 'Creative Dementia Research Group,' we invited a regional dementia worker from Dementia UK, who contributed to the recruitment of participants, alongside two people living with dementia, a person with carer experience and Professor Sue Jennings. Recruitment was not without challenges. As a 'hidden population' (Carter, 2022), reaching those who might benefit from our work was thwarted with difficulty, not least because of the lack of community-based services nationally that we might ordinarily work with to connect with potential participants.

What we did

The project involved delivering two 10-week creative workshop programmes to two cohorts of participants Dementia Quality of Life measures (DEMQOL and C-DEMQOL) by Brown et al. (2019), with group sizes of two and 11, respectively. Each session was video recorded and analysed using a video analysis protocol designed by Alison Ward (2019). The evaluation included pre-, post-, and 8-month follow-up assessments using several measures: the Revised Adult Attachment Scale – Close Relationships Version; Smith et al. (2005); and the Positive Psychology Outcome Measure (PPOM and PPOM-C) by Stoner et al. (2018) and Pione et al. (2022). Additionally, pre-, post-, and eight-month follow-up interviews were conducted, along with reflective notes gathered throughout the study. Data from these interviews were anonymised, transcribed, and thematically analysed Braun and Clarke (2006). Following analysis by the team, we invited the PPI consultation panel to an analysis day where the trustworthiness of our analysis was scrutinised by the consultation members.

Creating the workshop programme

Responding to key points raised in initial research findings, the project team began to develop a set of principles that would form the basis of a programme of work for responding to an adaptation of Neuro-Dramatic-Play and the Embodiment, Projection, Role model for adults living with young onset dementia and their close family and friends. Part of this included the necessity to explore the impact of creative problem-solving and social theatre on resilience building and attachment formation between the person with young onset dementia and a chosen partner who would attend the programme. Through this, we aimed to create an enhanced EPR model based on the findings of the research to support future extensions of the project.

We devised a series of 10 workshops deeply rooted in Neuro-Dramatic Play's association with attachment theory, sensory involvement, and the creative arts, aiming to foster resilience, communication, and connection in an accumulative manner. This series, designed by the team and reviewed by the PPI consultation panel, aligns with NDP's core principles, aiming to create a supportive environment where participants can explore their identities, build relational connections, and express themselves in novel and creative ways.

The principles

By employing the EPR framework in the context of nurturing identity, relational connection, and self-expression, the workshop series addresses the cognitive and relational needs of people living with young-onset dementia, encouraging engagement in creative and dramatic play that transcends verbal communication. This approach has the potential to create non-verbal and embodied ways of connecting, while for family members, it offers tools to build understanding, compassion, and attachment through shared experiences. The core components of embodiment, projection, and role were integrated into each workshop, allowing participants to engage in activities that encourage expression, movement, sensory exploration, and storytelling. However, the overarching trajectory that guided the journey over the 10 weeks was steered toward belonging – expressing ideas of safety and developing a sense of safety in the setting, identity – self-expression and developing new communication routes, and the present – remaining in the here and now and resisting narratives related to a past self or a lost future.

Structure and development of the workshop series

The series consists of 10 sessions, each lasting two hours and incorporating both structured activities and socialisation time. This setup is based on prior successful creative workshops for people with dementia, which demonstrated that regular, consistent engagement fosters a sense of routine and community among participants. Each session's theme is strategically designed to facilitate growth in communication, attachment, and resilience, with a gentle progression that builds on previous experiences. The 10 workshops were viewed as three progressive pillars that accumulated over time to offer a rich experience.

Pillar of belonging: the first three to four weeks, focusing on belonging, incorporated activities that built trust between group members and the delivery team and introduced relational practices and different communication styles. It also included topics on self-care and acknowledging what we need to feel safe.

Pillar of identity: once belonging had been established, the following 3–4 weeks of the programme focused on developing group cohesion and security among the group membership; the procedural aspect of the programme was well established by this point, but it was important to maintain consistency and name sections of the workshop to help participants recognise the shifts between activities and approaches. Collaboration became a key aspect of co-creation and co-creative problem-solving through expressive sounding, bodywork, story, and producing creative responses.

Pillar of the present (here and now): The final few weeks of the programme, while bringing the work to a close, combined several dimensions towards notions of building personal peace with dementia diagnosis; within these weeks, there is the encouragement of participants to take small risks and move out of perceived comfort zones trying new activities, more concentrated characterisation work and considering scenographic possibilities for performance, where imagined worlds or scenarios take seed.

Each workshop structure was divided into specific stages: introduction, main activities, reflective discussion, and toolkit development. This structure offers participants a safe, predictable environment where they can feel secure and open to creative exploration. The plans for each session include aims and objectives, rationales for the thematic pillar, and the element of EPR with a contextual statement relating to the NDP underpinning.

The following breaks down how the EPR framework is expressed across the range of workshops:

Week 1 – Introductions and Group Cohesion: The first session introduces participants to the workshop environment, the facilitators, and each other. Activities focus on group cohesion, using simple embodiment exercises like movement games to establish a sense of body awareness and connection. These initial activities introduce participants to the embodiment aspect, encouraging comfort within their own bodies.

Week 2 – Body as Home: This session explores the concept of 'body as home,' promoting self-acceptance and bodily awareness. Using exercises such as finger painting on large paper, participants visualise the qualities they need to feel at home within themselves. This continues to reflect the focus on embodiment as participants connect with their physical selves and explore concepts of self-care and identity.

Week 3 – Safe Places: In this session, participants create a 'scene in a box' to represent a place of safety. This activity emphasises projection, allowing participants to externalise and visualise concepts of safety, comfort, and belonging. Working with a partner, they build on the shared experience to cultivate understanding and mutual support.

Week 4 – Storytelling and Puppetry: Storytelling, as a central NDP tool, is used here to facilitate projection and encourage participants to imagine and narrate personal and group stories. In this session, participants create puppets as story characters, blending embodiment and projection to tell stories collectively. This exercise provides a playful way to explore identity and relationships within the group.

Week 5 – Soundscapes and Rhythms: Playing the strength of NDP's integral sensory focus, this session invites participants to bring in sound-making objects and explore soundscapes, using rhythm and sound to represent aspects of the story we are developing. This activity deepens the sensory experience and encourages non-verbal expression, which is essential for participants who may struggle with verbal communication.

Week 6 – Movement and Characterisation: Building on previous weeks, this session incorporates physical movement to embody the traits of their story characters. Through exercises like authentic movement, participants explore character traits and their relationships with the characters. This session further integrates the necessity of role, encouraging participants to take on new perspectives through movement.

Week 7 – Rehearsal and Role Exploration: As participants rehearse for a performance, they delve deeper into their characters, exploring movement, dialogue, and props. This invites participants to practice and refine their roles within the story, which in turn fosters confidence and expression.

Week 8 – Dress Rehearsal: The dress rehearsal consolidates all previous elements – embodiment, projection, and role. Participants practice their roles in a safe environment, preparing for the upcoming performance. This rehearsal process invites participants to experience the culmination of their journey.

Week 9 – Final Performance: In this commemorative session, participants perform their stories for one another or an invited audience. The performance serves as an expression of their shared journey, solidifying relationships and providing a sense of accomplishment. The act of performing offers a powerful means of building self-identity and community as participants witness each other's growth and creativity.

Week 10 – Reflection and Celebration: The final session focuses on reflection, allowing participants to revisit their journey over the 10 weeks. Through discussion, participants identify their favourite activities, reflecting on how they might integrate these into their lives. This session is a testament to NDP's impact on resilience and attachment, offering a concluding celebration that reinforces the relational bonds established during the programme.

Toolkit development and long-term impact

Each week, participants also develop a personalised toolkit – a collection of activities, objects, and sensory materials – that they can use outside the workshop to maintain a connection with the materials offered week to week. This toolkit aligns with NDP's emphasis on sensory engagement and attachment, providing participants with resources to sustain connection and creativity in their daily lives. By creating individualised toolkits, the work that takes place within the duration of the workshop extends into everyday life, where extended family and friends may also feed into the experience or witness the results and benefits of the programme. This contributes to fostering resilience and enhances the relationship between the person with young onset dementia and those closest to them.

The toolkit includes objects, photographs, poems, and activity cards, each reflecting different aspects of the workshop activities. For instance, the 'Heart's Desire' postcard or the 'Sound Maker' postcard, are activities that can easily be undertaken at home with just a few crafting materials, and the results can be brought into the following workshop to provide useful talking points or tangible reminders of creative experiences with others in one's life. By using the toolkit, participants can recreate moments of sensory and relational connection, maintaining the bonds developed during the workshop and nurturing bonds in other areas of their lives.

Research findings

The themes emerging from the project findings identified the common factors and experiences of people living with young onset dementia through background information and understanding of identity. Following the delivery of the sessions, the themes of Communication, Resilience, Attachment and Quality of Life were identified. Furthermore, the findings explored learning from this project that could support future delivery and the meaning of the NDP adaptation for this cohort. This chapter has focussed on the latter of these themes, that of the adaptation and the value of using NDP.

One of the key challenges faced by this project was that of recruitment. There are few dedicated services for people with young onset dementia, and, therefore, it can be challenging to find individuals or groups to promote this work with. We found a mixed approach, flexibility, and time were the most effective ways to reach our target group. As such, we delivered taster sessions and adapted our language around the use of arts and creativity to make the sessions more appealing and playful and to widen our geographical area of delivery. Consideration of time and location are key to engaging with this younger group, some of whom may still be at work, or find it difficult to access services before 10am, and require public transport to access venues. The choice of venue is also important, as this needs to be a space which encourages people to feel safe. Through our delivery, we worked in a room within a local repertory theatre and a space within a young-onset dementia service. Both had pros and cons, but both were accessible community venues that offered space for the participants to engage in a range of activities in a calm and quiet environment. While the physical space is important, space goes beyond this to create an atmosphere of trust and safety to enable people to be open to their creativity. As one participant reflected – 'obviously testament to the three of you [project leads], because you've created an environment that you felt comfortable in to open up.' The space is also what the group makes of it, and while the theatre venue, in particular, had a strong link to being creative and provided 'kudos' as one participant commented, it was also the way the group worked in the space that was important, it is what is done in the space and how people arrive in the space that helps to bring that creative spirit:

> I think because it was at the theatre, it's almost because that is a creative space, and I am not saying the room was particularly creative; we turned it into a creative space, didn't we?
>
> I don't think it particularly mattered because it's what you're, it's how your mindset is and the things you brought to it, and you know, you're thinking, you're not really thinking about what's there, you just think past that, don't you? Well, I did anyway . . . . As soon as you're stepping through the door, you're in a different head space, aren't you?'

Part of creating a space in which you can work creativity is also due to the materials and resources. This has partly to do with the quality of materials – paints, fabric, paper, etc. – but also the resources of the team delivering the sessions. How the team worked together was central to the success of the project, with each member prepared for the delivery, each monitoring and supporting the group, and working to the same ethos. This was picked up by the participants, who noted the way the session leaders worked together, providing a coherent and 'seamless' delivery. This can only come with planning, collaboration, and an agreed ethos to work with, which, basing the work on NDP, helped to provide.

> You have got it all planned in . . . . Sometimes one person would have led the whole session, . . . Even though I didn't really take it on board, but it seemed seamless. It was seamless from a participant point of view; there was no stop, start, or waiting around, like, 'What's happening now?' You know, I never felt that.

The NDP adaptation provided a theoretical underpinning for the project. This also enabled the team to align the project with the needs of those with young-onset dementia by using the EPR as the basis for this work. This supported the development of trust and a sense of security with participants, who were able to embrace being creative.

Through the creative activities, our participants were able to try different arts and test different ways to communicate through art. The use of the varied materials and approaches helped to provide stimulation and an exploration of what it means to be creative. This helped to build the social connections between the group members, enabling them to share experiences, connect with each other, and develop their sense of confidence and sense of self. The following comments show how this growing trust supported participation:

> [H]e [participant with dementia] was a bit anxious because he wasn't sure what is going to be happening, but the more we came, the more comfortable he became.
>
> [We] all worked together, like when we were all doing the poem and things, it was everybody's input that, that we're doing. You weren't doing it by yourself, and it was nice to have heard other people's opinions.
>
> I have made friendships, friendships, yes, and nice and, like, meeting [participant name], which I've never met before.

This sense of cohesion that developed was aided by the process of using NDP, especially with its focus on ritual. Each session had a similar framework, and each participant engaged in a welcome and a goodbye ritual to mark the start and end of sessions. NDP also provided a meaningful way to engage with the group, which was supported by using the EPR frame. Each activity had a clear objective that linked to one or all of embodiment, projection, and role, and these built over the weeks to lead our participants to the final week where they performed their own performance piece, having designed their own characters, story, props, and setting. This build-up across the weeks was noted by one participant, who commented on the 'gentle process' that allowed them to find meaning in the creative work and to gradually feel more and more comfortable each week in finding their own way through the sessions.

Participant 1: There was a meaning. We didn't sit down on day one, did we, and go, 'Right, at the end of week 10 we're going to do a performance.' We didn't do that.
Researcher 1: No, we worked up to it.
Participant 1: We did. It was how we worked up to it. It was really a kind of gentle process. Because I think if you'd have come in and said that [we] would have run a mile.

Finally, NDP's playfulness was a key element that helped the participants to engage; these were fun sessions that encouraged enjoyment and a light-heartedness that further encouraged people's engagement. This does not mean that people did not discuss or work on difficult subject matter, but that there were always moments of relief and playfulness to balance the sessions. As Sue Jennings writes: 'The use of sensory, rhythmic and dramatic playfulness of NDP assists the [individual] to reconnect with their capacity for healing play' (Jennings, 2012), and it was this healing play which was central to the way our participants engaged with this project.

Conclusion

The journey that we have been on with this pilot project over the last two years has, at times, been exciting and, at others, frustrating but tinged with moments of creativity and pure joy. Relationships have been formed, and support has been offered and received between group leaders, group members, and our expert panel. What the project has shown is that NDP, as a guiding principle, has both the flexibility and creativity built within it so that it can be used across diverse, difficult, and challenging populations across the lifespan.

As we have seen, people with young-onset dementia are in a uniquely challenging position from a diagnosis and support perspective. They fall between the gaps of both the general public and statutory service expectation of dementia as being a condition that only affects the old and the very old. Statutory services are not geared up in such a way to support such groups of people. Very limited research has been done in this field using creativity and the arts, and never before using NDP.

What this small pilot project has shown is that experienced facilitators with an understanding of NDP principles can work effectively with small groups of adults with young onset dementia and their family members and carers to offer supportive, creative, and fulfilling experiences using the arts, despite the many challenges this group of people face daily. It also has the potential to build and support the relationships the individuals have with their family members, carers, and support more generally groups of people with a diagnosis of young onset dementia together using the developmental creative processes that NDP offers at its core.

From everything that we have learnt, we very much hope to build on this project and develop a larger piece of work that will give even greater weight of evidence that NDP can be used across the life span and especially with groups such as people with young onset dementia who face challenges and difficulties on a daily basis.

We would very much like to thank Professor Sue Jennings for her undivided attention across the project and especially thank all our experts by experience and every group member and their family members and carers who supported us throughout the project.

References

Alzheimer's Research UK. (2024) *Prevalence and Incidence.* https://dementiastatistics. org/about-dementia/prevalence-and-incidence/

Alzheimer's Society. (2024) *Singing for the Brain.* https://www.alzheimers.org.uk/ get-support/your-dementia-support-services/singing-for-the-brain

Basting, A. (2022) *TimeSlips.* https://www.timeslips.org/

Bird, J., Bird, L. and Collard-Stokes, G. (2023) Social action art therapy and the enhancement of political imagination. *Journal of Applied Arts and Health*, 14, 47–61, March. https://doi.org/10.1386/jaah_00126_1

Braun, V. and Clarke, V. (2006) Using thematic analysis in psychology. *Qualitative Research in Psychology*, 3(2), 77–101. https://doi.org/10.1191/1478088706qp063oa

Brown, A., Page, T. E., Daley, S., Farina, N., Basset, T., Livingston, G., Budgett, J., Gallaher, L., Feeney, Y., Murray, J., Bowling, A., Knapp, M. and Banerjee, S. (2019) Measuring the quality of life of family carers of people with dementia: Development and validation of C-DEMQOL. *Quality of Life Research*, 28(8), 2299–2310.

Camic, P. M., Crutch, S. J., Murphy, C., Firth, N. C., Harding, E., Harrison, C. R., Howard, S., Strohmaier, S., Van Leewen, J., West, J. and Windle, G. (2018) Conceptualising and understanding artistic creativity in the dementias: Interdisciplinary approaches to research and practise. *Frontiers in Psychology*, 9, 1842, Online.

Carter, J. (2022) Prevalence of all cause young onset dementia and time lived with dementia: Analysis of primary care health records. *Journal of Dementia Care*, 30(3), 1–5.

Carter, J. E., Oyebode, J. R. and Koopmans, R. T. C. M. (2018) Young-onset dementia and the need for specialist care: A national and international perspective. *Aging & Mental Health*, 22(4), 468–473. https://doi.org/10.1080/13607863.2016.1257563

Collard-Stokes, G. and Irons, J. Y. (2022) Artist wellbeing: Exploring the experiences of dance artists delivering community health and wellbeing initiatives. *Research in Dance Education*, 23(1), 60–74. https://doi.org/10.1080/14647893.2021.1993176

Gerise, A. (1992) *Earthtales – Storytelling in Times of Change.* London: Green Print.

Glazer, G. (2024) *Alzheimer's Poetry Project.* https://www.alzpoetry.com/

Greenwood, N. and Smith, R. (2016) The experiences of people with young-onset dementia: A meta-ethnographic review of the qualitative literature. *Maturitas*, 92, 102–109. https://doi.org/10.1016/j.maturitas.2016.07.019

Hayo, H., Ward, A. and Parkes, J. (2018) *Young Onset Dementia: A Guide to Recognition, Diagnosis and Supporting Individuals with Dementia and Their Families.* London: Jessica Kingsley Publishers.

Hendriks, S., Peetoom, K., Bakker, C., Van Der Flier, W. M., Papma, J. M., Koopmans, R., Verhey, F. R., De Vugt, M., Köhler, S., Withall, A. and Parlevliet, J. L. (2021) Global prevalence of young-onset dementia: A systematic review and meta-analysis. *JAMA Neurology*, 78(9), 1080–1090. https://doi.org/10.1001/jamaneurol.2021.2161

Holmwood, C. (2021) Older people, dementia and neuro-dramatic-play: A personal and theoretical drama therapy perspective. *Drama Therapy Review*, 7(1), 61–75. https://doi.org/10.1386/dtr_00061_1

Holmwood, C. (2023) *Games for Building Secure Relationships in the Early Years.* Hinton House.

Jaaniste, J. (2016) Life stage and human development in dramatherapy with people who have dementia. In *Routledge International Handbook of Dramatherapy*, eds. Jennings, S. and Holmwood, C. London: Routledge, 262–271.

Jennings, S. (1993) *Play Therapy with Children: A Practitioners Guide.* Oxford: Blackwell Scientific.

Jennings, S. (Ed.) (2009) *Dramatherapy and Social Theatre – Necessary Dialogues.* London: Routledge.

Jennings, S. (2011) *Healthy Attachments and Neuro-Dramatic-Play.* London: Jessica Kingsley Publishers.

Jennings, S. (2012) *Neuro-Dramatic Play and Trauma: 'Towards Healing and Hope'*, collaboration with B. Braun Medical Industries Penang, Malaysia, Lai Fong Hwa and Mooli Lahad. Malaysia: B. Braun Medical Industries.

Jones, P. (1996) *Drama as Therapy Theatre as Life.* London: Bruner-Routledge.

Mayrhofer, A., Mathie, E., McKeown, J., Bunn, F. and Goodman, C. (2018) Age-appropriate services for people diagnosed with young onset dementia: A systematic review. *Ageing & Mental Health*, 22(8), 927–935.

Moiseyeva, D., Goodman, J., Heath, P., Harrison, L., Draper, C. and Astell, A. (2023) Together Stronger: A Creative Arts Program for Children of a Parent with Young Onset Dementia. *Alzheimer's Dement*, 19, e079990. https://doi.org/10.1002/alz.079990

Museum of Modern Art. (2024) *Meet Me. The MOMA Alzheimer's Project: Making Art Accessible to People with Dementia.* https://www.moma.org/visit/accessibility/meetme/

Palmiero, M., Di Giacomo, D. and Passafiume, D. (2012) Creativity, and dementia: A review. *Cognitive Processing*, 13, 193–209. https://doi.org/10.1007/s10339-012-0439-y

Pione, R. D., Spector, A., Cartwright, A. V. and Stoner, C. R. (2022) A psychometric appraisal of positive psychology outcome measures in use with carers of people living with dementia: A systematic review. *International Psychogeriatrics*, 33(4), 385–404. https://doi.org/10.1017/S1041610220003464

Rodda, J. and Carter, J. (2023) Highlighting the need for better care planning in young-onset dementia. *International Psychogeriatrics*, 35(9), 453–455, September. https://doi.org/10.1017/S1041610223000492. Epub 2023 Jun 1. PMID: 37259705.

Ross, S. D., Lachmann, T., Jaarsveld, S., Riedel-Heller, S. G. and Rodriguez, F. S. (2023) Creativity across the lifespan: Changes with age and with dementia. *BMC Geriatrics*, 23(1), 160, March 22. https://doi.org/10.1186/s12877-023-03825-1. Erratum in: *BMC Geriatrics*, 23(1), 307, May 17. https://doi.org/10.1186/s12877-023-03964-5. PMID: 36949404; PMCID: PMC10035174.

Smith, S. C., Lamping, D. L., Banerjee, S., Harwood, R., Foley, B., Smith, P., Cook, J. C., Murray, J., Prince, M., Levin, E., Mann, A. and Knapp, M. (2005) Measurement of health-related quality of life for people with dementia: Development of a new instrument (DEMQOL) and an evaluation of current methodology. *Health Technology Assessment*, 9(10), 1–93, iii–iv, March. https://doi.org/10.3310/hta9100. PMID: 15774233.

Stoner, C. R., Orrell, M. and Spector, A. (2018) The Positive Psychology Outcome Measure (PPOM) for people with dementia: Psychometric properties and factor structure. *Archives of Gerontology and Geriatrics*, 78, 204–212. https://doi.org/10.1016/j.archger.2018.06.004

Turtle Key Arts. (2024) *Turtle Song*. https://www.turtlekeyarts.org.uk/turtle-song

Ward, A. (2019) *Understanding Photography and Storytelling with People with Early-Stage Dementia to Understand Their Lived Experience and Enable Them to Tell Their Stories*. University of Northampton.

Ward, A., Schack Thoft, D., Lomax, H. and Parkes, J. (2018) A visual and creative approach to exploring people with Dementia's experiences of being students at a school in Denmark. *Dementia*. https://doi.org/10.1177/1471301218786636

World Health Organisation. (2024) *Dementia*. https://www.who.int/health-topics/dementia#tab=tab_2

Afterword

The momentum of *The Handbook of Neuro-Dramatic-Play*

Phil Jones

This book contains much that addresses and examines the current state of knowledge within Neuro-Dramatic-Play (NDP). Looked at from a slightly different perspective, many of the different chapters begin to anticipate new potentials and directions. This afterword aims to consider some of these and to build upon them: it explores the momentum present within this volume by identifying and then suggesting how these areas could further be developed. In the space afforded by a short afterword, it isn't feasible to go into detail: rather, I am going to use the space to form questions and sketch initial directions. These questions are:

- What dialogues can occur between different cultures of play and NDP?
- How can NDP further problematise and critique the 'development' element within its work?
- How can individual experiences contribute to wider knowledge within the field of NDP?
- How can NDP further enhance its engagement with, and empowerment, of participant responses and 'voices'?

What dialogues can occur between different cultures of play and NDP?

Chapters in this book address many contexts and how play, attachment, and development are being experienced by children, parents, adults, and those involved with them through different processes and professional roles. These vary from forensic settings (Chapter 15) to parent and child nature-based play therapy (Chapter 9), from water in art therapy (Chapter 8) to theatre of resilience for young adults (Chapter 6). One particular direction – of the reporting of play in NDP within different cultural contexts – is the momentum that this book is creating, and this seems a direction that can further be explored and critically engaged with. The chapters are based in,

DOI: 10.4324/9781003498209-23

or connect to, a variety of different cultures, for example, a junior school in the UK (Chapter 4); an early intervention service in India (Chapter 13); performance training in Greece (Chapter 12); and orphanages, or a Temiar village in Malaysia (Chapters 10 and 11): and we hear from the author-researchers about the different ways the play is experienced. Recent sources draw attention to the need to deepen reporting on play by developing analysis that involves particular kinds of reflective awareness and interconnection across and between cultural contexts. There are many ways that literature defines and problematises the 'cultural contexts' of play. In terms of developing this momentum within NDP, useful recent perspectives could be those of Van Oers (2019) and Courtois et al. (2024), as they help articulate questions for future research, indicating areas allied to NDP's concerns of becoming, as Jennings says in Chapter 1, 'more aware of the process of the drama theatre on our clients, and indeed on ourselves' (p. 9). Van Oers, for example, firstly positions culture and play as interconnected and complex, seeing:

> culture . . . as a family of historically developed expectations in the members of a community about acceptable varieties of acting in their community. These expectations are controlled, transmitted, maintained, and changed with the help of the shared cultural tools . . . within the context of cultural practices. Culture (i.e., its expectations about what is acceptable or not) is interactively represented in the ways of behaving of agents and most of the time implicit in current practices.
>
> (2019, p. 10)

He further argues that 'the study of the value of play and the relationship between culture and play, deepens the understanding and nature of enquiry and practice' *within* any culture and *between* cultures (2019, p. 10). Courtois et al. (2024) add a dimension to this that also holds potential for further NDP enquiry. Discussing the futures of research connected to play, they argue that 'play research' needs better to 'adapt to the places it seeks to understand, rather than map onto them foreign understandings as though they were universal' (2024, p. 246). The values of this include greater cultural awareness and responsiveness in order to benefit participants and deepen their facilitators' engagement. A future need and potential, they suggest, is to build questions and enquiry that attempt to identify, comprehend and respond to the 'complexity of the context: how the culture but also the social and economic disparities, drive differences in how play is valued and understood' (2024, p. 246). NDP might fruitfully build on this book's reporting of different contexts by developing these areas further. For example, future research could question and explore the ways in which NDP knowledge can be widened by examining parallels and differences, within and between, cultures concerning play and, in particular, play's varied contextual relationships to development, attachment, and neuro-dramatic-play. The following diagram summarises this potential direction:

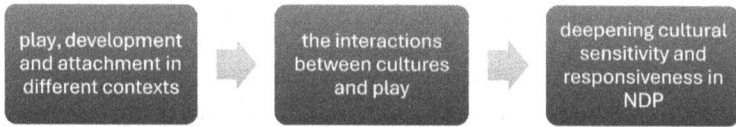

play, development and attachment in different contexts	➡	the interactions between cultures and play	➡	deepening cultural sensitivity and responsiveness in NDP

Figure Afterword.1 What dialogues can occur between different cultures of play and NDP?

How can NDP further problematise and critique the 'development' element within its work?

One of the challenges for any philosophy, theory, practice or model, such as NDP, that is based on development, is that it is situated within the histories and contemporary forces that affect how development is conceived of, understood, performed, or used. Often, development is drawn on with little or no reflective awareness of critique, for example (McDonald and O'Callaghan, 2008). Chapters in this book begin to explore a more nuanced engagement with how 'development' features in neuro-dramatic-play. They approach it – not as some neutral, 'useful' paradigm – but as something that is constructed in particular ways – and that these ways are different and varied, changing and changeable. For example, Chapter 2 explores its emergent, positive potential in dialogue with the new societal and psychological contexts of surrogacy and same-sex couples.

This means that 'development' is something that can be *critiqued*: this position makes it visible in ways that do not occur when those engaging with it simply draw on the concept and do not critically reflect on it. Particular disciplines and the dynamics at work in relation to certain professions do not encourage such questioning and reflexivity. For example, in many societies, the domain of mental health and psychological development is often presented by professionals and by researchers allied to health and education as unexamined certainties, with individual humans who differ from these norms being treated as 'deficits', rather than as individuals with differences (McDonald and O'Callaghan, 2008; van Zyl et al., 2023). An approach rooted in seeing development as constructed offers awareness that it is saturated in assumptions that are time and culture-specific and contain choices – a particular *version* of development, rather than an unexamined, neutral given. This more nuanced, critical perspective, building on the questioning within some of this book's chapters, would enable NDP to make visible and explore interconnected questions such as:

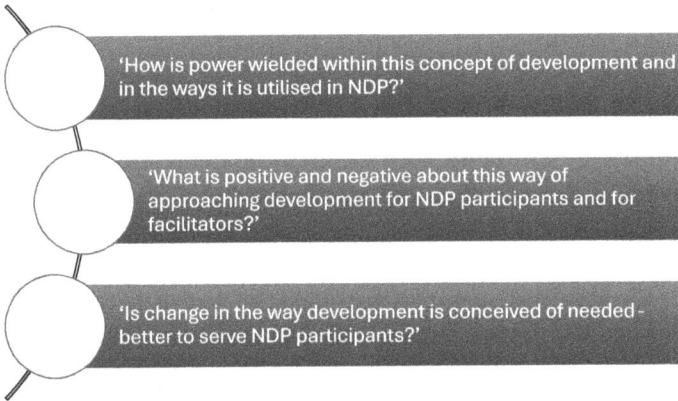

'How is power wielded within this concept of development and in the ways it is utilised in NDP?'

'What is positive and negative about this way of approaching development for NDP participants and for facilitators?'

'Is change in the way development is conceived of needed – better to serve NDP participants?'

Figure Afterword.2 Interconnected questions

Such attention enables us to examine how assumptions positively or negatively impact the people we work with, or whether the way development is understood and drawn on in practice needs to change better to respond to participants or clients. Within this book, there are many thoughtful and detailed examples of how development in NDP is being applied and offered. Some chapters, in particular, start to explore how development is not a given or constant and how contexts, a client's or participant's individual journey, are illuminated by the ways therapists or facilitators try to be as sensitive as possible to their *individuality*. Additionally, chapters illustrate well the importance of the individuality of the professional: they are *not* applying a monolithic, learned procedure – deliverers of a template of processes and activities that remove their individuality and creativity as facilitators. When looked at in this way, questions for future work in NDP can be formulated that assist in deepening awareness of the contextual nuances of development, which we might not initially see because we are too enmeshed within a set of assumptions. To me, this is a particularly rich area and dynamic to address – and one that this book gestures towards. The following diagram illustrates one way this momentum could further be realised:

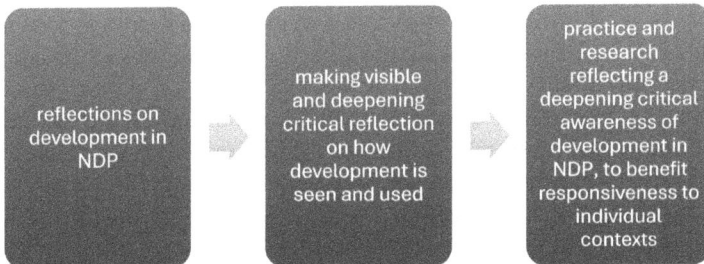

reflections on development in NDP

making visible and deepening critical reflection on how development is seen and used

practice and research reflecting a deepening critical awareness of development in NDP, to benefit responsiveness to individual contexts

Figure Afterword.3 NDP and development

How can individual experiences contribute to wider knowledge in NDP?

(i) Could the momentum of the knowledge being created by the many individual accounts of practice be developed by dialogue with particular ideas about 'case study'?

Different chapters contain many thoughtful and detailed accounts of practices and include a variety of means of seeing, and reporting, the work involved. A future direction for *some* practice might be to create dialogue between such individualistic approaches to recording and reporting within the chapters and recent arguments about the importance of developing case studies that reflect particular kinds of rigour and recording in research. There are different approaches to this but, for NDP, further exploration could involve developing accounts of practice which aim to enable dialogue between an individual facilitator's reporting and concepts and approaches linked to particular ways of seeing and communicating 'evidence'. One example might be designing and presenting practice in ways that form a 'case study'. McQuaid et al. (2023) might be a helpful support for further developing this dimension of NDP. They draw on a variety of sources to define and critique what a 'case study' is, to examine how it is useful, as well as reviewing what can most helpfully be included within case study design and reporting to assist in making cross-study understandings of 'value' and 'impact'. Drawing on Flyvbjerg (2006), Stake (1995), and Yin (2018), they define a case study as enabling descriptions that are rich in detail and depth, involving the study of the particularity and complexity of a single case, whilst coming to understand its work within particular circumstances and, often, drawing on multiple sources of data for triangulation (McQuaid et al., 2023, p. 8). These are complex areas, and a short afterword does not leave room for this – but, relevant to NDP, might be the further development of creating recordings as effective case study material to understand and communicate work and its impact. McQuaid et al.'s (2023) position echoes that of Keiller et al. (2023) on dramatherapy, in arguing that for a case study to be fully useful in such endeavour, it needs to include particular dimensions such as context, participant details, data collection methods and approach to analysis. This enables the case study to be usefully drawn on in building communal insights from the momentum of single studies. The work reported on within this volume might connect, then, to McQuaid et al., building on Yin (2018), as they argue that 'the accumulation of case studies may offer greater rigour, reliability and external validity of findings as a larger dataset is created' (2023, p. 13). They argue for a future 'valued position' to capture 'both the depth and breadth of practice':

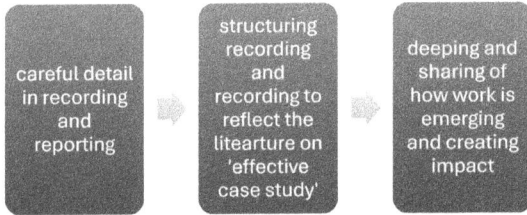

Figure Afterword.4 How can a case study approach contribute to wider knowledge in NDP?

Collecting and pooling case study research data from practice can capture these important elements and allow for pattern matching or synthesis. In this way, case study research can hold value for evidence building, just as the randomized controlled trial, or other larger-scale inquiry, does for generalizability with the potential to inform policy and practice.

(p. 13)

The thoughtful descriptions of work contained in this volume and the desire to understand and communicate the effect of work can, perhaps, be further developed by dialogue with such arguments and sources.

(ii) Could the momentum of the knowledge being created be further enriched by deepening attention to individual participant responses as challenges to help develop NDP theory?

McQuaid et al. also notes the importance of paying attention to 'why' an approach or 'intervention may not be working as expected' when reporting and analysing practice (2023, p. 13). Does the experience purely support the position of key texts and ideas – or is it possible to positively problematise the literature as a result of the work with participants? For example, there is a great deal of material in this volume that, rightly, shows how effective and useful the theory of NDP is and how the work with the client or participant simply illuminates this. However, only in a few instances do chapters reflect on how the experiences with participants modified, challenged, or created insights to modify those theories and beliefs about how change is created and held by the practitioner before their encounters with participants. Chapter 7, for example, fascinatingly records such a process whereby 'V' does not always accept the potential offered by his play therapist:

If I offered any props such as emotions cards these were quickly rejected. I did use commentary on his activities and some simple reflections and although I felt there was more understanding there than it might at first appear, he seldom responded.

(p. 82)

The inclusion of such details and building insight from them might helpfully be connected with the values of reflection on whether there is a danger of 'confirmation bias' – where researchers may 'evaluate evidence that supports their prior belief differently from that apparently challenging these convictions' (Kaptchuk, 2003, p. 1453). Olmos-Vega et al. (2022) have advocated an essential aspect of discussion of data in qualitative research to acknowledge the individuality of responses and to take into the act of reflection processes that are sensitive to the value of *dissent* or *divergence of response* from the professional's or researcher's expectations. They argue that 'discussion should reflect researchers' active interpretive work . . . this should not simply be an exercise of finding means of confirming the researchers' interpretations. Instead, we argue that seeking out and presenting' aspects of responses 'that might challenge researchers' interpretations' and that this 'constitutes important personal and methodological reflexive work' (2023, p. 248). An area to develop might be the ways in which the theory and framework of NDP are changed and modified by experiences that are *not* confluent with expectation and which stimulate change or develop new directions of the model and ideas drawn on by the facilitator. Achterberg and Vanderschuren (2023) have identified future questions for the field of neurobiology of social play behaviour to address – and it seems to me that NDP can be well positioned to explore how its insights into and between individual responses and experiences can build across examples of practice to contribute to changes and new developments in knowledge. For example, Achterberg and Vanderschuren indicate one such area of needed enquiry:

As the abundance and structure of social play changes from weaning to adulthood, do the underlying neural mechanisms change too? It is plausible to think that the answer is yes, but as far as our knowledge goes, there are no studies that have explicitly addressed this question. Clearly,

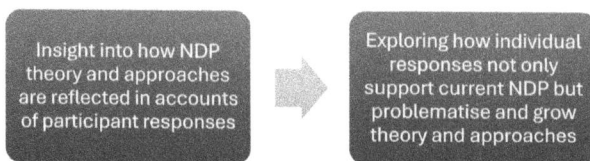

Insight into how NDP theory and approaches are reflected in accounts of participant responses

Exploring how individual responses not only support current NDP but problematise and grow theory and approaches

Figure Afterword.5 How can individual experiences contribute to wider knowledge in NDP?

information about the – changing – neurobiology of social play during development is likely to inform about its relevance and function as well.
(Achterberg and Vanderschuren, 2023, p. 23)

This seems to be a dynamic implicit in the book that could be powerfully built on by those involved – as a way of reflecting in supervision on practice with clients and with peers and in the process of reflecting upon and reporting research.

How can NDP further enhance its engagement with, and empowerment of, participant responses and 'voices'?

An emerging area in many areas related to NDP – of health, care, play, and education, for example, concerns how participant 'voices' are included and engaged with, how experiences are encountered, silenced, or listened to and taken into emergent discourse and practices.

Observation and care in reflection through training, note-taking, reflective supervision, and careful reflection on the meanings of what is experienced by the worker are important. However, recent developments in a number of fields are transforming how provision is being designed, practiced, and researched – with an emphasis on methods that work with participants differently. These include approaches carefully designed to access the experiences, evaluation, and views of those involved in services, rather than judgement of participant experience, impact, and meaning being the domain solely of the professional. The term 'voice' is often used in relation to these areas: 'a concept which describes an individual's capacity for self-expression, self-insight and agency' (Jones et al., 2020, p. xxii) and can involve verbal or arts-based communication. Finlay summarises an aspect of this process where researchers and practitioners are questioning ways of working and reporting that rely on professional accounts solely or only include their interpretation of material expressed through clients' physical expressions or artifacts without 'member checking', or a sense of ambiguity or the provisional about their interpretation. This developing approach is typified by:

> Researchers who take interpretivist paths and embrace more relativist positions that eschew the representational 'truth'. . . . These researchers are more explicitly creative, artful and/or reflexive. They use dialogical exchanges with participants to uncover (latent) meanings and, in their analysis, they try to make their interpretive process transparent.
> (2021, p. 104)

Munroe and Gauvain (2010) have noted that cross-cultural research concerning children tends to see them and work with them as 'passive recipients'.

Courtois et al. argue that such approaches in play-related practices tend to silence children:

> Evidence thus tends to come from parent reports and interviews, rather than from children themselves, and even when children are interviewed, questions tend to be centred on the researcher's ideas of what is important to childhood, rather than the children's.
>
> (Courtois et al., 2024, p. 245)

They situate this in recent approaches that approach children as actively constructing their knowledge and as full participants in their culture, arguing that 'cultural sensitivity in different contexts should start with children, not imposing foreign ideas of play but starting with the children's own play' (Courtois et al., pp. 245–246).

To ask a blunt verbal or written evaluative question may well be inappropriate in terms of the capacities of those involved or the process and language within the session, and chapters in this book demonstrate awareness of the potential of other approaches to this aspect of NDP research and practice. There are some fascinating examples in this book of facilitators being sensitive in their interpretations of creative and play work and the verbal, facial, or bodily expressions of those they work with in terms of how these might communicate or express feedback. Chapter 16, for example, has 'reflection' as part of the structure of sessions alongside the design and selection by each participant of a creative 'toolkit' to reflect on the work and to build bridges between the experience of NDP and their life outside (p. 227), Chapter 9, records how Hunter gives feedback verbally on the experience of his play experiences in nature – 'I still have this place that I can come back to' (p. 110). Chapters 5 and 2 interpret eye contact, bodily expressions, and responses to puppets or play objects as encounters that involve participant response and feedback. Some of the chapters begin to gesture towards participant and facilitator understanding the experience *together*, involving feedback on the process of the whole provision or the view of the participant on their overall experience of the NDP work. Recent research outside of NDP (Jones et al., 2020; Wall and Robinson, 2022) has developed much knowledge of this process and dialogue with such work on facilitating and responding to participants' 'voice' and their views could be fruitful. By innovating approaches that draw on play and the arts, further

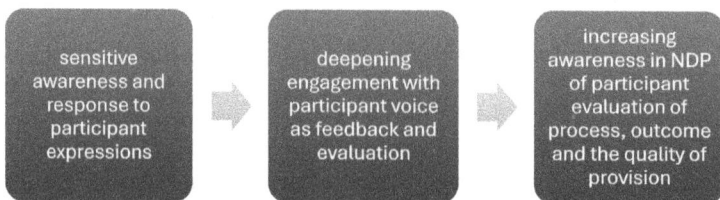

Figure Afterword.6 How can NDP further enhance its engagement with, and empowerment of participant responses and 'voices'?

expansion of the work of this book could form an exciting potential. NDP practice, accessing participant feedback and, for example, including some sense of whether there is any change in provision needed as a response to such feedback, could fruitfully be developed. The following diagram summarises this potential direction:

Conclusion

In their recent contribution to the *Neuroscience and Behavioural Review* concerning pretend play and development, Gleason and White identify 'future directions', noting that:

> While the preponderance of evidence reviewed here links pretend play and abstraction to development in the cognitive, emotional, and social domains, we are cognisant of both the lack of research demonstrating causal links between such play and child outcomes as well as the small samples and lack of replication of many of the findings presented here.
>
> (2023, p. 9)

The work within this volume is aligned with this consideration of future direction and connects to the concerns they identify: developing insight, building our knowledge and understanding, and exploring dimensions such as causality or replication. However, I think the view of future potentials within the chapters of 'The Handbook of Neuro-Dramatic-Play' is broader and richer than that identified by Gleason and White – and I hope that this afterword has articulated some of those: – exploring the dynamics between different cultures of play; examining development critically; looking at how individual experience can build upon and problematise 'given' assumptions; and how participants' voices can contribute to NDP knowledge.

Phil Jones PhD

Emeritus Professor of Children's Rights and Wellbeing, IOE, UCL's Faculty of Education and Society. Author of many books on children's rights and on the arts in health and therapy including' Child Agency and Voice in Therapy' (Routledge 2021) and 'Drama as Therapy' (Routledge 2007).

References

Achterberg, E. J. M. and Vanderschuren, L. J. M. J. (2023) The neurobiology of social play behaviour: Past, present and future, *Neuroscience & Biobehavioral Reviews*, 152(1), 1–28.

Courtois, S. L., Ezeugwu, C. R., Fajardo-Tovar, D. D., Nowack, Domnick, S. K., Okullo, O., Bayley, S., Baker, S. and Ramchandani, P. (2024) Learning through play in global majority countries: Reflections from the PEDAL centre on understanding and adapting the concept in four different contexts. *International Journal of Play*, 13(3), 228–253. https://doi.org/10.1080/21594937.2024.2388952

Finlay, L. (2021) Thematic analysis: The 'good', the 'bad' and the 'ugly'. *European Journal of Qualitative Psychology*, 11(1), 103–116.

Flyvbjerg, B. (2006) Five misunderstandings about case-study research. *Qualitative Inquiry*, 12(2), 2019–2245. https://doi.org/10.1177/1077800405284363

Gleason, T. R. and White, R. E. (2023) Pretend play as abstraction: Implications for early development and beyond. *Neuroscience & Biobehavioral Reviews*, 147(1), 105090, ISSN 0149-7634.

Jones, P., Cedar, L., Coleman, A., Haythorne, D., Merceica, D. and Ramsden, E. (2020) *Child Agency and Voice in Therapy: New Ways of Working in the Arts Therapies*. London: Routledge.

Kaptchuk, T. J. (2003) Effect of interpretive bias on research evidence. *British Medical Journal*, 326(1), 1453.

Keiller, E., Tjasink, M., Bourne, J., Ougrin, D., Carr, C. E. and Lau, J. Y. F. (2023) A systematic review of dramatherapy interventions used to alleviate emotional distress and support the well-being of children and young people aged 8–18 years old. *JCPP Advances*, 3(3), e12145. https://doi.org/10.1002/jcv2.12145

McDonald, M. and O'Callaghan, J. (2008) Positive psychology: A Foucauldian critique. *The Humanistic Psychologist*, 36(2), 127–142. https://doi.org/10.1080/08873260802111119

McQuaid, L., Thomson, K. and Bannigan, K. (2023) Exploring the contribution of case study research to the evidence base for occupational therapy: A scoping review. *Systematic Review*, 12(1), 132. https://doi.org/10.1186/s13643-023-02292-4

Munroe, R. L. and Gauvain, M. (2010) The cross-cultural study of children's learning and socialization: A short history. In *The Anthropology of Learning in Childhood*, eds. D. F. Lancy, J. Bock and S. Gaskins, 35–63. AltaMira Press.

Olmos-Vega, F. M., Stalmeijer, R. E., Varpio, L. and Kahlke, R. (2022) A practical guide to reflexivity in qualitative research: AMEE guide no. 149. *Medical Teacher*, 45(3), 241–251. https://doi.org/10.1080/0142159X.2022.2057287

Stake, R. E. (1995) *The Art of Case Study Research*. Thousand Oaks: Sage Publications.

van Oers, B. (2019) Culture in play. In *The Oxford Handbook of Culture and Psychology*, ed. Valsiner, J. Oxford: Oxford University Press.

van Zyl, L. E., Gaffaney, J., van der Vaart, L., Dik, B. J. and Donaldson, S. I. (2023) The critiques and criticisms of positive psychology: A systematic review. *The Journal of Positive Psychology*, 19(2), 206–235. https://doi.org/10.1080/17439760.2023.2178956

Wall, K. and Robinson, C. (2022) Look who's talking: Eliciting the voice of children from birth to seven. *European Early Childhood Education Research Journal*, 1(1), 1–7.

Yin, R. K. (2018) *Case Study Research and Applications: Design and Methods*. Thousand Oaks: Sage.

Index

Numbers in **bold** indicate a table. Numbers in *italics* indicate a figure. Numbers that are <u>underlined</u> indicate a box.

Achterberg, M. 240
ACT model (Acknowledge, Communicate, Target)107
addictive conditions 10
ADHD *see* Attention Deficit Hyperactivity Disorder
adoption 14, 19
Aegean Sea 144
aesthetic integration 58–60, <u>62</u>; EPR framework for 58–60
Argyraki, E. 13, 15; *see also* performativity
ASD *see* autism spectrum disorder
AEON program 15
Afghanistan 76
African theatre, postcolonial: NDP and 170–181; *see also Agbo Play*
Agbo Play: aesthetics of 170; Cowfoot 173–176, 178; Imùlè Theatre and 170, 171–172; Ayo (Ayodele Scott) and 170–176, 178–179; Ayo's mother 173; Kriolisation and the aesthetics of 176–177, 180; NDP and 174–176, 180; see also **Native Wit** (*Agbo Play*)
agbos (play spaces) 176, 180–181
Alzheimer's Disease 219–220
Alzheimer's Poetry Project 221
anxiety 14, 25, 32, 88; anticipatory 158; in children 155; COVID-19 and 39, 41, 161; fear/anxiety, as motivator to take action 57; feelings of 167; Hunter's feelings of 106; NDP's capacity to provoke 180; separation 17, 158, 161; social 45, 188; using VR to address 133
anxiety-based school avoidance 39; *see also* Emotionally Based School Avoidance (EBSA)
anxiety loop, anxiety isolation loop 40, *40*
Art Therapy 3; case study (Anna, an adult) 97–101; case study (Poppy) 93–97; contemporary trauma-informed 88; Dyadic model of 93; EPR and 90; interoception and 91; traditional 91; use of water in NDP-informed AT 87–101
attachment: addiction and 10; distorted 10; EPR and early play and 6; individual and social 9; loss of 10; Messy Play and 7; NDP paradigm based on 154; positive, developing of post-COVID 32–43; unhealthy 13; *see also* bonding
attachment-based play 9–11, 23; NDP as methodology of 116
attachment-based intervention: NDP as 142
attachment-based research project 223
attachment development 23
attachment difficulties 41
attachment disorder 43n13
attachment issues 10, 189
attachment-play intervention: NDP as 24
attachment story: Moose and Mouse get Muddy! 10–11, 12n1, 166

attachment theory 5, 75; NDP's association with 224; tenets of 104

Attention Deficit Hyperactivity Disorder (ADHD) 153; case study (Jim) 18; Jennings' own diagnosis of 5; as manifestation of neurodiversity 26–27; NPD for 27–29; subcategories of 26

autism 14, 43n13; children with 40; McClain (James) diagnosis of 109; as "special" 108

Autism Parenting Magazine 40

Autism Spectrum Conditions 154

autism spectrum disorder (ASD) 153: case study (George) 15–16; case study (Jim) 17–19; case study (Hunter) 104–105, 107–109; case study (John) 16–17

autistic children 40, 41, 105; *All My Stripes* story about 109

Ayres, J. 154

Bailey [no last name] 214–215

Bailey, S. 59

balloons, use in therapy of 49–50

bed-wetting 28, 92

Berry, C.: *Voice and the Actor* 150

Bilateral Body Mapping 91

Body Mapping *see* Bilateral Body Mapping

Bolton, G. 3

bonding: early, between infants and parents 104; early, between mothers and (unborn) babies 9, 218; Nesting Circle and 168; group 149

bongos and tambourines 51

Botting, N. 39

Bowlby, J. 5, 89

Bradley [no last name] 214

Brain Play 8

Braithwaite, J. 215

Braun, K. 106

Brechtian narration 61

British Association of Dramatherapists 33

British National Health Service 32

Bryson, T. P. 89

CAMHS *see* Child and Adolescent Mental Health Services

Carroll, B. 45, 51; *see also* relational safety; Wellbeing Program

CBT *see* Cognitive Behavioral Therapy

CF *see* Children First

Chaplin, C. 178–179

'Child Drama' (Slade) 33–34

Child and Adolescent Mental Health Services (CAMHS)(UK) 33

Children First (CF) India 153–169; Connect Model at 154, 168–169; NDP at 153–155, 161, 168; employing NDP principles in the pedagogy of 162–165; Nesting Circle at 168; NPD during COVID-lockdown at 156–161; NPD as COVID-lockdown ended and in-person learning resumed 161–162; a story about 168–169; Supervision Sessions of 165–167

circles of containment, care, and attachment 79

Clay Field 91

clay figures 68

Cognitive Behavioral Therapy (CBT) 187–188, 201, 202

Collard-Stokes, G. 223; *see also* dementia

collective: journey of learning in a collective in the context of COVID-19 153–169; *see also* Children First (CF)

Colors of Life session 192–193

coming-of-age ritual(s): case example 62; creating 69–70; designing and enacting 66; expanded EPR framework and theatre of resilience for young adults in response to social trauma and 53–73; personal, creating of 65–66, 69; *see also* rituals

connection to inner mysteries *see* inner mysteries

Cori, It Takes a Village (Carroll) 51

Courtney, R. 9

Courtois, S. L. 235, 242

COVID-19: Annie 36, 37; impact on children's education and social development of 37–39; impact on UK schools of 37–38; journey of learning in a collective in the context of 153–169; school absences in the wake of 39; using NDP in schools with children and young people post-Covid-19 32–43

creative arts 40, 41; dementia and 221–222; NDP and 43, 224
cultural considerations 205; displacement and 76–78
cultural contexts, of play 235
cultural ineptitude 173
cultural sensitivity 242
cyberbullying 32
Cyclades 144; *see also* Naxos

Dagher, R. 187
daydreaming 26
dementia 13, 28, 206; building bonds using play between caregivers and people with 223–227; creative arts and 221–222; overview of 219; younger-onset dementia and 219–221; *see also* young-onset dementia
Dementia UK 223
depression 41, 220; perinatal 185, 186, 187, 202; peripartum 187; postpartum 104
Devine-Wright, P. 75
disintegrative shaming 215
displacement 76–77, 158, 176
dissent 240
distorted attachment 10
distorted parenting 5
divergence of response 240
drama: child 33; 'for real' 9, 146
drama-making process 3
drama studio, Naxos 149
drama teacher 5
drama theatre 9, 235
Dramatherapists (dramatherapists): Holmwood 223; Jaaniste 222; Jennings 218; Krasanakis and Argyraki 13; Ng 56; Western 3
Dramatherapy (dramatherapy) 3–4, 219; child drama as form of 33; EPR paradigm for 5; in Greece 13; *Handbook of Dramatherapy* (Jennings) 34; Jennings and 33; NPD and 6, 34; Slade and 33; young adult dramatherapy across Four Seasons in Hong Kong 62–63, 63–66
Dramatherapy Institute 15
Drama Therapy Pie 59
Dramatic Play (dramatic play)(also Interactive Play) 6, 8, 13, 14, 28, 148; attachment and 10; attachment

as 10; as part of Neuro Dramatic Play 23, 28; puppet play and 8; on taking on the role of other (via Dramatic Play) 51; therapeutic effect of storytelling in 18
dramatic playfulness 5
dramatic process 148
drama work 3, 4, 161
drawing 27, 66; collage 68; finger painting and (Anna) 98; free drawing 67; sessions with K incorporating art and 159
dreamcatchers 201
dressing up 8, 90
DSM-5 187
dyspraxia 153, 161

EAP *see* European Association of Psychotherapies
early bonding between mothers and babies 9
early infant development 5
Early Child Development (early child development) 6, 9, 92
early childhood trauma 34
EBSA *see* Emotionally Based School Avoidance
embodied: approaches to dementia 222; art making 101; experience(s) 105, 109, 116, 122; play 41, 219, 174–175, 177, 219; sense of self 10; storytelling 171, 173; techniques 91; work 42
embodiment 34; NDP and 45
Embodiment Projection Role (EPR): aesthetic integration and 58–60; age range for 34; creativity and 39; developmental paradigm of 4–6; "E," "P," and "R" in 34; Dramatic Play and 51; in Early Child Development 9; expanded EPR framework and theatre of resilience for young adults in response to social trauma 53–73; how it can be used in schools post-COVID-19 40–42; Hunter's journey using 104–110; Jenning's definition of 53, 90; Jenning's development of 4–6, 34; Jenning's paradigm of 82; Jenning's positioning of EPR and NDP as Theatre of Body 82; and NDP and 34, 54; NDP stages using 27; paradigm of 82, 87; place

in schools for 42–43; purpose of
39; reversal of 222; second stage 27;
story-based 37; supervision sessions
using 166; tactical principles in
using EPR with young adults 60–66,
67–70
Emergency Shakespeare 206–214
Emotionally Based School Avoidance
(EBSA) 39
empathy **90**, 181; authentic 132;
building 131; development of 27;
Emergency Shakespeare and 212;
EPR and 166; healthy bonding and
104; genuine 132; lack of 45; NPD
and 143; recovery and 119; rhythmic
play and 175; showing 8; of Temiar
children 140; therapeutic virtue
of 133
EPR *see* Embodiment-Projection-Role
Erikson, E. 5, 48, 81, 89; *Identity,
Youth and Crisis* 5
European Association of
Psychotherapies (EAP) 13
Evans, D. ("D"): autoethnographic
account of NDP/African theatre and
friendship with Ayo 170–181
Exploratory Play 8

face-heart connection 46, 52
face-to-face: education 39, 42;
interaction 38; sessions 162
Farmer, M. (Lord) 206
Finlay, L. 241
Flyvbjerg, B. 238
Fox, J. 3
free drawing 67
Freetown, Sierra Leone 170, 171, 173

Gabriel (angel) 3
Gary [no last name] 213, 214
Gauvain, M. 241
Gersie, A. 218–219
Gifford, R. 75, 86
Gleason, T. 243
Good Enough Attachments session
198–199
Gooding, L. 26
Greece: Dramatherapy in 13; NDP and
performance in 143–144; NDP and
performance training in 142–152; *see
also* Naxos
Gyra, A. 151

Handbook of Neuro-Dramatic-Play (on
the momentum and future of NDP):
how can NDP further enhance its
engagement with and empowerment
of participant responses and 'voices'?
234, 241–242, *242*; how can
individual experiences contribute
to wider knowledge in NDP? 234,
238–240, *239, 240*; how can NDP
further problematise and critique
the 'development' element within
its work? 234, 236–237, *237*;
interconnected questions for *237*;
momentum and future of NDP
234–243; what dialogues can occur
between different cultures of play and
NDP? 234–236, *236*
Heathcote, D. 3
Henricks, T. 177
Henry, L. 39
Hide and Seek 8, 26, 107, 108
HMP Leicester's Talent Unlocked
Festival 204
Holmwood, C. 223
Hong Kong 56–57; EPR and theatre of
resilience for young adults in 53–70;
existential challenges faced by young
adults in 66; self-expression via the
arts in 63; session plan for final
session working with young adults in
(outlined in 8 stages) 67–70; young
adult dramatherapy in 62–63, 63–66;
see also young adults in Hong Kong
Hunter Heartbeat method 207
Hunter, K. 207
Hunter (a child)'s journey: ACT model
applied in 107; case study using NDP
and EPR 104–110
Hunter's mother: ACT model followed
by 107; bedtime and other routines
se by 109; as "Mummy bird"
108; nurturing of Hunter by 106;
postpartum depression of 104;
voicing of wishes for her son 105
hybridity 56–57
hyperactive daydreamer 26
hyperactivity 26
hyperactivity/inattention 38
hypermasculinity 205

inner dialogue **68–69**
inner mysteries 65, 66, **68–69**

integration: aesthetic 58–60, <u>62</u>;
coming-of-age ritual for 65;
communal <u>62</u>; dialectical 59; need
for 91; of NDP with Therapeutic
Metaverse 133–134; (psychological)
89; Sensory 143, 154, 156; societal
57; strategic 63
Integration therapy 154
interoception 91
Interpersonal Psychotherapy (IPT) 187,
188, 201–202
IPT *see* Interpersonal Psychotherapy
Iran 56
Israel 56

Jaaniste, J. 222
Jack, G. 76
Jennings, S. 15, 89, 155; on building
an emotional relationship with the
unborn 188; Dramatherapy and 33;
EPR as defined by **90**; *Handbook
of Dramatherapy* 34; *Healthy
Attachments and Neuro Dramatic
Play* 13, 34; "Managing Social
Anxiety in Children and Young
People" 188; as mother of Andy
Hickson 135, 140; Nesting Principle
of 46; NDP paradigm of 35; PhD
work among Temiar people by
135; as pioneer of Play Therapy 33;
Play Therapy with Children 34; on
pregnant women enjoying pregnancy
188; on taking on the role of other
(via Dramatic Play) 51; on Theatre of
Resilience 64, 82; on working with
puppets 47; *see also* Embodiment
Projection Role

Kagin, S. 89
Keiller, E. 238
Kinitras Studio and Performing Arts
Network, Greece 151

Landreth's Rule of Thumb 78
Lara, M. A. 186
Lester, K. J, 39
Living as a Symphony session 193–194
Low, K. 185
Lusebrink, V. B. 89

maladaptive behavior 187
Malaysian jungle *see* Temiar people

Malaysian orphanages: assessing goals
and needs of children in 121; children
in 118–119; companionship and
empathy of psychotherapists working
with 130–132; empowering children
with autonomy in 132–133; journey
of empowerment for children in
119–120; NDP in orphanages in
115–134; owning and alienation
128–130; practical considerations
and ethics of working with children
in 128–133; sample of planned
sessions with **124–126**; termination
of sessions with 123–127; therapeutic
sessions for children in 121–123;
transformative power of NDP for
children in 127–128
Malchiodi, C. 90, 91
Maldonado-Durán, J. 180
Manchester Camerata 221
mandala layout *197*
Mandala of Motherhood session
196–198, 199
Manzo, L. 75
Mary Magdalene 3
mask making 51, **124**, *130*, 167
masks (psychological) 118
masks (theatrical) 27, 51, 59, 145, 165
Mask Work *164*
McCarthy, D. 81
McClain, J. 109
McQuaid, L. 238–239
memory: ADHD and 26; dramatic play
and 14, 177; music and memory
project (Manchester Camerata) 221;
performing Emergency Shakespeare
and 214; poignant 127; trauma
and 88; traumatic 90; young-onset
dementia and 220
mental health 236; behaviorally-based
concerns 77; of children and young
people post-COVID-19 32–43; NDP
and 142; NDPP and 143; of pregnant
womens 185–187; of young adults
53–54, <u>62</u>, 66, 70
mental health services 53
Messy Play 6, 7, 10, *164*; between
therapist and client 14; case study
(Jim) and 17; Dramatic Play and 13;
Monster 7; NDP and 23, 27, 28, 34,
45; Outdoor Play and 8; teenagers
and 24

Michael 215
Michealson, D. 39
mime and miming 59, **61**, 171, 176, 178, 179
mimicry 6, 8, 128; before language 5
Minotaur 144, 150
Monkey King **125–126**, 127, 138–139
Monster Messy Play 7
Monster Projection (storytelling) **125**
monsters 35, 80; the Monkey King against 138; puppets as 151
morality 104
morality plays 3
Motherhood a Journey session 200–201
Motherhood a Landscape session *195*, 195–196
movement, in *movement, sound, storytelling and silence* 91
Mummer's plays 3
Mummy (mother) bird 108
Munroe, R. L. 241
Myanmar 56
mysteries *see* inner mysteries
mystery plays 3
mythology 65, **67**

Narradrama practices 201
Native Wit (*Agbo Play*) 170, 172–174, 176; 'Cowboys and Nigerians' scene 178–179
Naxos: adventure of journeying to 151; NDP on 144–145, 147, 148, 149, 152
NDP *see* Neuro-Dramatic-Play
NDPP *see* Neuro-Dramatic-Play and Performance
Nesting session 194–195; *see also* Nurture and Nesting (NaN)
nesting and breathing 49
Nesting Circle 167–168
Nesting Principle 46
Nesting Tree *108*
neurobiology 88, 153; of social play behavior 240
neurodivergence 45, 50, 155; NDP and 23–31
neurodiversity: defining 23
Neuro-Dramatic-Play (NDP) 87
Neuro-Dramatic-Play (NDP): application(s) of 24–25; as attachment-play intervention 24; basics of 1; CBT paired with 188;

Children First's employing of NDP principles in its pedagogy 162–165; Children First COVID-19 lockdown and 156–161; Children First COVID-lockdown lift and 161–162; children and young adulthood 21; defining 23; diverse populations and 183; foundation of 34; how it can be used in schools post-COVID-19 40–42; how a neurodiverse child can benefit from 27–29; importance of safety in 25–27; international perspectives on 113; meaning of Dramatic in 27; meaning of Neuro in 27; meaning of Play in 27; on Naxos 144–145, 147, 148, 149, 152; neurodivergence in children and young people and 23–31; paradigm 35, 154, 155, 156, 167, 170, 177, 188–189, 201; postcolonial African theatre and 170–181; roots and branches of 3–11; in therapy 73; three stages of 27; three phases of (NDP, EPR, ToR) 218; transcultural relevance of 170; in the Temiar jungle 135–141; two examples with children of 35–37; *see also* *Handbook of Neuro-Dramatic-Play* (momentum and future of NDP)
Neuro-Dramatic-Play and Performance (NDPP) 142–143, 146, 151
neurological effects 104
neuroscience: art therapy and 88; of early development 162; NDP and 34, 222; NDPP and 142; on plasticity of the brain 181
Neuroscience and Behavioural Review 243
Neurosequential Development of the brain 51
neurotypical: defining 23
Ng, P. Y. N. 57
Nillni, Y. 187
nursery activities 24
nurture: case study (Hunter) 106, 108; nature versus 32
Nurture and Nesting (NaN) 27, 115, 117, 119, **124**, 161

Oasis session 190–192
Obun, P. 207; cartoon book *210*, *211*, 212

Odysseus and the Odyssey 151
O'Herlihy, D. 45
Olmos-Vega, F. 240
Orang Asli people 135
orphanages 115–119, 121–123,
    126–127, 130, 132–133, 235
orphans: messy/rhythmic/dressing play
    and 117
Othello see Shakespeare, W.
Outdoor Play 8, 11
outdoors, freedom of 157
outdoor swimming 97, 100
Ovtscharoff, W. 106

Palestine 56
Payne, J. L. 186
Penelope (*The Odyssey*) 151
performative play 5, 6, 10, 23, 27,
    28, 174
performative ritual 180
performativity in the beginning of life:
    case study (George) 15–16; case
    study (Jim) 17–19; case study (John)
    16–17; psychotherapy and 13–19
perinatal depression 185, 186, 187, 202
peripartum depression 187
Perry, B. 52
Perry's Prescription model of offering 52
Piaget, J. 89, 147
pillars (NDP workshop) 225
Pimlico Opera 205
Pione, R. 224
place attachment 75–76, 85
place bond 75–76
play: Agbo 170–177, 180–181; 'as if'
    8, 96, 120, 122, **125**, **126**; Brain
    8; child-led sensory 154; cultural
    contexts of 235; differentiating
    early forms of 6; dressing 117;
    embodied 41, 219, 174–175, 177,
    219; different intermediary play
    organized according to types of
    transitional function **61**; flour **67**;
    intermediary **61**; mask **61**; mysterious
    61; NDPP and 143; Outdoor 8;
    performative 5, 6, 10, 23, 27, 28;
    pretend 147, 243; puppet 8, 27, **61**;
    sand 34; therapeutic 8, 18, 134, 159;
    trace **61**; *see also* attachment-based
    play; Messy Play; Projective Play;
    Rhythmic Play; role-play(s); Sensory
    Play; Water Play

play-based work 155
Play-Doh 94, *95*
Playing the Baby session 198
Play Therapy (play therapy): case
    study of V (child in the UK from
    Ukraine) 78–86; Jennings as pioneer
    of 33; nature 105; NDP and 143;
    NDP as variation of 24; parent and
    child nature-based 104, 234; as
    psychotherapy 13
Play Therapy with Children
    (Jennings) 34
'Polyvagel Theory' (Porges) 28, 88
Proges, S. 46, 49, 52; *see also* Polyvagel
    Theory; Social Engagement theory
positive autonomy 204, 205
Positive Psychology Outcome Measure
    (PPOM and PPOM-C) 224
postpartum depression 104
pregnancy and pregnant women's:
    attachment-forming during 9–10;
    Colors of Life session 192–193;
    Good Enough Attachments session
    198–199; heartbeats experienced by
    the unborn during 28; intervention
    proposal for (ten proposed sessions)
    189–202; Living as a Symphony
    session 193–194; mandala layout
    197; Mandala of Motherhood
    session 196–198, 199; mental
    health of 185–187; Motherhood
    a Journey session 200–201;
    Motherhood a Landscape session
    195, 195–196; mothers talking
    to their unborn children during
    8; NDP for 29, 187–189; Nesting
    session 194–195; Oasis session
    190–192; playful 92; Playing the
    Baby session 198; Rehearsing
    the Good Enough Attachments
    session 198–199; Rehearsing
    Reality session 199–200; stressors
    experienced by 186, **186**; taking
    care of pregnant women using NDP
    as model 185–202; among Temiar
    people 5; true knot cord during 104;
    the unborn and water 6; *see also*
    unborn; Water Play
pregnancy play 5, 23
prisons: emotions neuro-dramatic play
    in 204–215; Mackenzie's work in
    204; *see also* Emergency Shakespeare;

positive autonomy; Shakespeare
Unbound; Shakespeare, W.
Projection (as in EPR) 34, 45
Projection Play 50
Projective Play (projective play) (P) 8,
    13, 60, 63, 65, 97–98, 175, 177; *see
    also* EPR
puppet play 8, 27, **61**; dramatic play
    and 8; extended 27
puppets and puppetry 34, 59, **69**,
    90, 145; animal puppets 95; case
    scenario (Poppy) using 95, 96; EPR
    using 226; examples of NDP with
    children and god puppet 70; Kari the
    Puppet, working with 46–47; "How
    to Make a Puppet" (video)(National
    Theatre UK) 151; NDP and 242;
    NDPP course using 151; 'playing the
    baby' with 198; Sam the Puppet 35,
    35–36, 41; Shakespeare using 161;
    younger children's use of 147

RAW *see* Research Arts and Wellbeing
    (RAW) cluster, University of Derby
Reduced Shakespeare Company 214
Rehearsing the Good Enough
    Attachments session 198–199
Rehearsing Reality session 199–200
relational safety 45, 52
Research Arts and Wellbeing (RAW)
    cluster, University of Derby 223
resilience 27, 33, 128, 130, 131,
    152; children's cultivating of 134;
    emotional 122, 143, 204, 208; EPR
    and 166; ethos of 177; inherent
    116; NDP's building of 45, 50, 117;
    performing in postcolonial African
    theatre of 170–181; stories in
    orphanages of 118; V's journey of 82;
    see also Theatre of Resilience (ToR)
Revised Adult Attachment Scale 224
rhythm 14; *see also* rhythm and ritual
Rhythmic Play (rhythmic play) 6–7,
    13, 14; NDP and 23, 27, 28, 45, 63;
    orphans and 117; V's sessions with
    83–84
rhythm and ritual 155, 161
Riley [no last name] 212–213
rite de passage 3
'Ritual and Risk' (Jennings) 28
rituals 3, 9; aesthetic integration
    and 59; *agbo* as venue for 174;

of coming-of-age 62, 65–66, **69**;
    disruption by COVID of educational
    routines and 156; Enrichment
    sessions using 160; fertility rites 3;
    grief and 10; kitchen 173; potential
    68; rhythm and 155, 161; rhythmic
    play and 28; rules applying to
    180; water used in 87; *see also*
    coming-of-age ritual(s)
ritual space 65, 66, **70**
Rogerian principles 105
Role (as in EPR) 34, 45
Role Play (role play, role-play, roleplay):
    active storytelling and 90; 'as if' 145;
    attachment and 145; 'crazy' fictional
    63; embracing childlike wonder via
    145; embodying emotions through
    122; engaging children in 147;
    EPR and 116, 117; by Hunter 109;
    identifying patterns via 64; mask
    making and 51; NDP and 145; NDP's
    inspiration and child's role-play in
    the Temiar jungle 140–141; Piaget
    on 147; sand stories and 50; working
    with teenagers using 50–51
Role Projection Embodiment (RPE) 222
role reversal 8, 68
RPE *see* Role Projection Embodiment
Rosen, Michael: *We're Going on a Bear
    Hunt* 37

SafePlace 119–120, **124**, 133
same-sex couples 236
Save the Children 76
Scannell, L. 75, 85
Seigel, D. J. 89
self 9; dramatic 156; as soother 46
self-acceptance 226
self-actualisation 42
self-affirmation 48
self-assurance 146
self-awareness 51, 60, 62, 122, 133;
    working with young adults using
    different modalities of the arts on
    self-expression and 63
self-care 168, 193, 225, 226
self-confidence 35, 123
self-connecting 63
self-criticism 195
self-demanding 195
self-determination 132
self-development 210

self-direction 8
self-discovery 117, 127, 128, 131
self-esteem 35, 42, 45, 48, 51, 122; low 115; NDP as affirming 142; Emergency Shakespeare and 214; NDP as platform as 127; Shakespear UnBard and 204; ToR as tool for 146
self-exploration 65
self-expression 60, 62; EPR framework for 224–225; 'voice' and 241; working with young adults using different modalities of the arts on self-awareness and 63
self-harm 10
self-perception 62
self-reflection 48, 116, 164–165, 165
self-regulation 143
self-reliance 142
self-understanding 62, 122; via relationship and intimacy 63–64
Sensory Integration 143, 156
Sensory Integration therapy 154
sensory memory 90
Sensory Play (sensory play) 6, 45, 50, 63, 92, 124; Agbo Play and 172; child-led 155; Hunter and 109; language of messy play and 156; NDP and EPR and 122; relaxation promoted by 188; water and 95
Sensory Processing Framework 155
Shakespearean drama 145
Shakespeare UnBard 204, 212, 215; see also Emergency Shakespeare
Shakespeare, W.: King Lear 212; Midsummer Night's Dream (play) 123; Naxos NDP course built around 149–150; Othello 204, 212; the Tempest 207, 209–211
Sheridan, M. 89
silence, in movement, sound, storytelling and silence 91
Slade, P. 3, 5, 33–34; 'Child Drama' 33–34; Remedial Drama 33
Smith, S. C. 224
social media 32, 56, 58
socio-emotional-play-based work 155
social engagement 222
Social Engagement system/theory (Porges) 46, 52
soothing: back rubbing as being 25; bamboo flute music as being 136; essential oils as being 26; playing

with water as being 88; rhythmical patterns as being 193; rocking as being 7, 106; self-soothing 46, 84; sensory 91; water waves as being 92
sound, in movement, sound, storytelling and silence 91
Stake, R. E. 238
Steele, W. 90
Stoner, C. R. 224
story-making 64
storytelling 18, 27, 29, 61; agbo as venue for 174; by Ayo's mother 175; beauty of 146; by children 35, 116, 134; creating myths and 67; drama 34; Dramatic Expression and 143; Emergency Shakespeare and 206; emotion-based 122; exercises 64; family 174; four-part arts-based healing involving 91; impact on brain of 109; improvisational 69; by the Jennings-Hicksons among the Temiar people 138–139; Monkey King 125–126, 127, 138–139; in movement, sound, storytelling and silence 91; multi-sensory approach to 37; NDPP and 142–143; NDP as vehicle for 146; "Moose and Mouse Get Muddy" 10–11, 12n1, 166; Oseo and the Giant 50; TimeSlips 221; Together Stronger project 221; as tool of EPR and NDP 226; Water Play and enhancement of skills in 91, 101
story work: aesthetic awakening via 146–148
substance abuse 186
Sudan 56
surrogacy 9, 14, 19, 236
swimming 92, 97–98, 100–101, 107, 136
swimming pool 158
symbolic memory 90
symbolic space, creating 66, 68
symbols 65, 66, 67–68
sympathetic nervous system 52
Syrian refugees 76–77

Temiar people and Temiar jungle 5–6, 135; bamboo raft making in 137–138; building relationships with 139–140; child's role-play and NDP's inspiration among 140–14;

Senoi 34; storytelling and games among 138–139; Temiar jungle and 135–137
Theatre Art 9
Theatre of Body 82, 116, **124, 125**
Theatre of Cruelty (Artaud) **61**
Theatre of Healing (ToH) 54–55
Theatre of Life (ToL) 54–55, 59, 82, 116, 122, 123, **125**
Theatre of Resilience (ToR) 27, 34, 54–55, **125–126**; *Agbo Play* and 177, 180, 181; children empowered by 116; Early Child Development and 9; expanded EPR for young adults in response to local trauma and 53–70, 234; Jennings on 64, 82; NDP and 117, 123, 133, 146–148; NDP at CF and 161; pregnant womens' mental health and 189; as term 9; young onset dementia compared to usefulness of ToR for teenagers 219
Therapeutic Metaverse 133–134
Therapeutic Play (therapeutic play) 8, 18, 134, 159
Theseus and Ariadne 144
TimeSlips 221
Together Stronger project 221
Tony [no last name] 206
ToL *see* Theatre of Life
ToR *see* Theatre of Resilience
touchstone: aesthetic 171; therapeutic 104–105
Tripartite Model (Scannell and Gifford) 85
Tuan, Y.-F. 75, 76
Turtle Keye Arts 221

Ukraine: a young hero's journey to the UK from (case study of V, a child in the UK from Ukraine) 78–86
unborn children: mothers building an emotional relationship with 188; mothers talking to 8; NDP and 34, 79, 142, 218; "Oasis" session with 190–191

vagus nerve 49, 51
Vanderschuren, L. 240
Van Niel, M. S. 186
Van Oers, B. 235
virtual reality (VR) 133

Vlaicu, C. 148
voice(s) 51, 241; actors' 150; alternative 151; creating, for dolls 9; echoing group chorus voices **68**; finding one's own 36, 127; loud 167; for Moose and Mouse 30; movement and 27; NDP and use of 145; storytelling in monkey voice 139; teen puppet 47
Voice and the Actor (Berry) 150
voicing of opinion 105
VR *see* virtual reality
Vygotsky, L. 89

Waite, P. 38
Wall, M. 176
Ward, A. 223, 224; *see also* young-onset dementia
water: Annie placing figures in a puddle 36; attachment-based play and 10; case scenario (Anna) working with 97–101; case scenario (Poppy) working with 93–97; case study (George) playing with 15, 16; case study (John) playing with 17; case study (V) playing with 81, 83; childbirth and 7; children's approach to 19, 42; clay as soil and 14; developmental stages (of children) and 89; different and changing states of 88–89; fundamental importance of 87–88; Messy Play with 24, 66; integrating stages and states using NDP-informed Art Therapy and 89–91; in NDP-informed Art Therapy 87–101; metaphor of 88; themes of 87; themes in Art Therapy of 91–92; *see also* Art Therapy; swimming
Water Play 10, 15, 28, **67**, 79; bubble play as part of 28; case scenario (Poppy) and 97; Embodiment Stage 101; infants/babies and 6, 28; NDP and 23, 27, 28, 34, 92–93, 117
Wellbeing Programme (Ireland)
Wayne, J. 177
Way, B. 3
wellbeing: dementia and the creative arts and 221; emotional 45; impact of COVID-19 on 32, 35, 38; "Imùlè" ritual and 181n1; nesting in the maternity process and 194; perinatal depression and 187; water and 87, 88, 94

White, R. E. 243
window of tolerance 110
Winnicott, D. W. 14, 51, 105
Wu Cheng'en: "Journey to the West" 123
Wyn [no last name] 207–209

Yin, R. K. 238–239
young adulthood: shifting understanding of 55–56; as socio-political-economic construct 66
young adults in Hong Kong: case study (dramatherapy across Four Seasons) 62–63, 63–66; chaos in developmental trajectories of 58; contradictions faced by 57; crises of fragmentation/disorientation/detachment of 56–58; distinctive needs of 53; expanded EPR and aesthetic integration for 58–60; expanded EPR in response to local trauma and 53–70; fear/anxiety as motivators for 57; hopelessness felt by 56, 57; mental health challenges faced by 70; need for an aesthetic/imaginative/playful reintegration for 58; powerlessness felt by 56, 57; reclaiming integration for 58; tactical principles using EPR for 60–66; waiting for a revised developmental horizon for care of 53–55
young-onset dementia: building bonds using play between caregivers and people with 223–227; community-based approaches to 221; creative arts and 221–222; defining 220; EPR framework applied to 224, 229; global prevalence of 220; NPD research project focused on 218–231; research findings and participant comments regarding 227–230; themes of Communication, Resilience, Attachment and Quality of Life identified in workshops for 228; toolkit development for 227; unique challenges of 220, 230; workshop pillars of 225; workshop series for, structure and development of 225–227

For Product Safety Concerns and Information please contact our EU
representative GPSR@taylorandfrancis.com
Taylor & Francis Verlag GmbH, Kaufingerstraße 24, 80331 München, Germany

www.ingramcontent.com/pod-product-compliance
Lightning Source LLC
Chambersburg PA
CBHW050341270326
41926CB00016B/3551